THE STATE OF THE WORLD'S CHILDREN 2000

ISBN 92-806-3532-8

The Library of Congress has catalogued this serial publication as follows:
The state of the world's children 2000

UNICEF, UNICEF House, 3 UN Plaza,
New York, NY 10017, USA.

E-mail: pubdoc@unicef.org
Web site: www.unicef.org

UNICEF, Palais des Nations,
CH-1211 Geneva 10, Switzerland

Cover photo
UNICEF/92-702/Lemoyne

Back cover photo
UNICEF/91-0906/Lemoyne

THE STATE OF THE WORLD'S CHILDREN 2000

Carol Bellamy, Executive Director,
United Nations Children's Fund

unicef
United Nations Children's Fund

Contents

Foreword

There is no trust more sacred than the one the world holds with children. There is no duty more important than ensuring that their rights are respected, that their welfare is protected, that their lives are free from fear and want and that they grow up in peace.

The State of the World's Children 2000 is a rallying call to us all. It is a call to governments, civil society, the private sector and the whole international community to renew our commitment to children's rights by advancing a new vision for the 21st century: a vision in which every infant has a healthy beginning, every child a quality education and every adolescent the opportunity to develop his or her unique abilities. It is a call to families and communities – and to children and adolescents themselves – to make their voices heard in helping translate this vision to reality in their daily lives.

This report tells of the many ways the world's commitment to children has been translated into action – particularly since the adoption of the Convention on the Rights of the Child in 1989 and the World Summit for Children the following year. More children are born healthy and more are immunized; more can read and write; more are free to learn, play and simply live as children than would have been thought possible even a short decade ago.

But as *The State of the World's Children 2000* so eloquently tells us, this is no time to stand on past achievements. Millions of children continue to endure the dreadful indignities of poverty; hundreds of thousands suffer the effects of conflict and economic chaos; tens of thousands are maimed in wars; many more are orphaned or killed by HIV/AIDS.

The State of the World's Children 2000 begins and ends with the premise that the wellspring of human progress is found in the realization of children's rights. It spells out a vision in which the rights of all children, without exception, are realized. The challenge, as so often, lies in the implementation of good intentions. Let us summon all our courage and commitment to make it so. Because a child in danger is a child who cannot wait.

Kofi A. Annan
Secretary-General of the United Nations

A vision for the 21st century

A girl from Mozambique stands by a tree trunk in a transit camp.

An urgent call to leadership

As the 21st century begins, the overwhelming majority of the people in the world who live in poverty are children and women. They are also the overwhelming majority of civilians who are killed and maimed in conflicts. They are the most vulnerable to infection with HIV/AIDS. Their rights, as set forth in the Convention on the Rights of the Child and the Convention on the Elimination of All Forms of Discrimination against Women, are violated every day in numbers of such magnitude as to defy counting.

But the pall that these abuses of poverty, conflict, HIV/AIDS and gender discrimination have cast on lives around the globe can be lifted. The conditions are neither inevitable nor immutable. Nor is the international community about to abandon women and children to them. Government bodies and civil groups, organizations of the United Nations system and non-governmental organizations, philanthropies and responsible corporate citizens – as well as children and adolescents themselves – have formed alliances to redress these wrongs.

Ready to take the necessary next step in advancing the well-being of the world's children, representatives of these various groups are to gather in an extraordinary meeting in the New York autumn of 2001, that will be linked to a Special Session of the General Assembly. Together, they will form a grand global coalition committed to fully meet the goals of the 1990 World Summit for Children. And they will begin the 21st century with a new agenda, clear and passionate about what needs to be done – for all women and all children – before the first decade of the new millennium ends.

Taken as a whole, these many organizations and the millions of people they represent – neither cowed nor intimidated by the challenges ahead – will form an unprecedented international movement on behalf of children. Many have worked long years to better the lives of children, adolescents and women: bringing the Convention on the Rights of the Child into being in 1989, setting goals and plans of action the following year at the World Summit, striving in the decade since then to be true to their promises. Others have embraced the cause of child rights more recently, drawn by a particular issue such as child soldiers, child labour or the trafficking of children for prostitution.

Together, they share a belief that human progress and overall development lie in the progress of women and children and the realization of their rights. They are animated by what has already been accomplished: the proven child survival gains of the 1980s and 1990s, the tenets of the Convention on the Elimination of All Forms of Discrimination against Women (CEDAW), the law and spirit of the Convention on the Rights of the Child and the achievements in nearing the World Summit goals.

Humanity has seen stunning advances and has made enormous strides for children, many of them in the last decade, many others in just over the span of a generation. Children's lives have been saved and their

Two girls enjoy lunchtime at the Angela Landa primary school in Havana.

suffering prevented. Millions have grown healthier, been better nourished and had greater access to a quality education than ever before. Their rights as put forth in the Convention have been acknowledged and laws to protect them enacted and enforced.

Polio, once a global epidemic, is on the verge of eradication, and deaths from two remorseless child killers, measles and neonatal tetanus, have been reduced over the past 10 years by 85 per cent and more than 25 per cent, respectively. Some 12 million children are now free from the risk of mental retardation due to iodine deficiency. And blindness from vitamin A deficiency has been significantly reduced. More children are in school today than at any previous time.

The momentous social movement that is needed for children is too important – and the urgency too great – for it to be led by a traditional few.

Despite the many stunning steps forward, a number of the goals remain out of reach for hundreds of millions of children throughout the world. Their lives and futures are threatened in a world marked by deeper and more intractable poverty and greater inequality between the rich and poor, proliferating conflict and violence, the deadly spread of HIV/AIDS and the abiding issue of discrimination against women and girls.

These problems are not new, but they are more widespread and profoundly entrenched than they were even a decade ago. Interwoven and reinforcing, they feed off one another and abrogate the rights of children and women in compounding ways. In some countries and regions, they threaten to undo much of what has been accomplished.

Intergenerational patterns of poverty, violence and conflict, discrimination and disease are not unconquerable. They – like other challenges before them – can be met. What is more, given the resources that the world has at hand, these deadly cycles can be broken within a single generation.

The world must now direct its efforts towards those points where the potential for change and impact will be greatest: the best possible start for children in their early years, a quality basic education for every child and support and guidance for adolescents in navigating the sensitive transition to adulthood.

The State of the World's Children 2000 seeks to fan the flame that burned so brilliantly for children a decade ago. It is a call to leaders in industrialized and developing countries alike to reaffirm their commitment to children. It is a call for vision and leadership within families and communities, where the respect for the rights of children and women is first born and nurtured and where the protection of those rights begins.

And it is a call to all people to realize a new world within a single generation: a shared vision of children and women – indeed of humankind – freed from poverty and discrimination, freed from violence and disease.

UNICEF/90-0003/Tolmie

In Colombia at the beginning of the decade, 3.5 million children under five years old were reached through a network of health clinics and the dissemination of health messages. A woman weighs a boy in a sling scale in her home.

PANEL
1

South Africa: Helping children by helping families

A group of young South African children files into the park, their eyes wide with anticipation. Suddenly, 2 four-year-old boys dash over to a bright red climbing structure, their squeals of glee piercing the din of traffic. The boys scramble up a ladder, while several girls, their black hair in short pigtails and colourful beads, bolt for the swings. Soon the play equipment is swarming with giddy children, while their caregivers chat on a nearby bench. The scene looks utterly normal, like many playgrounds the world over. Which is what is so remarkable: because Joubert Park is so much more than a playground.

The park is a swatch of green in the crime-ridden inner-city neighbourhood of Hillbrow in Johannesburg, one of the world's most violent cities. Until last year, the formerly 'whites only' park was a magnet for everyone from hawkers to squatters, and its sidewalks served as a crowded taxi stand for commuters. The Johannesburg Art Gallery, located here, was largely abandoned as its former well-heeled clientele fled the inner city.

A renaissance is now under way in the heart of Johannesburg, and it is being spearheaded by, of all things, an innovative child-care centre. The Joubert Park Child and Family Resource Service, housed in a low-slung building beneath shade trees in a corner of the park, is part of the Impilo (meaning 'life') Project. Managed by the provincial Gauteng Department of Education (GDE), Impilo is a series of linked pilot projects that are developing new multi-service approaches to early childhood care and development. The Joubert Park Service, led by Cynthia Ndaba, is building partnerships, including one between the Service and the health clinic, to help families and communities meet the needs of young children for health, safety and nutrition.

But this is not simply a crèche. Aimed at providing opportunities for poor people and rejuvenating a blighted neighbourhood, it is a model of comprehensive care for children that promotes the major pillars of children's rights.

The idea for a crèche-cum-empowerment centre came about after South Africa's first democratic election in 1994, which ended a half-century of white minority rule that had entrenched striking inequities for children. The province of Gauteng, which includes the cities of Johannesburg and Pretoria, is home to about 1 million children below the age of six. Fifty-nine per cent of Gauteng households are classified as poor, and 6 out of 10 mothers of school-age children are unemployed. Early childhood care has been nearly non-existent for black children: 80 per cent of pre-schoolers in the province were not being served by any programme. "We needed a new framework that overcame the inequalities of the past," asserts Carole Liknaitzky, Impilo Project manager for GDE.

UNICEF/95-1112/Pirozzi

Children in a playground in Johannesburg.

Since opening in 1998, the Project's pilot programme has striven to be a catalyst for providing a broad range of services to lower-income families. At its heart is the centre that provides day care for the poorest children in the neighbourhood, many of whom had been shuttered inside high-rise apartment blocks that ring the park. The crèche is adjacent to a mother-child health clinic that offers care to children, their families and the community.

PANEL
1

In an ambitious effort, the Project has also taken on the challenge of making the neighbourhood child- and family-friendly again. It is working with the police to improve safety around the park and has joined with the provincial Department of Agriculture, Conservation, Environmental and Land Affairs to clean up the park and provide nature outings and education to children and their families. Even the Art Gallery, once a bastion of white privilege, is now involved, offering arts education to caregivers from the Project. This 'web of linked services' is Impilo's holistic approach to early childhood care.

Jobs first

Inside the Joubert Park Service one morning, 30 children, ranging in age from three to six, are busy at different stations. The room is divided into areas for fantasy play with dolls and dress-up clothes, stations for math and puzzles and other areas for science, blocks, art and books. "These children are working freely, making what they want to make," explains Liza Titlestad, an artist and Montessori educator from the provincial Curriculum Development Project. "Most people assume children can't think for themselves. In fact, they are much more stimulated and creative when they can choose how to express themselves."

The caregivers in the Service meet monthly with parents, encouraging them to be involved in their children's education. The meetings are also designed to learn what parents need in order to help their families. During initial meetings, parents repeatedly highlighted their biggest concern: jobs. It became clear that the best way to help the children was to ensure that their families had steady incomes. "The idea was to help the child by helping the family," explains project coordinator Leon Mdiya. "Once they have a source of income, it is then more relevant for us to talk about the child's education and health care." So the parents conceived of the idea of opening a bakery.

A few blocks from Joubert Park, the Itsoseng ('wake yourself up') Community Bakery is catering to a steady stream of lunchtime visitors. The bakery, which was set up with support from the Urban and Rural Development Education Project, the US Wheat Board and the Open Society Foundation, serves hot lunches and will eventually sell fresh bread and other baked goods. Within one month of its May 1999 opening, the storefront was bustling with enthusiastic customers. The bakery employs 17 people, all of whom have children at the Joubert Park child-care centre. One of the parents is Catherine Bosoga, 27, whose five-year-old son takes part in the centre's activities while she bakes. Ms. Bosoga had been unemployed for five years before participating in the bakery cooperative. Noting that she is paid R200 ($33) per week, she says, "Now we have food in the house."

Ms. Bosoga motions to the queue of people waiting to buy the food that she, along with other parents, cooked this morning. "I think we are going to make it," she says.

About early childhood care

- Assuring the best for children throughout their lives depends on assuring them the best beginnings: The health and well-being of their mothers are essential, as is the care and attention children receive during their earliest years, from birth to age 6.
- A child grows and develops holistically, with his or her physical, emotional and intellectual needs interrelated and interdependent.
- Early childhood care is one of the best ways to assure the child a smooth transition into primary school. It is also a critical factor in the child's subsequent transition to adulthood, influencing both social skills and behavioural choices.
- The family and immediate community environment are fundamental to ensuring the rights of the child.
- Attention to early childhood is a critical aspect of anti-poverty strategies to break intergenerational cycles of chronic poor health and suboptimal human development.

Teaching the caregivers

The township of Kathlehong, just outside Johannesburg, appears an unlikely place to look for creative approaches to early childhood care. The landscape is dominated by small cinder block homes and shacks. In the early 1990s, this township was a war zone, the scene of deadly faction fighting between rival political groups vying for power. Just surviving was challenge enough for families and children in those days; development was a luxury. This was the urgent dilemma that confronted the Impilo Project when it arrived in 1998.

In Kathlehong and the neighbouring townships of Thokoza and Vosloorus, the Impilo Project has reached out to the numerous 'informal' services in shacks and hostels, offering training, resources and funding to upgrade facilities. "Services in informal settings do not qualify for legal recognition," says Sophia de Beer, the early childhood development officer for the province's Department of Education. Day-care providers routinely hid children from apartheid government inspectors, fearful that their crèches would be discovered and closed down. As a consequence, Impilo Project workers have to seek out the unregistered services – often finding them by sighting brightly coloured drawings in windows – and reassure them that the Government is there to help.

As part of its mission, the Impilo Project carries its philosophy of child-centred learning down a rutted dirt road where, at the end of a row, a gaily coloured metal shack has the words 'Teboho Child Care' (*teboho* means 'a gift') painted on the side. Some children run around the sandy lot, while others sit outside on a veranda working with measuring utensils. "I made this for the love of the kids," says Emily Serobe, 48, dressed in a brilliant red dress and blue scarf, as she motions to her small, neatly kept crèche. She and three other women look after 29 children up to age five. "The kids were running in the streets, and they were victims of child abuse. There was much fighting here in 1994. I saved the children by taking them inside."

Ms. Serobe now receives an annual subsidy from GDE of R4,000 ($670). She has used it to expand her space and to buy art supplies, toys and teaching resources. The Impilo Project also provides Ms. Serobe with training in how to care for children. "I used to beat and yell at the kids if they didn't respond," she acknowledges candidly. "They were crying, making noise, and I didn't know what to do. Then I learned to talk to them quietly and not beat them." She motions to the youngsters who are absorbed in drawing pictures and measuring seeds. "Now they have things to keep them busy. You can see the change," she says proudly.

The Impilo Project has made a similar difference at the nearby Vulindlela Crèche in Kathlehong, a formal child-care centre with 42 children. Principal Beatrice Radebe explains, "Impilo has been teaching me that children must learn through what they need, not through what I want them to do." She walks over to Jabu, a five-year-old girl who has drawn a picture of a woman with green legs. The small girl stands proudly next to her creation. "I like it here. I can draw and write," Jabu says with a shy smile.

Ms. Radebe holds up the picture and recalls how at one time she would have corrected the girl's choice of colours. The principal declares, "I mustn't tell her that it is wrong. Now, they can do what they like with the drawing. The children learn through their senses."

UNICEF/99-1005/Goodman

Emily Serobe with a child at the Teboho Child Care crèche in South Africa.

Other components of the Impilo Project include an 'action research project' in Kathlehong and neighbouring townships that is trying to identify what families need to support their children's development. Their research found that deep poverty and schools that are not child-friendly proved to be major reasons why more than 100 school-age children in the community were not attending school. A 'back to fast track' initiative brought 100 out-of-school children, ages 7 to 14, back to school and helped them catch up with their peers.

The most important contribution of the Impilo Project may simply be that it recognizes the hard and lonely work of child-care providers in poor communities. In the back room of a flower shop in Kathlehong one day, a dozen local caregivers are attending a training session with Fanny Ntuli from the Learning Project, who is working with all Impilo practitioners in the district. Ms. Ntuli observes, "The Department of Education never gave funds to informal crèches. Now they realize that even an auntie in a shack is important to children. They just needed some guidance on how to do things better."

Freda Thusi, a tall, matronly crèche owner who is attending the training, stands up and declares, "This training has really empowered us, and it will help the children. It has given us the real *impilo* in our future."

Promises to keep

To tell the story of how well the cause of human rights was advanced over the course of the last century is not simple. An honest narrative would raise questions of what became of the promises made for children and women, or of those pledges for international peace and commitments to universal human rights.

Some of the most dramatic and compelling stories of our times are of the significant gains in social development when the ideals of human dignity, justice and equality became reality through the actions of governments, organizations and individuals. Millions of people who might have died from communicable diseases and preventable illnesses in the past 50 years were saved because of public health measures such as immunization, improved access to safe water and sanitation facilities, and mass information campaigns.

Hundreds of thousands of women are alive today because of well-spaced and healthy pregnancies. Many more women than before are emancipated from illiteracy, largely because of political commitments to educate girls, commitments that were followed by global campaigns and local reforms.

Millions of children, born of healthy mothers, well-nourished and immunized against childhood diseases, have survived, whereas others, born before the child survival and development revolution of the 1980s and its life-saving programmes, did not. Thousands of children and adolescents, boys and girls alike, are now in school rather than trapped in exploitative and hazardous labour, or living on the streets and train platforms, or being trafficked for prostitution.

Nearly half of the children in the least developed countries of the world do not have access to primary education. Girls and boys share textbooks at a community school in Bhutan.

UNICEF/96-0543/Charton

But there are also sombre accounts of the 20th century about actions and inaction and times when not even the slightest shadow of the ideals of human rights could be seen. Clearly, not all have enjoyed the fruits of progress – and children and women especially have been denied.

Over the last 20 years, at the same time that the world economy increased exponentially, the number of people living in poverty grew to more than 1.2 billion, or one in every five persons, including more than 600 million children.[1]

In the last 15 years, denial and an unconscionable silence have allowed the HIV/AIDS pandemic to kill millions and decimate societies, especially in sub-Saharan Africa.

And in the last 10 years, the rape of women and girls and the systematic slaughter of civilians, including children, have become conventional weapons of war in every region of the world where conflicts rage.

How can one era hold such disparate and conflicting realities? Why has progress been possible in some countries and not in others? And what distinguishes countries where the rights of women and children are protected and promoted from those where children and women languish in poverty because the commitment to their rights was a hollow promise?

Clearly, not all have enjoyed the fruits of progress – and children and women especially have been denied.

Answers to these questions turn on the point of leadership. Where leadership for children and women is just, their rights can be protected. Where leadership is abdicated, abuses and human rights violations follow.

Many countries have begun the task of building a society around the best interests of children, and the benefits are evident. In Uganda, where political leaders invested in basic social services, infant mortality and child mortality rates were reduced by 5 percentage points between 1992 and 1997. In 125 countries, nearly 80 per cent of an entire generation of children were immunized against common childhood killers such as measles and tetanus through the collaborative actions of governments, civil society and international organizations. More than two thirds of all the world's children under five years old – 450 million – were immunized against polio in 1998 alone. In India that year, health workers and volunteers vaccinated 134 million children during National Immunization Days.

Even in countries at war, the commitment to immunize children has been honoured. In the Democratic Republic of Congo, for instance, National Immunization Days held since 1998 have reached 96 per cent of the children in more than two thirds of the country.

Though national efforts and large-scale campaigns are more visible, examples also abound of vision, solidarity and social change at every level. Because such actions often break with traditional power structures and relations, they call for courage and an impassioned motivation. Indigenous women in Chicontepec (Mexico), for example, formed a women's network in their community and installed a water pump, built a school and helped develop a gender-sensitive curriculum. They also engaged the men of the village in their workshops and provided skills training for them.

Similarly, young people across Africa and South-East Asia, like the teenage counsellors in the Zambian capital of Lusaka, have taken the initiative and volunteered in support groups to provide confidential counselling about HIV/AIDS in youth-friendly health services. And in many parts of the world, people are refusing to accept violence against women as inevitable, creating shelters and hotlines for women and raising awareness. In Bangladesh, young women have organized a movement that speaks out against the horror experienced by hundreds of the country's girls and women who are injured in brutal acid attacks by spurned suitors and hostile relatives every year.

BOX 1 Children's rights: From chattel to citizens

To start from the contention that all children possess rights is to challenge many of the world's most long-held beliefs. One thousand years ago, children were all but invisible as individuals, regarded as property and made to work as soon as they were physically able to. Adults paid little attention to their special needs.

By the turn of this century, when the deadly scourges of cholera, typhoid and influenza were rampant throughout the world, children were no closer to gaining their basic rights than they were during that earlier period. It took the world's horror at the First World War and the commitment of the newly formed League of Nations to peace and rehabilitation to transform charitable approaches on behalf of children into the recognition that children had rights as well as needs.[1]

The important but still limited benefits of charity frustrated many child advocates, including Eglantyne Jebb. The dynamic Briton, who established the Save the Children Fund in 1919, drafted the first document in history endorsed by the international community to state that children have rights. Writing in 1923, Jebb noted, *"The moment appears to me to have come when we can no longer expect to conduct large relief actions. If we wish nevertheless to go on working for the children . . . the only way to do it seems to be to evoke a cooperative effort of the nations to safeguard their own children on constructive rather than on charitable lines. I believe we should claim certain rights for the children and labour for their universal recognition, so that everybody . . . may be in a position to help forward the movement."*[2]

Throughout the 20th century, a burgeoning field of experts and grassroots children's advocates mounted a movement to recognize children's special needs as inalienable rights and to guarantee those rights under law. In 1989, this 'child rights movement' resulted in the Convention on the Rights of the Child, a landmark in international human rights legislation that incorporated the full array of rights embodied in the 1948 Universal Declaration of Human Rights and the twin Covenants on Civil and Political Rights (1966) and Economic, Social and Cultural Rights (1966), international humanitarian law and the rights of refugee children.

In an unprecedented collaboration, governments and NGOs from around the world hammered out the most comprehensive human rights instrument in history. On item after item, the drafters reached a consensus on such sensitive issues as child labour, child soldiers and the sexual exploitation of children. Child rights advocates were successful in insisting that paramount importance be given in the document to the principle of "the best interests of the child."

When the United Nations General Assembly unanimously adopted the Convention on the Rights of the Child on 20 November 1989, groups of children looking on from the gallery burst into applause.

An altered landscape

When the story turns to leadership on behalf of children's rights, there are no more exhilarating chapters than those that tell of the 1989 Convention on the Rights of the Child and the 1990 World Summit for Children. With its full spectrum of civil, political, economic, social and cultural rights, and the overwhelming consensus seen in its nearly universal ratification, the Convention positioned children squarely at the forefront of the worldwide movement for human rights and social justice. It altered the landscape for children by clarifying the vital and distinct roles to be played by State signatories, NGOs, international organizations, communities, parents and children themselves in realizing children's rights (Box 1).

The Convention on the Rights of the Child put forward several principles to guide the world's work on behalf of child rights, including one with the most expansive potential: that the best interests of the child shall be a primary consideration in all actions concerning the child. Moreover, another compelling clause made it clear that a partnership of rich nations and poor is vital so that resources are committed to the extent possible at the national level and assistance is pledged internationally to ensure that children have the opportunity to enjoy their rights.[2]

Following closely on the adoption of the Convention by the UN General Assembly, the World Summit for Children was convened in New York City in September 1990. The 71 Heads of State and Government and others assembled drafted an ambitious plan for the closing decade of the century, with 27 goals, 7 of them considered major, to be accomplished by the year 2000 (Box 2).

No one who took part in these momentous events on behalf of children could have anticipated the extent to which the Convention and the Summit goals would suffuse every significant summit and conference that followed.[3] In particular, they informed the agenda of the 1995 World Summit for Social Development and were reflected in the *Human Development Report* of 1994.[4] And they can be seen in the goals of the Development Assistance Committee (DAC) to cut poverty in half, reduce mortality by two thirds among children under five years of age and ensure universal access to primary education by the year 2015.[5]

Nor could those present in 1990 predict how much the World Summit and the Convention would galvanize the energies of many thousands of individuals and groups around the world for years to come. So although human rights abuses against children still persist in all parts of the world, remarkable progress has been made for children in country after country.

In 1990, for example, the member States of the Organization of African Unity drafted their own Charter on the Rights and Welfare of the Child and, since then, countries have used it in conjunction with the Convention on the Rights of the Child in their programming and advocacy activities. Since 1990, 117 countries have developed a national plan of action for children, and 17 countries in Central and South America have passed significant child rights legislation.[6] Many other countries have revised their national legislation in response to provisions of the Convention on matters ranging from public health to juvenile justice and female genital mutilation. And national reports on such subjects as 'The State of Our Children' and 'Children's Budgets' are now issued in countries around the world.

The United Nations has made its own commitment to keep children's rights at the centre of its peacekeeping and peace-building activities. In 1993, Graça Machel, former Minister of Education of Mozambique, was appointed by the UN Secretary-General to undertake the first comprehensive assessment of the multiple ways children suffer in armed conflict. Following Ms. Machel's compelling study, the Secretary-General appointed Olara A. Otunnu in 1997 as Special Representative for Children and Armed Conflict to serve as a public advocate and moral voice on behalf of children caught in war's chaos. Today, children hold a regular place on the agenda of the UN Security Council as it considers the effects of its actions – whether, for example, to intervene in the Democratic Republic of Congo, Sierra Leone or East Timor – on the rights and welfare of children.

In the UN General Assembly, too, the plight of children receives attention. In opening remarks to the 54th General Assembly, President Theo-Ben Gurirab, Foreign Minister of Namibia, identified the future of children as one of the seven main challenges facing the world today: "... their lives are at daily risk of being snatched away by the cruelty and indifference of adults." GA President Gurirab added his endorsement to designating the first decade of the new millennium as the International Decade for a Culture of Peace and Non-violence for the Children of the World.[7]

Perhaps most significant of all, the spirit of the Convention and of the World Summit has stirred a remarkable level of interest and participation on the part of children and adolescents. They have addressed

BOX 2 Major goals of the 1990 World Summit for Children

To be achieved by the year 2000:

- Reduction of mortality rates for children under five.
- Reduction of maternal mortality rates.
- Reduction of malnutrition among children under five.
- Reduction of adult illiteracy rates.
- Provision of universal access to basic education.
- Provision of universal access to safe drinking water and sanitary conditions.
- Improved protection of children in especially difficult circumstances.

national parliaments, and in several regions, 10 countries in West and Central Africa, for example, they have formed their own Children's Parliaments or similar structures. Millions have participated in referendums on children's rights in Chile, Ecuador, Mexico and Mozambique. In Colombia, riven by war and violence for over 30 years, children and adolescents have taken the courageous lead in launching a nationwide peace movement.

The price of failure

For all the gains made, the story of the 20th century is also about failed leadership – a lack of vision, an absence of courage, a passive neglect. The number of violations of children's rights that occur around the globe every day are staggering. They range from acts of omission – such as the failure to register births or provide access to health care services and primary school – to the deliberate abuses of armed conflict, forced labour and sexual exploitation. They are often hidden in families, rich or poor. They lead from one violation to another, exponentially.

Every day that nations fail to meet their moral and legal obligations to realize the rights of children, 30,500 boys and girls under five die of mainly preventable causes, and even more children and young people succumb to illnesses, neglect, accidents and assaults that do not have to happen.

Every month that the full-scale campaign needed to stop the terrifying HIV/AIDS pandemic is postponed, 250,000 children and young people become infected with the fatal virus.[8]

UNICEF/99-0607/Pirozzi

The devastating effects of war continue long after the conflict ends. This Iraqi woman lost her right hand and injured both legs when she mistakenly picked up a landmine.

Every year, 585,000 women die of complications of pregnancy and childbirth that could have been prevented.

In the last year alone, approximately 31 million refugees and displaced persons[9] – mostly children and women – were caught in the conflicts that ravaged the world, searching in vain for a safe haven, fleeing inhumane circumstances and ruthless attacks by mortar and machete, rape and dismemberment.

And every year that governments fail to spend what is needed to support basic social services and that development assistance is slashed, millions of children throughout the developing world are deprived of the access to safe water and sanitation facilities, and school and health services that are vitally necessary for them to survive and develop.

These are gross violations of the rights of children and women and as long as they persist – and the circumstances that give rise to them remain unchanged – human development will be compromised.

UNICEF/98-0201/Lemoyne

More than 150,000 children and women were forced from their homes during the civil conflict in Yugoslavia. This woman stands with her children in a temporary settlement of displaced ethnic Albanian Kosovars.

UNICEF/99-0109/Pirozzi

In Uganda, Umaru, 8, and Avisa, 10, who lost their father to AIDS and whose mother is sick with the disease, watch as Maxim Vengerov, internationally renowned violinist and UNICEF Envoy for Music, shares a light-hearted moment outside their house.

Alliances for children

To shift the way the international community assumes its responsibility towards children requires political will and an unwavering commitment on all levels to social action. It requires the rededication of those who have been working for children over long years and the building of new alliances. The momentous social movement that is needed for children is too important – and the urgency too great – for it to be led by a traditional few.

The leadership called for in the next millennium extends beyond traditional sectors and governmental structures, to engage all those who share a concern for human progress – people's movements, community-based organizations, youth movements, women's groups, professional networks, artists and intellectuals, the mass media. It is a global leadership that will work bottom-up as well as top-down, involving Heads of State, leaders in the political, business, academic and religious communities and children and adolescents themselves who are already working towards positive change in their families and in their communities.

This expansive leadership, set to gather in 2001, will be the catalyst to the profound social transformations that are necessary to improve the world for children and women and to advance human development.

Undeclared war

Despite the progress made on many of the goals set at the 1990 World Summit for Children, this has been a decade of undeclared war on women, adolescents and children as poverty, conflict, chronic social instability and preventable diseases such as HIV/AIDS threaten their human rights and sabotage their development.

Each of these obstacles is compounded for women and girls by the discrimination against them that infiltrates all sectors of society in every country. Gender discrimination, so entrenched in social norms as to escape notice, keeps young girls from school and women from active and equal involvement in their communities. This discrimination is at the base of many of the violations of women's rights, including the physical duress of domestic violence or the strategic use of rape and forced pregnancies as weapons of war. And where women's rights are at risk, children's rights are too.

The poverty trap

Poverty is a world of darkness, where every day is a struggle to survive. The poor are the majority in nearly one of every five nations in the world. In rich countries, they are increasingly concentrated in minority communities. They endure lives of hunger, malnutrition and illness and are denied their right to education, to receive good health care, to have access to safe water and sanitation and to be protected from harm.

The number of people living in poverty continues to grow as globalization – one of the 20th century's most powerful economic phenomena – proceeds along its inherently asymmetrical course: expanding markets across national boundaries and increasing the incomes of a relative few while further strangling the lives of those without the resources to be investors or the capabilities to benefit from the global culture. The majority are women and children, poor before, but even more so now, as the two-tiered world economy widens the gaps between rich and poor countries and between rich and poor people.

To be a girl born into poverty is to endure discrimination many times over in pervasive and insidious patterns. From the moment of girls' conception, their rights are in peril. There may be as many as 60 million 'missing women' in the world who, except for the gender discrimination that starts before they are born and continues throughout their lives, would be alive today.[1]

Although discrimination against girls and women is found on every continent of the world, for the sheer scale of its population and the cultural strictures against gender and class, few regions compare with South Asia, where every year millions of girls are born into poverty, debt servitude and dehumanizing birth castes. Poor pregnant women, worried about the future dowry costs of a daughter, increasingly seek the services of travelling 'sonogram doctors', and female foeticide has been reported in 27 of India's 32 states. In some communities of Bihar and Rajasthan, birth ratios, naturally expected to be 100 females for every 103

In a camp for displaced persons in Sierra Leone, two girls stand outside their mud house while armed soldiers pass by.

males, are dramatically lower at 60 females for every 100 males.[2]

These girls, children of poverty, often begin their lives passed over in favour of their brothers for food, medical attention and schooling. At the mercy of the men in their families and communities, they suffer the isolation of ignorance and illiteracy, the agony of beatings. For girls and women of the lowest caste, public humiliations are frequent.[3]

And where women's rights are at risk, children's rights are too.

Caste poverty persists throughout the vast region, defying the laws that prohibit its practice and stripping well over 160 million people in India alone of their rights.[4] A particularly cruel burden falls on the children, as parents take out meagre loans in exchange for consigning or selling a child to a factory or plantation owner. An estimated 20 million, and perhaps as many as 40 million, girls and boys in South Asia toil in this debt servitude,[5] hunched over looms, making bricks, or rolling cigarettes by hand. Countless others spend their childhood and adolescence in domestic servitude, sweeping floors and scrubbing pots and pans.

It is disturbing to imagine what awaits a child of six when his parents place him in debt bondage in exchange for a loan for seed or shelter. It is almost unfathomable to think of a girl from the Nepalese mountains who, sold by her impoverished parents to an agent offering employment in a carpet factory, instead finds herself in a windowless room in Calcutta or Mumbai with other girls, forced to have sex with as many as two dozen adult clients a day. Like the debt-trapped countries in which they live, the children rarely succeed in paying off their parents' debts, even after 10 or 12 years, and they perpetuate their families' servitude by handing it down to a younger sibling or to their own offspring.[6]

Poverty's deep pockets

Slave-like also describes the lives of millions of other children throughout the world. There is no way to calculate the exact number of young boys and girls whose lives are endangered by their sale and trafficking, by debt bondage, serfdom, forced or compulsory labour, forced or compulsory recruitment

Figure 1 **The growing gap between rich and poor countries**

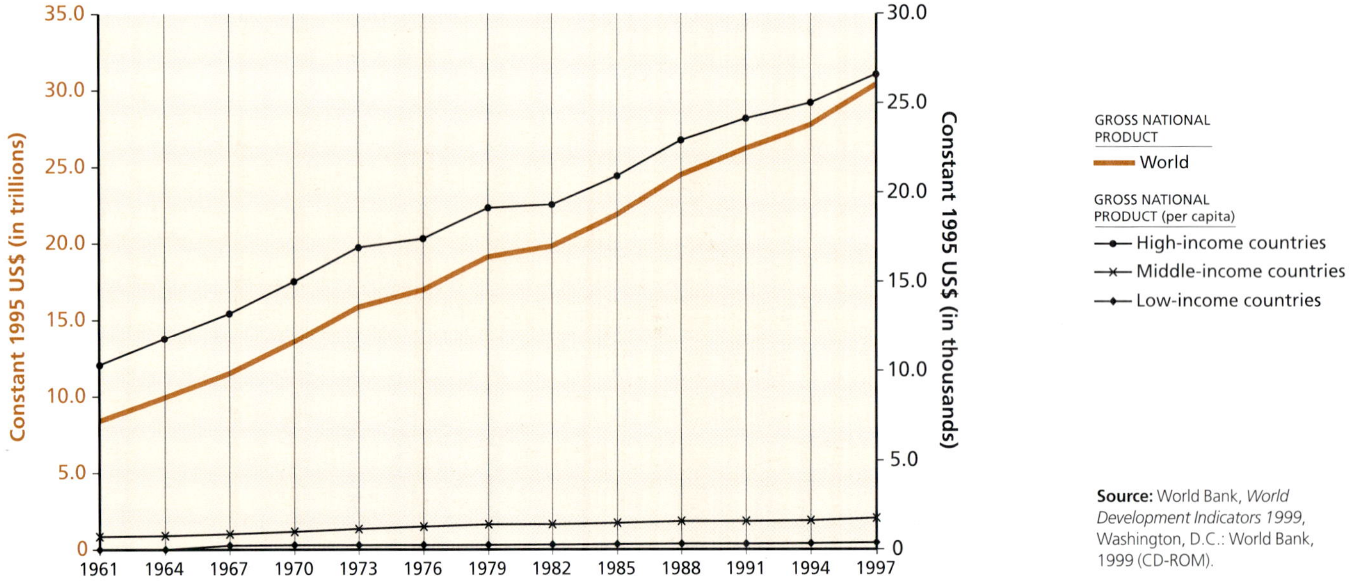

Source: World Bank, *World Development Indicators 1999*, Washington, D.C.: World Bank, 1999 (CD-ROM).

PANEL 2

Indonesia's despair

Rini is a 13-year-old girl who lives in a working class neighbourhood on the outskirts of Jakarta. For many years, Rini's father worked in a printing shop. Money was always tight, but it was enough to support Rini, her mother and her younger brother and sister. Then, in January 1998, the family was dealt a major blow. The printing shop closed without warning and her father was thrown out of work, turning Rini's world suddenly upside down. With the future so uncertain, Rini's parents worried about not being able to afford to send her to school.

Rini's loss and those suffered by millions of other Indonesian children in the Asian economic crisis that began in 1997 reflect the downside of globalization. Such disasters can seem almost unthinkable in countries where financial and legal mechanisms, solid infrastructures and decent living standards buffer people from extreme financial vagaries.

With protections in place, globalization seems benign at worst and beneficial at best, an explosive opportunity for growth, as ideas, technology, goods, services and people criss-cross the planet in search of new markets. More than $1.5 trillion changes hands in the world's currency markets each day – an eightfold increase since 1986. This progressive potential is great, as jobs are created and economic and political barriers fall.

Certainly, Indonesia's encounter with globalization began well. The world's fourth most populous nation, with its rich natural resources and masses of poor people desperate for work, was an attractive port of call as capital began to roam the globe in the 1980s. Overseas investors flocked to Jakarta and, by January 1997, foreign investment in Indonesian stock stood at $59 billion. The average annual income for an Indonesian rose from $50 in 1967 to $650 in 1994.

However, the gains of this 'Asian Tiger' vanished like vapour, as global opportunity yielded to global carnage. In 1997, when the Thai economy collapsed, the dominoes fell rapidly throughout East Asia. Indonesia's currency lost 70 per cent of its value in one year, and by the end of 1997, its stock market had fallen by nearly 40 per cent.

UNICEF/99-0807/Lemoyne

Indonesian children pick through garbage at a dump in Jakarta.

PANEL 2

In 1998, the International Monetary Fund (IMF), the World Bank and other international agencies loaned Indonesia more than $50 billion. But the bailout came with stringent restrictions, including high interest rates and the mandated closure of 16 banks. The IMF-imposed austerity measures exacerbated the mushrooming social crisis. Soon, food riots and ethnic violence exploded in the streets. In May 1998, the Government fell.

Suffering the greatest setback of any country in East Asia, Indonesia saw its gross domestic product fall 12.2 per cent in the first half of 1998, compared to the same period in 1997. Between 1997 and 1998, according to the World Bank, the number of Indonesians living in poverty nearly doubled. The 20 million newly poor Indonesians – those earning $1 per day or less – could populate a medium-sized country. The International Labour Organization estimates that nearly two thirds of Indonesia's total population will be living below the poverty line at the start of the new millennium, a reversal that the World Bank has characterized as "the most dramatic economic collapse anywhere in 50 years."

The human costs of the debacle have been high, particularly for the poorest women and children. Many families, reeling from business failures and the loss of a million jobs nationwide, cut back from three meals per day to just one. The Indonesian Government estimates that 100 million people – nearly half the nation's population – cannot afford adequate food. More than 2 million Indonesian children below the age of five are already malnourished. Some people, in utter desperation, are giving up their children, creating a large population of 'economic orphans'.

With parents unable to afford school fees, about 20 per cent of all girls and 14 per cent of the boys in the poorer areas of Jakarta dropped out of junior secondary school in 1998. The rising number of uneducated children threatens to create a 'lost generation', ensuring that the fallout of the current crisis will endure for generations.

Although the financial crisis appears to be subsiding in East Asia, the human crisis continues. Twelve per cent of the populations of both the Republic of Korea and Thailand have fallen into poverty. Once again, women and children have borne the brunt of the losses: Between April 1997 and April 1998 in the Republic of Korea, employment dropped by 7 per cent among women, compared with a 3.8 per cent job loss for men. Among students, the high school drop-out rate in the Republic of Korea rose 36 per cent, while in Thailand, as many as 130,000 students left school.

As for Rini, the way out of poverty remains uncertain. Her father has been unable to find a steady job as the Indonesian economy continues to teeter. Her mother, Maida, has begun work as a seamstress in order to keep the family clothed and fed. Yet the family has been relatively fortunate: Maida has managed to earn just enough money to pay Rini's school fees.

About 4 million other children in Indonesia have been kept in school by the Aku Anak Sekolah – Back to School – Campaign. A collaborative effort of the Government of Indonesia, the World Bank, the Asian Development Bank and UNICEF, the campaign provides scholarships for students in primary and secondary schools and 130,000 block grants for schools to help maintain enrolment and teaching quality. Because of Aku Anak Sekolah, far fewer than the 6 million children it was feared might end their studies have actually left school. Nevertheless, 2.5 million children are no longer in class.

About inequities between the rich and poor

- As the world's currency markets exchange $1.5 trillion each day, more than 1.2 billion people in the world live on less than $1 a day – more than 600 million of them children.
- While the average per capita income in 40 countries has grown by more than 3 per cent each year since 1990, 55 countries have seen a decline during the same period and more than 80 countries now have per capita incomes lower than a decade ago.
- The richest fifth of the world's population enjoys a share of global income that is 74 times that of the poorest fifth.
- Income inequality has increased in most OECD countries since 1980.
- An estimated 12 per cent of the people living in the richest countries in the world are affected by poverty.

Sources: UNICEF; UNDP; *Human Development Report 1999*, World Bank 1999.

Equity in a global economy

Indisputably, the global market place has been bountiful for a small minority with capital and skills. The 200 richest people in the world, for instance, more than doubled their net worth between 1994 and 1998, to more than $1 trillion. Meanwhile, disparities continue to grow: In 1960, the income gap between the richest fifth of the world's population and the poorest fifth was 30 to 1; in 1997 it was 74 to 1.

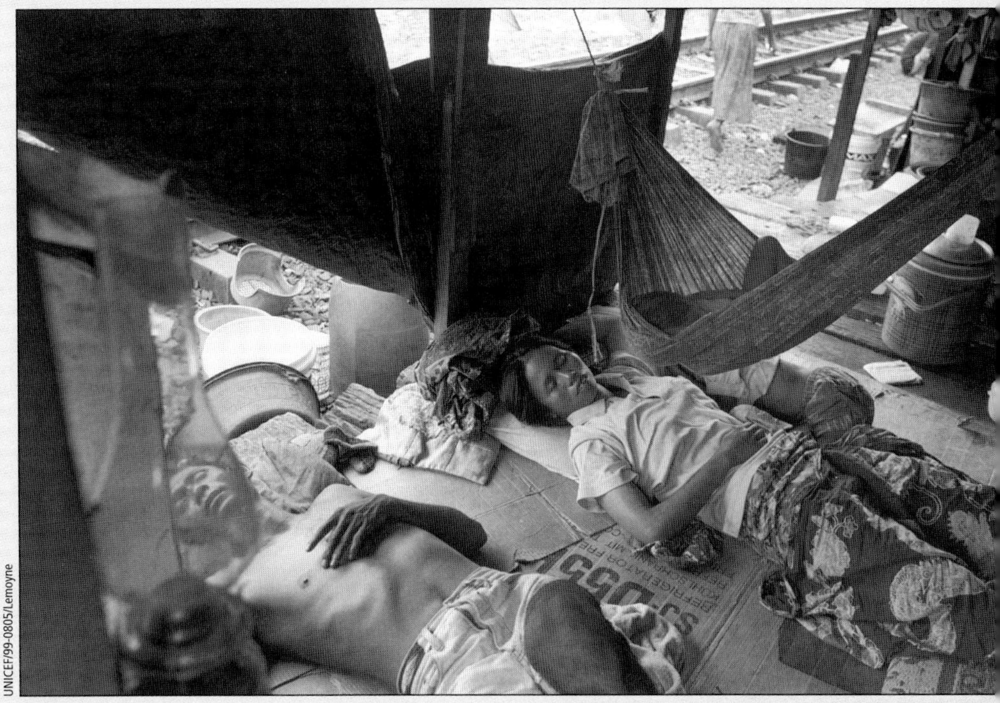
UNICEF/99-0805/Lemoyne

A family of squatters sleeping in their makeshift home along the railroad tracks in Jakarta's central district.

The problems and inequalities engendered by globalization demand both global and national responses. Among the global measures suggested in the *Human Development Report 1999* are mechanisms to help calm international market volatility before a crisis ensues and to ensure a steadier and more equitable investment stream for developing countries. On the national level, a number of countries have already instituted macroeconomic, social and political reforms and systems from which others can learn to prevent or modulate extreme fluctuations.

A fundamental and inescapable step in strengthening countries' capacity to participate equitably in the global economy is to ensure people's access to sound basic social services such as health, education, family planning and water and sanitation. These services make sustained and stable economic progress possible, help people achieve greater productivity and form an especially crucial buffer for children and women in difficult times. Basic services are financially feasible if, in the spirit of the 20/20 Initiative, developing countries allocate 20 per cent of their budgets to these services, and if donor countries similarly earmark 20 per cent of their official development assistance (ODA) to the same task.

"In the wake of the Asian financial crisis, both governments and civil society feel that the 20/20 Initiative is needed, essential and feasible," declared Horacio Morales, Agrarian Reform Secretary in the Philippines, in a keynote address to the Hanoi Meeting on the 20/20 Initiative, held in October 1998. "The Initiative does not promote merely a safety net. In addition to helping protect the gains in human development, it can contribute to economic recovery," he asserted. Insisting that the Initiative was feasible, Mr. Morales noted, "In a $25 trillion world economy, universal access to basic social services by the year 2005 will require less than 0.2 per cent of world income, or around 1 per cent of developing countries' income."

The 20/20 Initiative offers a practical way forward. But it is bucking a disturbing trend: ODA from donor countries, rather than increasing to a target level of 0.7 per cent of the gross national product (GNP), has declined by one third since 1986, standing at an average of 0.22 per cent of GNP in 1997, the lowest point since 1970. Meanwhile, external debt for the least developed countries has rocketed from 62.4 per cent of GNP in 1985 to 92.3 per cent in 1997. A recent UNICEF study of 30 developing countries indicates that nearly two thirds of these nations allocate more for debt payment than for basic social services. The solution to this zero-sum game is clear, according to Hilde Johnson, Norwegian Minister of International Development and Human Rights: "Breaking the vicious circle of poverty also requires eliminating the unsustainable debt burden."

into armed conflict, prostitution, pornography or by the production and trafficking of drugs. Efforts to eliminate these gross violations have been ongoing and have been energized by the 1999 Worst Forms of Child Labour Convention.[7] But, according to estimates by the International Labour Organization (ILO), some 250 million children between the ages of 5 and 14 work in developing countries and some 50 million to 60 million children between the ages of 5 and 11 work in hazardous circumstances.[8] The challenges of preventing and eradicating these extreme violations of children's rights illustrate the layers of want, discrimination and exploitation that drive humanity's poorest children into obscure and dangerous worlds.

Children and women are among the first to suffer when crises rip the covers off seemingly prosperous countries to reveal the poverty that exists. The effects of the recent financial crash in South-East Asia, for example, show that the absence of a social safety net has particularly devastating consequences for children's rights and human development. Similarly, the economic turmoil in the former Soviet Union and in Eastern Europe has caused 120 million people, almost 30 per cent of the people in the region, to sink into poverty since 1990. Again, children figure prominently among the victims: In the Russian Federation, 50 per cent of families with three or more children and 72 per cent of those with four or more children are impoverished.[9]

Even in countries that have robust economic growth, poverty is paralysing ever greater numbers, as in parts of Latin America, where the poorest 20 per cent of people share less than 3 per cent of national income.[10] In contrast, countries such as Costa Rica, Cuba, Sri Lanka and Viet Nam have shown that, even against international political odds, consistent policies aimed at providing a solid foundation of social services pay off in better health conditions and higher literacy rates than those found in many countries with greater economic resources.[11]

In still other countries, deepening pockets of poverty are masked in average national statistics. Only by disaggregating the national averages can the poor who are huddled in the margins be located. In New York City, for example, the percentage of children born into poverty rose from 44 per cent to 52 per cent from 1990 to 1996, a 20 per cent increase, and the number of homeless children rose 21 per cent during the same period.[12]

Figure 2 The distribution of income in three large economies

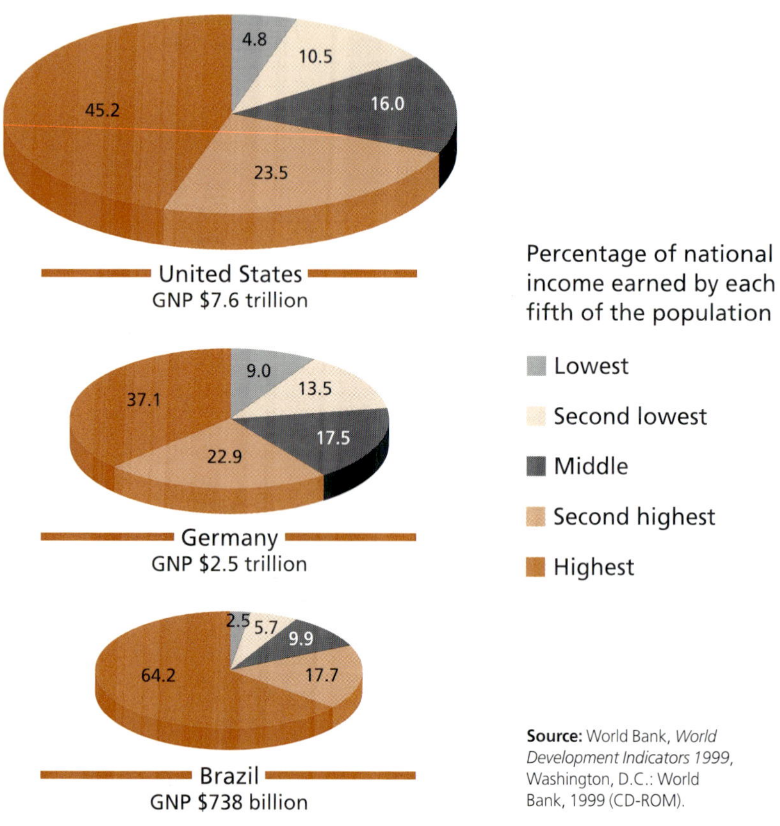

Source: World Bank, *World Development Indicators 1999*, Washington, D.C.: World Bank, 1999 (CD-ROM).

Conflicts and violence: No haven for a child

Changing the rules of war along with the battlefields, 20th century conflicts have shattered historians' theories of combat as a disciplined affair prosecuted by sovereign States. Nearly all of today's conflicts churn within national boundaries, and 90 per cent of war's victims are civilians, mainly children

PANEL
3

Children's risks in societies on the edge

In Fatsi, a small village in Ethiopia's northern province of Tigray, Hadgu Michaele, 12, still manages to attend school every day, a feat testifying to his own and his community's courage and determination. Fatsi is 10 kilometres from the border with Eritrea, and since hostilities between the two countries began in 1998, the primary school has moved three times to avoid the shelling. Teachers and students now trek up a steep and treacherous footpath to classes held in a cave, deep within cliffs of a rocky plateau, safe from gunfire.

That footpath is both harsh reality for the children of Fatsi and a metaphor for the steep struggles facing hundreds of millions of children like them throughout the world today. Over the past 10 years, armed conflicts, economic and political crises, natural disasters and AIDS and other diseases have grown in strength, frequency and complexity, posing daunting new threats to children's lives and rights.

When a society's foundations are laid on the shallow soil of poverty and underdevelopment, it can crumble quickly. Health clinics are destroyed in a hail of bullets, education is derailed in an economic crisis, flood waters wash away homes and hope. And with only the slimmest of margins between stability and social meltdown, the health and well-being of women and children are almost invariably the first assets a country loses – or sacrifices – when a crisis occurs.

Currently, an estimated 540 million, or one in four, children in the world live with the ominous and ever-present hum of violence that might erupt at any time, or are displaced within their countries or made refugees by conflicts that are already raging. Hundreds of thousands are buffeted by floods and droughts in repetitive

UNICEF/Ethiopia/Faye

In northern Ethiopia, children attend classes held in a mountain cave.

patterns. Many of those same children are among the more than 600 million children already beset by unyielding and merciless poverty.

The losses they face are hard to imagine, let alone capture statistically. The child risk measure developed by UNICEF in 1999 goes some of the way towards quantifying the toll complex forces such as conflict and AIDS take on the most vulnerable and least visible, the children. In 30 of the 163 countries in which it was calculated, the risk is an ominous 20 points above the world average, and 24 of the 30 countries are in sub-Saharan Africa. There, risks confronting children are 10 to 13 times those faced by a child in Australia, Norway or the United States. A child in Angola faces the greatest risks of all.

More time and resources need to be devoted to developing and sharpening measures such as this one, to gauge the changing and increasingly complex risks to children abroad in the world. Only through such analysis can children be protected better in present crises and can future ones be prevented.

Instability at century's end

Childhood is especially perishable in war. In the past 10 years, in much of the developing world, children have endured losses far out of proportion to their years and strength, of family and community members, of time to grow and learn, of the sense of hope.

In one of the most horrific human cataclysms, an estimated quarter of a million children in Rwanda were slaughtered in 1994 in the genocide that took, by some accounts, a million lives over the course of weeks. Scores of thousands more children were tortured, some by their schoolteachers, some in their churches, others while they lay in hospital beds. Hundreds of thousands more watched in agony and fear as their parents and families and friends were stalked and massacred by people they had known and trusted for years.

Landmines, too many to count, waste lives and limbs. Girls and women are raped as a

Healing games

Living through chaos can scar children's psyches and strangle their development, making programmes to address their psychological needs as necessary as those to bandage their physical wounds.

One such programme is 'The Return of Happiness', which was first developed in Mozambique during the 1992 civil war and engages traumatized children through music, art and play. Adaptable in various situations, it has been used in Ecuador with the children of soldiers, in Colombia after the 1998 earthquake and in Nicaragua following Hurricane Mitch.

That storm killed thousands in floods and mudslides. It wiped out roads, farmlands, water and sanitary infrastructures, health and educational institutions and left families destitute and homeless in Central America. But the ruins it left were the result of generations of chronic poverty, civil strife and social exclusion in the region, as much as they were the effects of that particular storm.

In Nicaragua, where three quarters of the people were already living in poverty and the nation was still healing from its earlier civil war, the rural poor were most affected. When the storm finally subsided, more than 100 health centres, as well as 512 schools and 17 per cent of all homes, had been partially or completely destroyed. Of the hardest hit, 45 per cent were children under the age of 14.

An estimated 10 per cent of children in the most affected communities suffered serious emotional trauma. Many saw family members carried off by flood waters or buried in landslides, others were separated from their families or made homeless.

Addressing their mental health needs became a priority for relief workers, who saw children traumatized by loss and languishing in refugee camps with no schooling and nothing to do. Like children affected by war, they experienced insomnia, nightmares, headaches, fear and dependent behaviour. With food shortages and the stress of family separation, violence among families increased in the camps.

Less than three weeks after the hurricane, in a refugee camp in the municipality of Polsotega, the Ministry of Health and the Ministry of Education, with support from UNICEF, launched 'The Return of Happiness' programme, which uses structured activities, including sack races, singing, puppetry, art and a trust-building exercise called 'l Lazarillo', in which children lead each other with their eyes closed. The goals were twofold: to entertain the children while preparing them for the new school year and to identify those who were withdrawn and in need of follow-up care from psychologists. As of June 1999, more than 30,000 children had been reached in villages and camps in affected areas.

weapon of war; in Sierra Leone, amputations of arms and legs were a common horrendous alternative to outright massacre. Children have been coerced or lured into armed conflicts in more than 30 countries in recent years.

In 11 other countries in the same period, the blunt instrument of economic sanctions has taken a toll easy to miss without exploding shells or body counts. In Iraq, under sanctions since 1990, the infant mortality rate in the southern and central parts of the country, where over 85 per cent of the people live, has more than doubled since 1989. Under-five mortality rates are also more than twice what they were before sanctions were imposed.

Even in the absence of war, the lives and futures of children in a number of countries are endangered by political and economic crises. Some 150 million children in the countries of Central and Eastern Europe and the former Soviet Union suffered during the region's precipitous decline in the early 1990s. Child mortality rates soared and diseases once conquered – diphtheria, polio, cholera, tuberculosis – returned.

In the East Asia and Pacific region, the economic meltdown of the late 1990s has begun to turn around for international investors and financial markets, but its effects on children will be of longer consequence.

These facts of children's lives can be so overwhelming as to paralyse anyone who might seek to make conditions better for them. That ways are found in such a world to help protect the rights of children and women – education and counselling are two – is testament to the power of the human spirit.

UNICEF/99-0717/Lemoyne

An ethnic Albanian adolescent in Pristina, who lost both legs in a landmine accident after the end of the bombing in Yugoslavia, in tears while reading a letter from her brother.

To learn under fire

As the border conflict between Eritrea and Ethiopia grinds on into its second year, the commitment to children's education remains unshaken.

"For the first time in the history of Tigray, we are trying to provide universal access to education," says Dr. Solomon Inquai, adviser to the Regional President for Social Affairs. "We see it as a source of pride that parents continue to think of education as a priority."

This is despite the fact that in the eastern, central and western zones of Tigray, 34 schools, more than half of the 58 in the region, have been destroyed or need repairs, and approximately 16,000 schoolchildren have been displaced. Supported by UNICEF, educators and officials have used an array of creative approaches to keep children learning and classrooms functioning – in shelters, under trees and, like the one in Fatsi, in caves.

To accommodate displaced children in schools in those areas not affected by the war, extra classes on weekdays and weekends are added. Some schools offer a morning and afternoon shift to make it easier for children who must work part-time for their families to attend.

In Fatsi, young Hadgu, a second grader, attends classes on an alternating schedule of mornings and afternoons with his 16-year-old sister so that each can help on the family farm. "I do my homework in the pastures while I'm tending the cattle. Some people have been hurt by the shelling, but no schoolchildren. Still, I'm scared whenever I hear it," Hadgu says.

Figure 3 Increase in number of complex emergencies

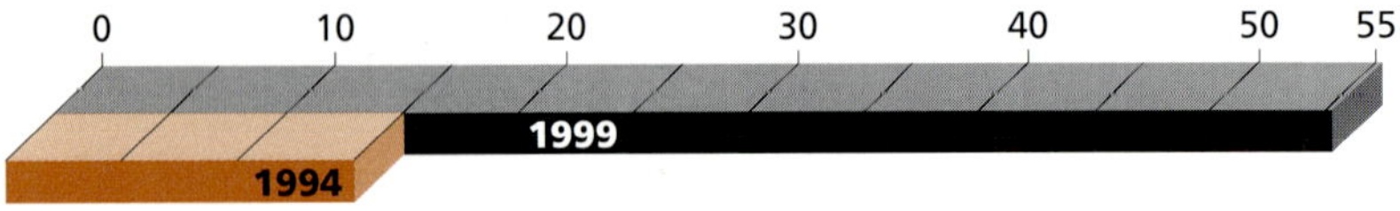

Source: UNICEF.

and women.[13] Soldiers, rebels and marauders target and slaughter children and women with impunity, while children kill other children and women other women. At times, it appears that this is an age of madness, as we witness 'ethnic cleansing' in former Yugoslavia, wanton amputations in Sierra Leone or militias on the rampage in East Timor.

In the decade since the adoption of the Convention on the Rights of the Child, more than 2 million children have been killed and more than 6 million injured or disabled in armed conflicts. Tens of thousands were victims of landmines.[14] In violation of their human rights, hundreds of thousands of children were forced into armed conflict as soldiers, sex slaves or porters. Scores of millions have been scarred psychologically by the violence they endured or witnessed at intimate range,[15] and countless others have died for lack of food or health services.

With the breakdown of many official nation-states and an unbridled international trade in weapons, the 'internal wars' of the late 20th century are arenas of chronic human insecurity and flagrant atrocities, with increasingly large populations governed and terrorized by rogue groups. In Africa alone, over 30 wars have sullied that continent since 1970, mostly within States. These accounted for more than half of all war-related deaths worldwide in 1996 and caused more than 8 million people to become refugees, returnees or displaced persons.[16]

Consider the conflicts of the past decade, among them those in Afghanistan, Angola, Bosnia and Herzegovina, the Democratic Republic of Congo, Eritrea, Ethiopia, Rwanda, Sierra Leone, Somalia, Sri Lanka and Sudan. And the recent brutality that enveloped Kosovo and East Timor. These and other flash points challenge overstretched relief and development efforts, undermine the rights of children and women and pose grave risks on a daily basis to humanitarian workers. Like the ravages of poverty, the festering conflicts of today, many masked

Figure 4 Prevalence of violence against women by an intimate male partner in any relationship

Percentage of adult women who have been physically assaulted, not including sexual abuse or rape.
Country studies are not necessarily comparable.

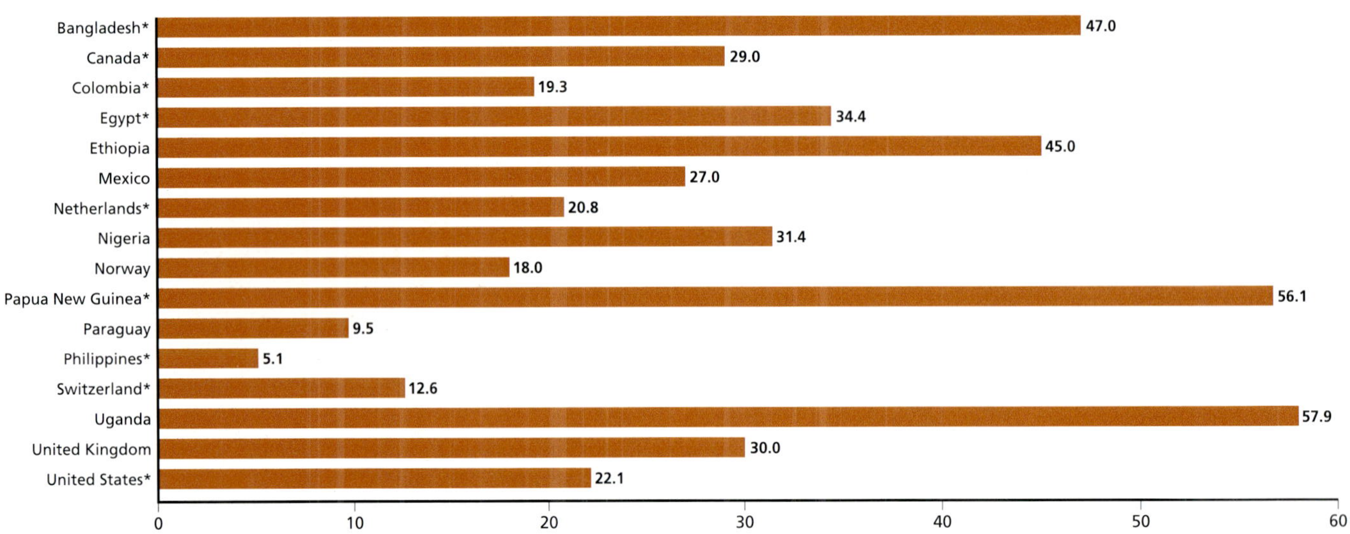

*National coverage

Source: WHO database on violence against women (1984-1998).

as 'political instability', threaten many of the remarkable achievements in health and education that governments, the international community and local citizens have laboured long decades to attain.

At the same time, there is pervasive violence in both the industrialized and developing worlds that runs through the lives of children and women – sometimes a subtle subtext, other times a pattern of explosive moments – in their families and communities, in mass media and entertainment. The incidence of violence within a family, though hidden from public sight and statistics, is almost certainly the most persistent, sparing no society or culture as it trickles down from one generation to the next, turning children reared on violence into violent adults. And in some industrialized countries, small arms and light weapons – used by children – have found their way from manufacturers to schoolrooms with tragic results.

The sustainability of conflict

What makes the ruthless conflicts that tear at the world so sustainable, apparently more durable than any solutions that have so far been devised? The fact is that poverty, protracted instability, greed and a vacuum of leadership set the stage for many of these wars and the malnutrition, maternal and child deaths, illiteracy and discrimination they spawn.

It is no accident that more than half of the world's poorest countries are embroiled in ongoing or incipient crises. These conflicts, fuelled by a mix of local territorial claims and the proliferation of light weapons, are stirred up by the insatiable hunger of outside parties for land and the natural bounty of

UNICEF/96-0620/Maillefer

A boy sifts for diamonds from a mine in the Democratic Republic of Congo.

gems, oil and, in Asia, opium. In Angola, Congo, Sierra Leone and Sudan, the landscape is thick with competing oil prospectors, gold and diamond miners and private security firms hired by prospectors and governments too weak to provide their own security.

The arms trade, indeed, has flourished since the start of this decade, as cold war stockpiles became available on the world market. The proliferation of light, inexpensive weapons has contributed to the increased use of children as soldiers and has been responsible for the vast majority of casualties in modern warfare. During a trip to southern Sudan in 1997, a UN mine assessment team found landmines from Belgium, China, former Czechoslovakia, Egypt, Iran, Israel, Italy, the former Soviet Union and the United States.[17]

Figure 5 Poverty and HIV prevalence

HIV prevalence among the 10 countries with lowest per capita GNP

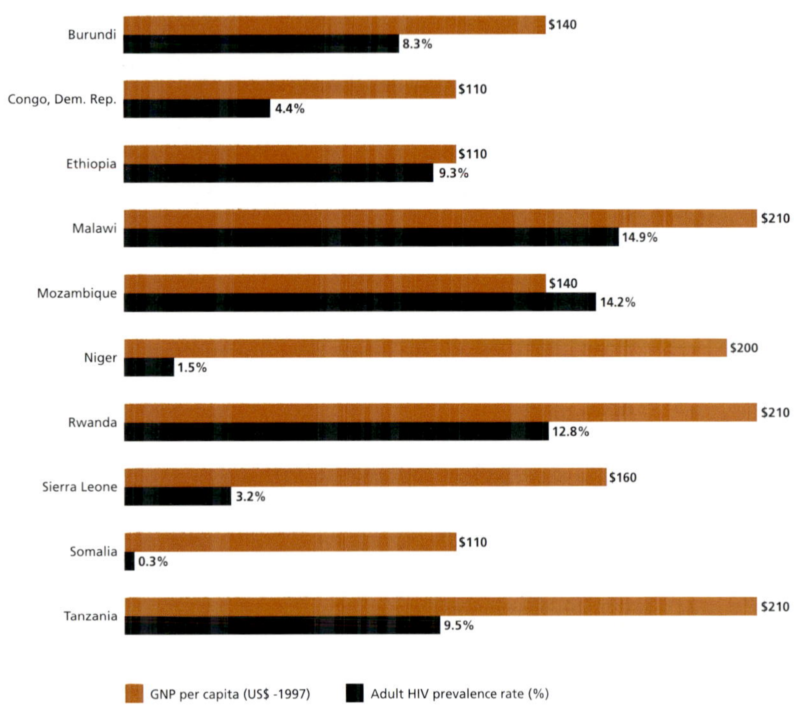

Note: A generalized HIV/AIDS epidemic exists when HIV prevalence is 5% or higher.

Sources: UNICEF, UNAIDS.

AIDS: A deathly, deadly silence

Each day 8,500 children and young people around the world are infected with HIV[18] and 2,500 women die from AIDS.[19] In 1998 alone, the number of women killed by HIV/AIDS was 900,000 – more than three times the death toll of the war in Bosnia.[20]

In Africa, the social and economic devastation caused by HIV/AIDS in the last decade is greater than the combined destruction of the continent's wars: an estimated 200,000 Africans, most of them women and children, died as a result of conflicts in 1998 while 2 million people were killed by AIDS. The pandemic wipes out families, villages, professions and age groups. From country to country, it has marched through sub-Saharan Africa where 22.5 million people now live with HIV.[21] Early in its assault the disease cut down the educated: professionals, administrators, teachers. Today, in sub-Saharan Africa as all over the world, HIV/AIDS preys on the young, poor and powerless – girls and women in particular.

While the educated have access to the knowledge needed to protect themselves from the virus, the life-saving information is not finding its way to those with little or no education. According to a study of 35 countries, the uneducated, whether men or women, were five times more likely to know nothing about the disease than were those with post-primary schooling. The uneducated were four times more likely to believe that there is no way to avoid AIDS, three times more likely not to be aware that the virus can be transmitted from mother to child, and three to four times more likely not to know that HIV-positive persons might look quite healthy.[22]

Any visitor to villages where AIDS has been an aggressive invader finds a legacy of huts deserted, fields fallow, children stunned and orphaned.[23] Equally haunting are the trauma and the long-term devastation.

PANEL 4

Zambia: Hope in the AIDS epicentre

In Zambia, where one out of five people are HIV positive, local health educators say everyone is either affected or infected by HIV/AIDS. Virtually everyone you meet has lost friends or relatives to AIDS. Some 360,000 children have lost at least one parent, most of them to AIDS. Many of the orphans exist at the mercy of friends or relatives. Life expectancy at birth in Zambia has dropped from 50 to 40 years since 1990, and child mortality rates are rising to levels not seen since the early 1970s, erasing a quarter-century of progress on children's health and welfare.

In the grip of this calamity and against sobering odds, some Zambians have chosen to live hopefully even as many struggle with their own poverty and difficult life circumstances. They brave a stigma by their association with AIDS and often are themselves discriminated against as they work to spare future generations from the ravages of this disease. Among the determined are the energetic members of the Anti-AIDS Club of Chibolya.

"Save Your Life – Learn About AIDS" proclaims a slogan on the side of the white truck as it bounces along the dirt lanes of the rambling shanty community of Chibolya, in Lusaka, the Zambian capital. Loudspeakers mounted on the truck bark in all directions, "Come hear the Anti-AIDS Club of Chibolya – performance in five minutes. Learn about AIDS – protect yourself!" Children race out of cinder block homes, jumping on the rear bumper of the truck, laughing and screaming in anticipation of the show.

The vehicle, covered in a thick coat of grey dust, stops in an open area where five young men and one woman, all dressed in green plaid pants and T-shirts, stand waiting. A crowd, numbering about 350 and including many young children, gathers in a large circle around the performers and breaks into song. The mood is festive although the message is clearly serious.

Three drummers signal the start of the performance. "Now we have come to teach you about HIV/AIDS. *Woza*! [Come!]" they sing. A teenage boy and girl sprint out and dance amid the swelling circle of young onlookers. The rapt audience roars with laughter as the dancers give way to a young man dressed in big red shoes, overalls and a funny hat. He is playing the part of a father who is scolding his teenage daughter, "You mustn't go out with so many men!"

The girl struts around the dirt ring and retorts, "That is my own business. You have old-fashioned ways. I will do as I want!" Besides, the girl tells the audience, "Where do I get the money? Because my father is not paying for my school fees."

UNICEF/99-1004/Goodman

A man from one of Zambia's Anti-AIDS Clubs delivers AIDS-prevention messages.

An older woman lectures the young actress, "These days, there are sexually transmitted diseases like HIV, so you must stop moving about the way you are doing. You must listen to your father! He is experienced with life." In the end, the girl heeds her father's advice, reappearing in a school uniform with a book bag over her shoulder, promising to take better care of herself.

After the performance, audience members crowd around the truck asking for information about AIDS and for condoms. This hunger for information is itself an accomplishment. The stigma associated with the disease means that there is a remarkable silence about AIDS in Zambia. Relatives will often say that an AIDS patient simply died of pneumonia, or tuberculosis, two of the many secondary infections that afflict AIDS patients. AIDS is sometimes referred to as 'the slimming disease', masking the true cause of the problem.

"We are making a difference," asserts Levy Kafuti, the 23-year-old coordinator of the troupe. "More people come to our performances every time. By the time kids reach puberty, they will know exactly how to protect themselves. It gives us much hope."

The Anti-AIDS Club of Chibolya, formed in 1995, is one of 1,760 such clubs in Zambia spreading AIDS-prevention messages through a variety of activities. The Chibolya Club's boys' soccer team and girls' netball team, for instance, deliver HIV/AIDS-awareness messages at their games. Performances of the 10-member drama troupe are staged in conjunction with visits of the Family Health Trust 'AIDSmobile', which distributes free condoms, advice and literature.

Poverty at the root

In another part of the city, Jayne Kunda Mwila is also working to check the deadly march of disease among young people. The 25-year-old social worker is a peer educator at the Youth-Friendly Health Service in the Kalingalinga Health Centre in Lusaka, one of 11 youth-oriented clinics in the city. The programme was launched in 1996 as a way to encourage young patients, who range from 10 to 24 years of age, to learn about their health and about AIDS. The Youth-Friendly Health Service is supported by governmental and non-governmental organizations and UNICEF, and jointly coordinated by the Family Life Movement and the Lusaka District Health Management Team.

"We don't judge the young people," Ms. Mwila explains, as adolescents queue patiently outside. Still in its pilot stage, the programme is increasingly known in Zambia and in other African countries for the supportive environment that the peer educators provide as they counsel both girls and boys about general health issues and those related to sexual and reproductive health and HIV/AIDS.

Ms. Mwila insists that the AIDS crisis is not simply a public health issue. "We can't deal with the root problem, which is poverty. If I go into a home and the only food coming in is from a sex worker, do you think that family will stop that person? I don't think so," says the health counsellor, a red AIDS ribbon adorning her black lapel. She says that the hope for turning the tide of AIDS rests with "finding a cure soon, and in reducing poverty."

The link between disease and poverty is particularly stark in Zambia, where 70,000 formal sector jobs were lost between 1991 and 1995. The country's dramatic socio-economic decline has provided fertile ground for AIDS to flourish. Young women are especially vulnerable and many succumb to the temptation of the 'sugar daddies' who linger around schools, offering money for sex.

Zambia now has one of the highest HIV infection rates in the world. Yet, resources to combat the disease are being hamstrung by foreign debt: debt servicing – amounting to $110 million in 1998 – accounts for more than the Zambian Government's health and education budgets combined.

About HIV/AIDS

- HIV/AIDS killed 510,000 children under the age of 15 in 1998.
- An estimated 1.2 million children under the age of 15 are living with HIV/AIDS.
- Young people (15 to 24 years old) make up the age group most vulnerable to HIV infection. More than 11 million are living with HIV. Five young persons are infected every minute, 7,000 every day, and, in 1998, nearly 3 million were infected with HIV.
- Nearly half of all people living with HIV/AIDS are women and girls. In many countries the infection rates are much higher among girls than boys; in some countries the rates for 15- to 19-year-old girls are 3 to 6 times higher than for boys.
- When a mother becomes debilitated by AIDS, her children are more likely to miss immunizations against childhood disease, eat fewer and less-nutritious meals and be taken out of school, especially if they are girls, to assume domestic responsibilities.
- Nearly 13 million children have been orphaned by AIDS.

Refusing to give up

People in rural Chikankata in south-eastern Zambia, with support from donors including UNICEF and the Salvation Army, have responded to the AIDS pandemic with the most powerful resource available: community. Today, Chikankata Hospital is sponsoring its first life skills workshop for children orphaned by AIDS. Wisner, a 17-year-old, listens attentively in a makeshift classroom. Posters line the walls with the lesson topics scrawled across them: Teenage sexuality. Rights of children. Assertiveness. Child abuse. Wisner, along with 19 other children in the class, has first-hand experience with these issues. He is one of 1,183 children in the five surrounding villages who have lost a mother or both parents to the disease in the last few years.

"Life is very difficult since my mother passed away in 1996," he says quietly. He lives with his grandmother, but she does not have enough money to pay his school fees. The elderly woman has lost five daughters to AIDS and now struggles to care for seven school-age grandchildren. "If I can go back to school, I can have hope," says the adolescent.

"The goal of this programme is to enhance the community's protection of orphans," explains Patrick Haachintu, coordinator of the Community-based Orphans' Programmes. He notes that orphans are often neglected or treated poorly by overburdened families, and they are frequently exploited for labour and sex. "They don't know their rights as children," says Mr. Haachintu. The workshop is part of an effort to support the orphans, which includes teaching them income-generating skills and basic agriculture. In this morning's lesson, the youths watch a video on how to resist aggressive sexual overtures from adults.

Walking through the wards at Chikankata Hospital, one sees surprisingly few patients – despite the fact that AIDS has ravaged the surrounding rural communities, killing 300 people between November 1998 and March 1999 alone. In another of its pioneering efforts, the hospital sees to it that AIDS patients and orphans are cared for in their communities, maintaining some semblance of continuity and stability in their lives. "Even if people have lost all their family members, we are encouraging them to see that other people within the community are their family," says Elvis Simamvwa, the hospital director.

In the nearby village of Ngangula, 150 villagers volunteer in the Children in Need (CHIN) programme to look after the orphans and provide health education to schoolchildren. Ngangula offers a microcosm of what is happening around Zambia: In 1996, surrounding villages, with a total population of about 4,200 people, had 231 AIDS orphans; by 1999, the number had risen to 550. In response, CHIN is trying to pay school fees for the children by running a small shop that sells basic goods. UNICEF has helped by paying to repair the school roof, which has enabled the school, in turn, to waive fees for 96 orphans.

Life for orphans in Ngangula remains difficult. Maxwell, 12, barefoot and wearing torn clothes, stands with a ragtag group of children during a school lunch break, some of the dozens of orphans at the Ngangula Basic School. "When my father was alive, I had shoes and decent clothes. Now, other children laugh at my clothes," Maxwell says shyly, as he lowers his voice and diverts his gaze when he speaks. He says he often goes the whole day without food.

A Ugandan boy, whose father died from AIDS, reads with his sister.

Byron Mwemba, the CHIN coordinator for Ngangula, is championing the cause of the village's most vulnerable from his base in a mud clinic with a cement floor. "Some guardians were harsh. They used orphans to collect wood and water and the children were overworked. Now we have educated the guardians." He says the community has provided the guardians with fertilizer so that they can grow food to feed the children, and a woman cooks lunch for the orphaned schoolchildren each day. He is trying to raise funds for a grinding mill, which would generate a small, steady income that could pay the orphans' school fees.

"You don't lose hope," asserts Mr. Simamvwa back at Chikankata Hospital. His gentle smile seems incongruous, given the magnitude of the crisis that he and his community are facing. But he insists, "This disease has taught communities a few lessons about themselves and how to live with each other." He adds, "Thinking negatively can kill you. But thinking positively can actually give you hope – and life."

Parents fall ill and waste away; children, and particularly adolescents, are often forced to drop out of school to care for their dying parents and then their orphaned siblings. Often, they lose claim to their parents' property and are shunned and ostracized by the community. Nearly 10 million of these children under the age of 15 live in Africa today,[24] their childhood forsaken and their rights to be nurtured in a family, to grow, to study and to develop to their full human potential denied them.

At times, the impact of the HIV/AIDS pandemic on children and women in this hardest hit of continents is difficult to grasp. In many countries, overall life expectancy is declining to levels last known in 1960, and even earlier.[25] Of the nine countries with the highest adult HIV prevalence, Botswana, Namibia and Zimbabwe are the most affected. Botswana, which had consistently allocated resources to basic services over the years, seemed poised for a public health breakthrough: It had been projected, in the absence of AIDS, that life expectancy would exceed the age of 69 by 2000-2005. Now, life expectancy is predicted instead to plumb new depths to 41 years by this same period.[26]

There can be little doubt that the same catastrophic combination of stigma, taboo and silence that continues to fuel the deadly epidemic in sub-Saharan Africa is repeating itself in South Asia. Since HIV/AIDS appeared in South Asia in 1986, more than 5 million people in the region have been infected with the virus, about half of them women.[27] There too, the social powerlessness of women means large numbers are being infected with HIV by their husbands. In a study of nearly 400 women attending clinics in the Indian city of Pune, nearly one fourth had a sexually transmitted infection, although 91 per cent said they had only had sex with

UNICEF/97-0073/Horner

In Thailand, a woman sick with AIDS holds her baby daughter.

their husbands; 13.6 per cent tested positive for HIV.[28]

One of the most outrageous dangers to children in South Asia is their invisibility in the HIV/AIDS pandemic. Whatever information is collected is not disaggregated to show the disease's effects on children. This makes it all the more difficult to identify those whose rights are most at risk and protect them from further harm.

Meanwhile, around the globe, AIDS is tightening the web of poverty and chronic insecurity in many societies, especially those burdened by heavy national debt. The stress on their limited social services is unbearable. Food production declines, leading to poorer nutrition and more vulnerability to illness. Lower education budgets mean less schooling for boys and girls, who later are less able to defend themselves against violence and abuse.

* * * * *

The obstacles to realizing the rights of children in the 21st century are daunting, it is true. But it is in the significant achievements of the last decades, many in the face of considerable constraints, that hope for the future is found: improvements in child survival rates and the nutritional status of children, strengthened systems of basic education and health services, improved conditions for water and sanitation.

It is from these accomplishments and from the vision and language of possibility that surround the 2001 meeting of global leadership that optimism springs: The barriers to all children everywhere realizing their rights can and will be broken within a single generation.

A Lebanese girl stands at the doorway of her home.

In a single generation

The principles of the Convention on the Rights of the Child provide the world with a vision of what the 21st century could bring – children and adolescents living in stable and nurturing homes and communities where, with adult guidance and protection, they have ample opportunities to develop the fulness of their strengths and talents and where their human rights are respected.

With this guiding vision, much can be done to break the intergenerational patterns of poverty, war, HIV/AIDS and discrimination that are robbing children of their rights and stripping countries of their progress. Significant work continues to be done within and across nations: The global efforts of UNAIDS, for instance, to prevent the transmission of HIV at the same time as it works towards mitigating the consequences of this apocalyptic pandemic. The Office of the United Nations High Commissioner for Refugees (UNHCR) has taken particular care in addressing the rights and needs of refugee children and adolescents as it leads the coordinated response to emergencies, with partners such as UNICEF and the World Food Programme. And in the last half of this decade, the International Monetary Fund and the World Bank worked together, as they have since 1944, to contain the Asian financial crisis, to assist the Russian Federation in its economic transitions and to reduce the debts carried by the majority of the poor countries in the world.

A mother talks to her baby son while they wait at a neighbourhood health clinic in Shanghai (China).

Success will depend as it always has on political commitment and additional resources at all levels. And success will also depend on the visionary leaders who will meet in 2001, ready to move forward with urgency and passion, determined to make lives better for children within the next generation.

Poverty does *not* always have to be with us

The patterns of poverty that are passed from one generation to the next can and will be broken when the poor have the means and opportunity to be healthy and well-nourished enough, and educated and skilled enough, to fully participate in the decisions that affect their lives. Because such needs are most efficiently met through public services, universal access to an integrated set of basic social services is one of the most effective ways of reducing poverty in any society. Access to basic health, education, family planning and water and sanitation services is what makes sustained and stable economic progress possible, helps people achieve greater productivity and forms an especially crucial buffer for children and women in difficult times.

The services, in light of their great benefits and certainly in comparison with most weapons of destruction, are modestly priced. By redirecting $70 billion to $80 billion a year in a global economy that is more than $30 trillion, the world could ensure access to the basics for everyone. The 20/20 Initiative is one way to do it.

An idea championed by then UNICEF Executive Director, James P. Grant, 20/20 was launched at the 1994 International Conference on Population and Development, held in Cairo, and pursued the following year at the World Summit for Social Development, convened in Copenhagen. It builds upon the Convention's mutual obligations for both rich countries and poor to come up with adequate resources for basic social services for human development. The Initiative suggests as a guiding principle that developing countries commit 20 per cent of their budget and donor countries 20 per cent of their official development assistance (ODA) to build and buttress these services.

ODA, however, has declined alarmingly in recent years, jeopardizing resources and creating strains on development goals. It dropped 21 per cent between 1992 and 1997, and among the leading industrialized countries, it dropped almost 30 per cent in the same time. Given the fact that the GNP in these countries jumped by almost 30 per cent, the retreat from assistance seems particularly egregious.

Figure 6 Growing wealth and declining ODA

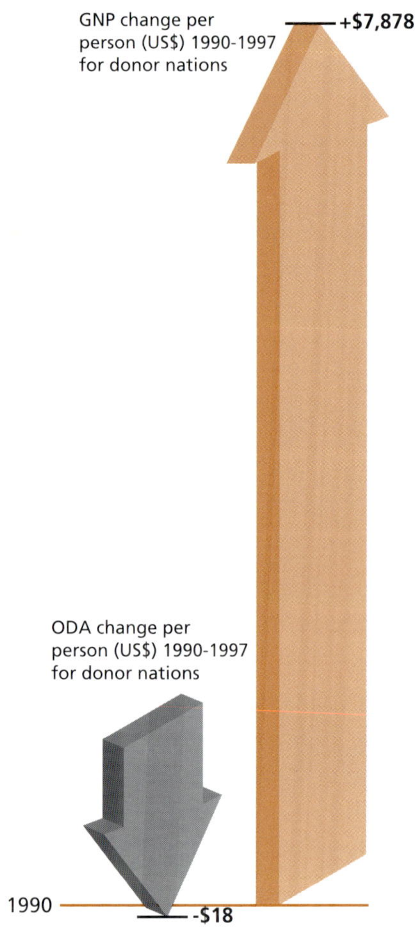

Sources: UNICEF, *The Progress of Nations 1999*; UNDP, *Human Development Report 1999* and *Human Development Report 1993*.

But governments in the developing world must answer as well for their budget decisions. Of 27 developing countries recently surveyed, only 5 – Belize, Burkina Faso, Namibia, Niger and Uganda – allocate virtually 20 per cent of their budgets to basic social services. Most governments spend only about 13 per cent of their budgets this way, significantly short of what is needed.

It is crucial for people on every continent to speak out against such uninformed priorities and misdirection of resources, as did Archbishop Desmond Tutu, when he criticized South Africa's plan to buy $5 billion worth of fighter aircraft, corvettes, helicopters and submarines from Canada, France, Germany, Sweden and the United Kingdom: "*Our country needs teachers and books, clean water and clinics. Billions spent on fighter aircraft should be spent on the upliftment of our people.*"[1]

Of course, some responsibility for the failure to meet fundamental obligations to children needs to be laid at the door of international creditors and those rich nations that have done little to ease the debt burden that drains the national resources of indebted countries. The rights of children throughout the world are not likely to be realized as long as governments remain trapped in debt bondage. In 1996-1997, for example, 4 per cent of Cameroon's central spending went towards basic social services while 36 per cent went towards debt service. In the United Republic of Tanzania, four times more is spent in repaying debt than on primary education, and nine times more than on basic health.

There is a growing international consensus to reduce the crippling external debts of the poorest countries in order to enable those governments to fulfil the rights of their citizens to basic health, nutrition and education services. And heads of the leading industrialized nations took a step in that direction when, at their May 1999 meeting in Cologne (Germany), they agreed to reduce the debts carried by the 41 most heavily indebted poor countries. More recently, IMF has proposed a plan to cancel $27 billion of the more than $220 billion owed, freeing that amount for investment in basic social services. Both are promising overtures that are still to be played through.[2]

Finally, efforts are needed to regulate the powerful forces of globalization without which it will continue to serve the expansion needs of global markets at the expense of equity between and within nations. As a result, the poor and vulnerable in the world will reap increasingly fewer benefits, leading to their further marginalization and social exclusion.

UNDP's *Human Development Report 1999* calls for stronger governance at the local, national, regional and global levels in order to ensure that globalization works for the benefit of people.[3] In keeping with the intent of article 3 of the Convention on the Rights of the Child, any attempts to regulate globalization should address the best interests of children through a 'child impact analysis'.[4] Such an analysis would review any proposals for their impact on children, taking into consideration, for example, whether changes in economic policies protect the rights of children to education and health services or whether changes in labour policies specifically address the issue of child workers.

All wars are wars against children[5]

The UNICEF 1996 Anti-war Agenda stated: "*Children need be the victims of war only if there is no will to prevent it. Experiences in dozens of conflicts confirm that extraordinary actions have been taken and can be taken to protect and provide for children.*"[6]

Since that time a number of significant measures have helped ensure higher visibility and greater protection of children, even as conflicts and atrocities seem to build.[7] Recommended in 1996 by Graça Machel, expert of the United Nations Secretary-General, a programme of humanitarian mine clearance, mine awareness aimed at women and children, and child-centred rehabilitation has become the standard in conflicts around the world.[8] There are ongoing international efforts supporting an Optional Protocol to the Convention on the Rights of the Child that would raise the minimum age for children's recruitment into armed forces and participation in armed conflict from 15 to

UNICEF/94-0286/Press

Rwandan children line up for water in a refugee camp near the town of Goma.

18 years. In 1997, 123 nations signed the Convention on the Prohibition of the Use, Stockpiling, Production and Transfer of Anti-Personnel Mines, and on Their Destruction. And in 1998, the International Criminal Court, another mechanism for international accountability, was accorded the authority to prosecute as war criminals those conscripting and using children under 18 in hostilities.

The humanitarian tradition of attempting to protect children from the gravest harm in armed conflict has other proud consequences. For nearly two decades, UNICEF has built a peace and security agenda on its belief that children – whether in their homes, in the streets, in their schools or in camps for the displaced – should be respected by all as a 'zone of peace', a concept first advanced to UNICEF by the distinguished Swedish humanitarian, the late Nils Thedin. It is a commitment recently reaffirmed by the United Nations Secretary-General.[9] Ceasefires have been negotiated for 'days of tranquillity' and 'corridors of peace' to bring food and vaccines to children trapped in wars, including those in Afghanistan, El Salvador, Lebanon, Sudan and Uganda, ground-breaking efforts that saved millions of children from malnutrition and disease. Other heroic efforts have been routinely made in active war zones, including quickly restoring education in order to help children regain some sense of normalcy and security.

Another little-known but promising initiative began in response to the overlapping crises of war and famine that decimated life in southern Sudan for so many years. Linked to Operation Lifeline Sudan, the remarkable effort established a set of humanitarian principles as Ground Rules – new standards by which combatants agreed to protect the rights of children.

The Convention on the Rights of the Child was the perfect instrument for the Ground Rules, owing to its constellation of human rights and humanitarian principles, and the fact that nearly 50 per cent of the population in southern Sudan was under the age of 18. Even military commanders who spurned discussions about human rights were willing to talk about the well-being of children. Under the Rules, local communities and military commanders were to be actively engaged in monitoring and addressing the acute problems in child health, education and forced military recruitment that occur during war.

It is also crucial that world leaders, who have been willing to bear the expense of militarization, not shrink from the costs of peace and demobilization.

The Ground Rules were signed in 1995 after months of intensive negotiations with all parties, a vital development in a situation like that in Sudan, where 4 million civilians lived in areas under rebel control. UNICEF followed up with an exhaustive campaign carried to the most remote communities, gathering under trees and in thatch huts with elders, health workers and military representatives to disseminate information about the Convention on the Rights of the Child and to train people in human rights and humanitarian principles. The goal was to identify the points in common between prevailing traditional values and international standards prohibiting war crimes and the abuse of children and women. This process revealed the frequent convergence between the Convention's principles and village traditions.

It will be the work of historians to determine how great and lasting an impact this effort will have but through it, thousands of people learned of rights they did not know they had, and the military significantly shifted its targets away from schools and other places where children might have been. The idea has set a precedent in introducing the use of international human rights standards by entities other than governments and offers valuable lessons as a prototype for working in other conflict settings.

Because the immediate crises caused by war are dramatic and pressing, they can obscure longer-term needs. Helping children and communities cope with the traumas and tensions that continue after fighting subsides is vital. Post-conflict communities, beset with poverty and high unemployment, must be prepared in advance to receive demobilized soldiers, and programmes for children must include measures such as foster care to prevent children from being dragged off again by armed forces. Girls, who were forced to serve as 'wives' and servants to the combatants, require especially vigilant care to ensure that they are not shunned or driven into further sexual exploitation, prostitution and the risk of HIV/AIDS.

It is also crucial that world leaders, who have been willing to bear the expense of militarization, not shrink from the costs of peace and demobilization. Experience in countries such as Angola, Liberia, Mozambique and Sierra Leone has taught us that without a long-term commitment to the retraining and reintegration of combatants, post-conflict societies risk careening into anarchy and crime.

PANEL 5

Seeds of peace: Young people in Colombia

The rural town of Aguachica Cesar in eastern Colombia has been in the crossfire of conflict between guerrillas, the paramilitaries and the Colombian army in recent years. In 1996, Juan Elias Uribe, then a 14-year-old boy who lived there, became convinced nevertheless that peace was possible and that young people could help bring great changes to his country.

Juan Elias is one of many teenagers in Colombia and thousands around the world who bring the idealism and intense energy of their adolescent years to a cause. Juan Elias's cause was peace. The more he talked publicly about peace in his country, the more certain he became that it could be had.

His father, a dentist and a respected member of the community who often led public health campaigns in poor areas of the town, was proud of his son's peacemaking efforts and let it be known. One morning, Señor Uribe was in his office with his 19-year-old niece, who hoped to become a doctor one day. Three men strode into the dentist's office and barged into the exam rooms. Gunshots rang out and the men exited quickly. Señor Uribe and his niece were found lying in a pool of blood, and both died several hours later.

Murders are common in Aguachica and killers are rarely caught. But this one was different – Señor Uribe was a popular public figure. Community members came forward to identify the killers, who were arrested and jailed for two years but never brought to trial. "They've never told us why they did it," a saddened Juan Elias says of his father's assailants. "Sometimes people in Aguachica don't talk about why things happen."

Beginnings of a movement

Since 1992, the number of political homicides in Colombia has jumped by more than a third, from about 4,400 people in 1992 to more than 6,000 people killed in 1997. Shockingly, the murder of children has also soared: In 1996, 4,322 children were killed, a 40 per cent rise in just two years.

War in Colombia began a half-century ago with *La Violencia*, a brutal struggle between the two main political parties that lasted 16 years and in which 300,000 people lost their lives. Today, half the country is controlled by two guerrilla armies, the Revolutionary Armed Forces of Colombia (FARC) and the National Liberation Army (ELN), which have a combined force of about 20,000 combatants. There are also believed to be about 8,000 individuals organized in paramilitary groups under the United Self-Defense Force of Colombia (ACU).

In Colombia, two adolescent boys from the Children's Movement for Peace join armed soldiers in a group handshake.

In the last decade alone, the war in Colombia has forced more than 1 million people – about 1 in every 37 Colombians – from their homes. Most of the displaced come from poor rural communities, and a disproportionate number are indigenous or Afro-Colombian. Over 70 per cent of the displaced are women and children who flee to the cities and are then plunged into abject poverty. Children are the main victims of the war and are among the chief perpetrators of violence, as more than 2,000 of them under the age of 15 have been recruited into guerrilla and paramilitary organizations.

Against this grim backdrop, the young people of Colombia decided to do what few dare to do: Work for peace.

PANEL

5

In 1996, Graça Machel, an expert appointed by the Secretary-General of the United Nations, completed a global study on thc 'Impact of Armed Conflict on Children'. Her investigation took her to Colombia, where she visited Apartadó, a town in the heart of the war-torn Uraba region where guerrillas had been fighting for more than 30 years. Farliz Calle, the 17-year-old daughter of a banana plantation worker, was president of the student council at the local high school and remembers the visit. "For the first time," recounts Farliz, gesturing animatedly to emphasize her message, "the authorities asked children to think in a constructive way about what was happening to us, about the violence and what we wanted to do about it."

The young people of Uraba had a lot to say: 5,000 of them, from more than a dozen townships in the area, wrote stories, poems and letters, painted pictures and constructed sculptures to create a grand exhibition for Ms. Machel. The student council also drew up a Declaration for the Children of Apartadó, which Farliz presented to Ms. Machel. The Declaration asserted, "We ask the warring factions for peace in our homes, for them not to make orphans of children, to allow us to play freely in the streets and for no harm to come to our small brothers and sisters...." Farliz and the other children demanded a right to play a more active role in solving problems in the community "so that our children do not suffer as we have."

The story might have ended there, but the students pressed their case. Embracing the Colombian Constitution, which had been rewritten in 1991 with guarantees for citizens to participate in their democracy, the students claimed a right to form a 'local government of children'. With the blessing of her embattled municipality, Farliz was elected the first 'child mayor' of Apartadó. This experience was to change her forever.

"To have peace you need to solve poverty, and children cannot do that," says Farliz, bubbling with energy and enthusiasm, "but we found other things." The group named themselves the Children's Movement for Peace in Apartadó, and they began organizing 'peace carnivals' for children from poor communities. They felt that finding ways for children to have fun was itself a way of making peace.

After Ms. Machel's visit, UNICEF invited the children and adolescents from Apartadó to take part in a workshop where young people from all around Colombia, including Juan Elias, came together to describe how violence was affecting them and to talk about how they could work for peace. "I realized that we in Apartadó were not alone," recalls Farliz. Out of this conference was born the Children's Movement for Peace.

The first goal of the Movement was to organize 500,000 youths to vote in a special referendum – the Children's Mandate for Peace and Rights. UNICEF provided funding and technical support for REDEPAZ (the National Network of Peace Initiatives) to help organize the voting, with assistance from the national Government. Many other groups became involved, including religious and children's organizations, the Catholic Church, the Colombian Red Cross, the Colombian Scouts and the YMCA. The intention was to empower the young people of Colombia as peacemakers and encourage the nation to listen to their voices.

About adolescents

- More than 1 billion people of the six billion in the world are between the ages of 10 and 19.
- Working with adolescents provides a unique opportunity to break a number of vicious, intergenerational cycles, such as gender discrimination, violence and poverty.
- Adolescents have a profound and direct influence on the next generation because of their roles as older siblings, heads of households, parents and members of civil society.
- They are filled with fresh ideas and know how we can best reach them with relevant interventions; they represent one of any society's most underutilized resources.
- Ensuring that teenagers participate in their communities and civil society is fundamental to protecting their right to development and to ensuring that their rights are protected and met.
- Providing adolescents with skills, information, support and services increases their capabilities to avoid or overcome many of the problems they are likely to encounter, such as violence, accidents, substance abuse and unwanted or unsafe sex.
- Adolescents are not a homogeneous group; they live in different circumstances and have varying needs. Recognizing their differences and responding to them will help ensure the rights of all adolescents – including those who are among the disadvantaged.

What happened next stunned the country: Six months after the plan was conceived, nearly 3 million children and adolescents turned out – roughly one third of the total population between the ages of 7 and 18. In many municipalities, the voter turnout was over 90 per cent. Of the dozen rights they could vote for, two thirds of the young voters chose the rights to survival, peace, family and freedom from abuse.

Several months following the election, Farliz and Juan Elias presided at a summit meeting with representatives from every organization that had supported the Mandate. Over three days, young Colombians aged 7 through 16 shared their ideas about what they should do in the name of peace and how young people could participate in a global peace process.

On 7 December 1996, Juan Elias Uribe – just a few months after his father's murder – presented the Declaration of the Children's Summit for Peace and Rights to Colombian President Ernesto Samper. Juan Elias declared, "We hope that you, Mr. President, and all adults in this country will look for all practical and feasible means to do away with violence and war, so that the children of Colombia will no longer be badly treated."

Peace: A universal cause

The Children's Movement for Peace inspired a war-weary and despairing nation to redouble efforts to end violence. The fragmented Colombian peace movement unified, and in January 1997, REDEPAZ, UNICEF and the anti-kidnapping organization País Libre announced that a Mandate for Peace, Life and Liberty would be placed before the Colombian people that October, during the regional elections. One hundred 'peace points' were established around the country where local governments and NGOs publicized and explained the Mandate. Young children and teenagers continued to feature prominently in the campaign.

One year after the children's election, on 26 October 1997, more than 10 million adults went to the polls – over twice the turnout of previous elections. Their votes expressed their desire for an end to the war and to atrocities and to involving children under 18 in warfare.

The vote for the Mandate was symbolic but the political impact was real. Warring factions were finally denied their claim to represent 'the people', since 10 million citizens had overwhelmingly voted for peace. The Mandate succeeded in making peace the central focus of the 1998 presidential campaign. President Andres Pastrana took office in August 1998 wearing a green ribbon on his lapel, the symbol of the Citizen's Mandate for Peace, Life and Liberty.

José Ramos-Horta, winner of the 1996 Nobel Peace Prize for his efforts to win independence for East Timor, visited Colombia in 1997 and met Farliz Calle, Juan Elias Uribe and other participants in the Children's Movement for Peace. He was so struck by the tenacity and vision of the young people that he nominated them for the 1998 Nobel Peace Prize. "The process initiated in Colombia has a chance to mobilize people and the world into a potent force for peace," declared Mr. Ramos-Horta, surrounded by a group of children. "The cause they represent," he said, motioning to the young faces around him, "is not only a Colombian cause. It is a universal cause."

Once viewed only as the victims of war, children are now seen as the purveyors of peace. Leaders of the Children's Movement for Peace, including Farliz Calle and Juan Elias Uribe, travelled to New York to visit the United Nations and, joined by 14-year-old Mayerly Sanchez, visited The Hague in the Netherlands to discuss their peacemaking strategies with children from other nations.

The emblem for the Children's Mandate for Peace in Colombia, 'hands' appeared all over the country on buttons, decals, flyers, walls and television screens.

For Juan Elias Uribe, the tragic death of his father inspired him to work harder for peace: "My father's death hit me very hard," he says. "I thought that all the work I was doing for peace was worth nothing, because it had not saved him.... In the end, my father's death gave me a more realistic attitude towards peace. I realized that if they did not stop me when my father was alive, they could do nothing to stop me now."

Mayerly Sanchez explains, "Children have a special gift for convincing people about the truth of what is happening. People never used to care about the war unless they were directly affected by it. But when children talk about pain and sorrow, we make adults feel the pain as if it was their own. Children are the seed of the new Colombia. We are the seeds that will stop the war."

HIV/AIDS will *not* have its way

Faced with the huge obstacle that HIV/AIDS places in the way of children's right to survive and develop, a truly global alliance for children has a rare opportunity – one missing from many other crises facing humanity. It can help prevent HIV/AIDS from spreading with a full-scale campaign to educate all people – adolescents and youth in particular – in how to break the patterns of discrimination and coercion that put them at risk.

The world has little valid excuse for not embarking on a strategy that is known to stop the spread of the virus: relevant information that is readily available, educational and health services that are accessible and cater to adolescents, and the direct involvement of young people in their own health, development and protection. Nor has the world an excuse for failing to undertake the specific actions recognized as crucial: teaching prevention to young people and teaching mothers how to reduce mother-to-child transmission, providing care and support to orphans and children affected by HIV/AIDS, and providing care and support to those AIDS workers and volunteers who are themselves HIV positive.

There are more than 10 million AIDS orphans living in Africa. This 12-year-old Ugandan girl lives with her elder sister since their mother died of the disease.

UNICEF/99-0307/Pirozzi

But no strategy or plan of action can prevent the spread of the disease by focusing only on personal behaviour. A range of measures, including testing, counselling, drug treatments and condom distribution, are needed, as is further research for vaccines and more affordable drug therapies and the identification of the best practices for reducing mother-to-child transmission of the virus. Counselling and social services are also needed to protect infants from infection and to support their HIV-positive mothers. And people and resources are crucial to provide compassionate care to those sick and dying from the disease and those children, immediate witnesses to its devastation, left orphaned.

Tragically, there is no indication that the resources needed will be forthcoming. If the international funds for poverty reduction have been a disgrace over this decade, the outlays to fight the global HIV/AIDS pandemic are an outrage. In 1996 and 1997, donor nations gave an estimated $350 million each year to combat HIV/AIDS.[10] In comparison, during the Asian financial crisis, IMF, the World Bank and rich countries gave $60 billion to bail out the Republic of Korea. And in 1999, the cost of NATO's military operation in Kosovo and of rebuilding the shattered country of Yugoslavia is an estimated $40 billion and growing.[11]

International and national leaders faltered when they did not respond as swiftly and forcefully to the HIV/AIDS crisis in Africa as they could have 15 years ago. They now have a rare second chance to marshal their resources to block the ongoing spread in Africa and similar outbreaks in other regions of the globe. What was indefensible before would be unconscionable today.

Within a single generation: The global agenda

There is renewed fervency on behalf of children as the 21st century begins, a clearer sense of what has to be done to promote and protect their rights and a surer sense that whatever needs to be done will be done. What children and all people need is well known: a world where rights are secure and people can thrive without injustice, disease and untenable poverty.

Research and practice have revealed that opportunities present themselves during early childhood, the primary school and adolescent years that are unmatched in their potential for beneficial change. Support and interventions at these points hold enormous promise for helping to break the intergenerational cycles that threaten children and women. And they present the exciting possibility of breaking the cycles within a single generation.

Early childhood care

Science now tells us that optimal neural development in a child, which affects physical, mental and cognitive development, depends on the good nutrition and loving stimulation the child receives during the first months and years of life. Research also clearly illustrates the powerfully positive effects of the bonding and interaction between infants and young children and their parents and caregivers on all aspects of the child's survival, growth and develop-

Figure 7 **Money spent on HIV/AIDS (1996 – US$)**

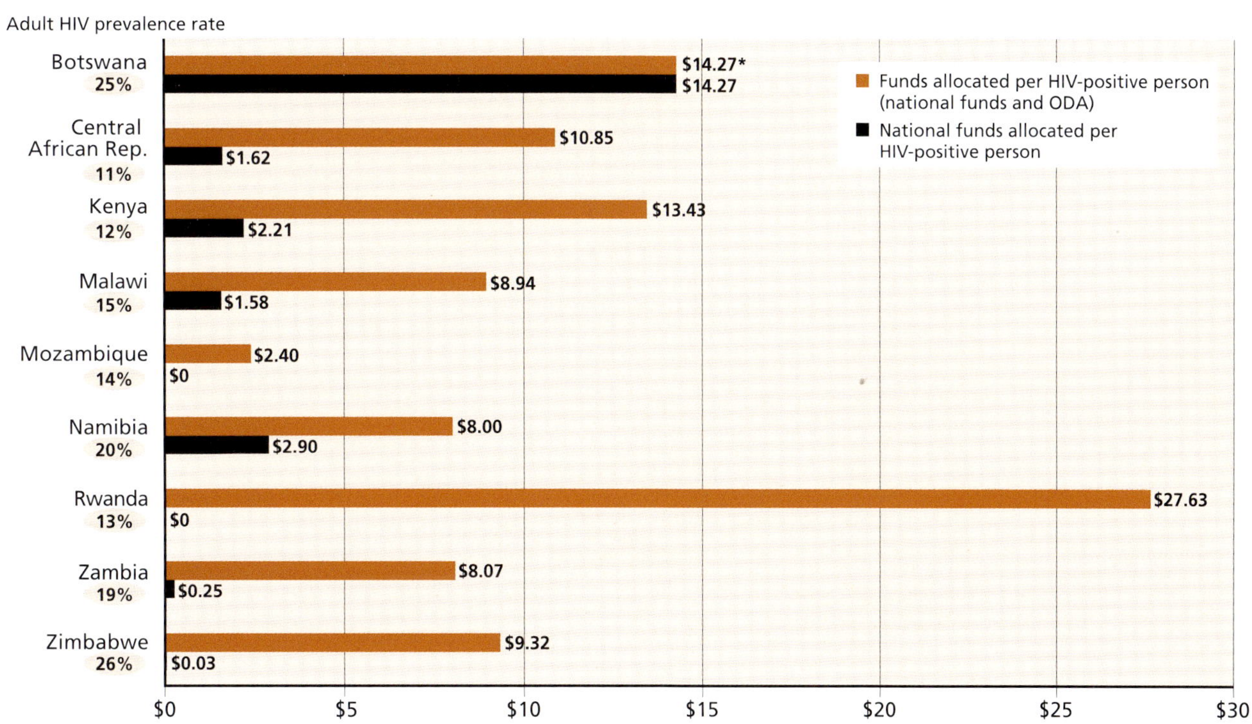

*No ODA funds for HIV/AIDS

Source: UNAIDS and Harvard School of Public Health, *Level and flow of national and international resources for the response to HIV/AIDS, 1996-1997.*

ment. On the negative side, it demonstrates that poor nutrition may trigger a downward spiral for the child as malnourished infants, lacking energy, appetite and curiosity, may be less able than healthy babies to elicit their caregiver's attention and affection.

The long-term benefits of good prenatal care and breastfeeding, and especially the rich effects of talking and playing with infants from their earliest days, are commonly acknowledged. Communities and governments are increasingly committed to the idea that the best way to care for children is to ensure their access to integrated health and social services based in the community, in which the child and family are the focus.

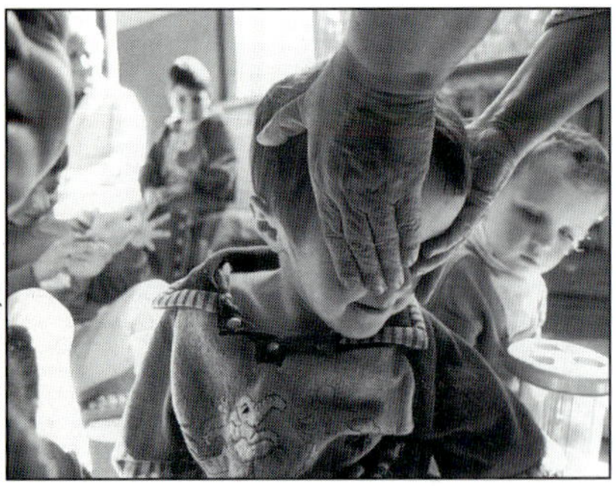

UNICEF/97-0611/Lemoyne

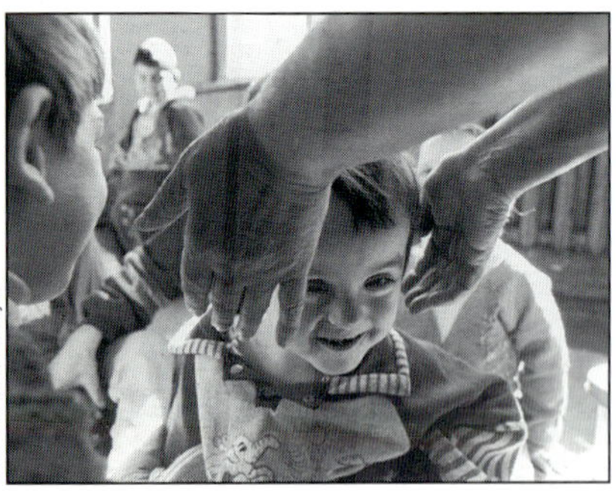

UNICEF/97-0612/Lemoyne

A health worker playfully covers the eyes of a boy with her hands in a village near Tbilisi (Georgia).

These ideas are catching fire in communities around the world. In many of these settings, parents and local health, nutrition and education workers have embraced a broad perspective on children's well-being. Much of this work takes place without fanfare, but, every day, significant changes in consciousness and practice are occurring somewhere.

In the Lao People's Democratic Republic, the Lao Women's Union on the Early Childhood and Family Development Project is a village-based community initiative in which traditional caregivers are taught about health, nutrition and the value of play and child-to-child activities. This vital training, provided both in centres and in the home, is a core feature of many other programmes in countries that include Jamaica, Nepal, Sri Lanka and Turkey.

The Community Childcare Project in Malawi is another pioneering effort integrating early childhood care with play in 216 community-based centres. Families attend the centres where they receive training in nutrition and learn about opportunities for generating income. In addition, they receive play and teaching materials and tools for community gardens. There has also been a focus on broader issues of childcare sparked by widespread concerns about the situation of children orphaned by HIV/AIDS in the country.

Communities such as these are demonstrating that early, low-cost interventions can both help secure children's rights and save millions of dollars in later costs to society.

Quality education

The ability to claim and enjoy the rights of an informed and responsible citizen rests squarely upon a child's access to a good basic education. A quality education – one that encourages children's participation and critical thinking and is infused with the values of peace and human dignity – has the power to transform societies in a single generation. Furthermore, the fulfilment of a child's right to education offers protection from a multitude of hazards, such as a life consigned to poverty, bonded labour in agriculture or industry, domestic labour, commercial sexual exploitation or recruitment into armed conflict.

While the majority of the world's children are attending school, more than 130 million are not. Reasons and excuses for this failure abound: tuition and other fees overwhelm family incomes; teachers are poorly trained; and curricula are dull and irrelevant to children – and in this regard the industrialized countries are not spared. For girls in certain cultures, the lack of separate facilities, primarily or exclusively male teaching staff and the belief that girls need little education to be wives and mothers all keep them from getting a solid basic education.

The yearning and reverence for education, however, run deep in societies around the world. Thousands of communities have devised ingenious ways to improve education

PANEL 6

The education age, past due

The sights and sounds of learning are unmistakable and unforgettable. Children's voices swell and subside animatedly, as the teacher guides, encourages and supports the questioning and discussion, drawing everyone in and inviting their participation. Faces are intent, minds engaged, reticence overcome and equality encouraged. Ideas are shared and opinions and differences are respected.

A good school releases more energy than any laboratory with all its chemical and physical transformations. Education – more than any other single initiative – has the capacity to foster development, awaken talents, empower people and protect their rights. Investing in education is the surest, most direct way a country can promote its own economic and social welfare and lay the foundation for a democratic society.

Yet for far too few children is school as exciting and energizing as it could and should be. And millions more have no chance to attend any school at all: worldwide, more than 130 million school-age children are out of class. So while steam and atomic energy have lent their names to eras of human advance, the powerful age of education has yet to dawn in much of the world.

The best hope for garnering these benefits and ushering in the long-delayed age of education is child-friendly schools. Gaining momentum since the World Conference on Education for All, held in Jomtien (Thailand) in 1990, the child-friendly school movement is driven by the challenge of enrolling all children in primary school, matched by that of keeping them there. Improving the quality of education is crucial if the relentless economic, social and cultural pressures to drop out are to be resisted. This is particularly true for girls, who represent nearly 60 per cent of all children not enrolled in school, in violation of their right to education and a loss of talent and capacity that no society can long afford.

Girl-friendly = child-friendly

One prime gauge of educational quality is how narrow the classroom gender gap is. A school is truly child-friendly when both girls and boys find it a safe, welcoming and healthful environment, centred on the rights of the child, where teachers demonstrate respect for those rights and where students discover that education is not only relevant to their lives but also a source of joy.

UNICEF/96-0528/Noorani

Two girls share a textbook in a multi-grade public school in Davao, on the island of Mindanao (Philippines).

Slowly – some may say painfully so – the gender gap in primary education is narrowing, especially in sub-Saharan Africa, the Middle East and North Africa and South Asia – regions where it has historically been the widest. Persistence and creativity have brought this vital change, through measures such as the African Girls' Education Initiative, which UNICEF helped launch in 1994. With its support, for example, more girls are in school throughout Zimbabwe thanks to community discussion groups on gender issues and life skills workshops that are helping break patterns of gender imbalance and inequity.

In the Islamic Republic of Iran, it is high-level political commitment, backed with adequate resources, that is improving gender parity in primary schools: Since 1986, the primary school enrolment rate of girls has climbed from

80 per cent to 96 per cent nationally. Even in rural areas – where enrolment rates are lowest for all children – girls' enrolment rate has gone from 60 per cent to 80 per cent in the past five years.

More heartening is the fact that nearly 95 per cent of girls who enrol in primary school complete this level of education. And a new milestone was reached in 1999 when, for the first time, girls comprised 52 per cent of the students accepted into Iran's public universities.

Golnar Mehran, a professor of education in Teheran, credits government policies, especially since 1985, with the increases. One simple but highly effective strategy has been the training of more women teachers, a vital measure given Iranian social and cultural views on the segregation of the sexes. Many families are reluctant to send their daughters to schools with male teachers, and in fact all schooling up to the university level is separate for boys and girls. Now, with more women teachers, girls have more role models, and schools have become less threatening for both parents and students. Education officials have also sought to locate schools closer to communities to reduce the distances girls must travel.

More changes are needed, though, if schools are to become fully girl-friendly. These will entail revisions in texts and curricula so that they no longer stereotype girls and changes in teaching methods so that girls are encouraged to think critically and act independently. Their physical safety and security also must be ensured, and facilities must be built to meet their need for personal privacy.

Other, more resistant barriers to girls' full participation in education remain. A survey in three Iranian provinces found that 25 per cent of those families whose daughters do not attend school believe that education is irrelevant for girls in their future roles as wives and mothers. Another 34 per cent said that poverty kept their daughters at home, because while education is compulsory and free through high school, there are always costs for supplies and uniforms – and thus daughters are likely to be kept at home so that sons can attend.

Nevertheless, Iran's achievements are impressive, especially the changes in girls' own thinking. Says Professor Mehran, "When we ask them what they want for their future they say, 'I want to work, but if I don't, I want to be educated.'"

About education

- Free access to a quality primary education is the right of every child without exception.
- The State is accountable and all of society is responsible to ensure that the right to education be realized for all children and all adolescents.
- For the child's right to education to be fully realized, strong links must be maintained among service providers in education, health, nutrition, hygiene and sanitation, and child protection.
- Education systems and programmes must be designed with the best interests of the child and adolescent foremost. They must:
    - be healthy for children and adolescents;
    - protect all children and all adolescents;
    - assure gender equity in access and quality;
    - involve families and communities;
    - include family literacy programmes and parent and caregiver education in early childhood care;
    - be unified and comprehensive, diverse and flexible;
    - be efficiently managed and equitably financed;
    - use both formal and non-formal pedagogies;
    - assure that all students graduate with the essential skills, knowledge and values to succeed; and
    - use information and communication technologies to reduce disparities in access and quality.

The multiplication factor

The child-friendly schools initiative has taken off in earnest in the Philippines. The aim is to stem student attrition in a country where primary school enrolment rates are high for both boys and girls – 97 per cent and 96 per cent, respectively – but on average only 70 per cent of children will reach the milestone of fifth grade.

Poverty and geography conspire to thwart even the most committed students in the rugged mountainous terrain of rural areas, where children must trek to and from distant schoolhouses, sometimes for hours. And, while education is free and compulsory through the elementary grades in the Philippines, the cost of books and supplies can strain a poor family's limited budget. Even in urban areas, where access to schools is easier, the lure of the streets or the need to earn income for the family leads many children to drop out of school.

The Philippine child-friendly schools initiative was launched by the Government and UNICEF in 1999 to counterbalance these factors, and it has already earned the enthusiastic support of teachers, administrators, parents and local officials. The welcome has been so warm that what started out as 24 multigrade model schools in 12 provinces has now mushroomed to 120 schools in 20 provinces and five cities. The child-friendly schools are scheduled to open for the school year in June 2000.

The Philippine approach has much in common with the Child-Friendly Schools Programme in Thailand, which began in 1998, supported by Save the Children (USA), UNICEF and other organizations. Introduced in 23 primary and middle schools in six provinces, the initiative was part of the sweeping educational reforms enacted to stem the haemorrhaging of students from schools in the face of the national economic crisis. In some villages, as many as 10 per cent of primary-school-age children have dropped out, raising the spectre of exploitative labour and crushing hopes for brighter futures built on education.

A 1997 constitutional guarantee of a free 12-year education provided by the State was an acknowledgement that, to thrive as a society, Thailand must ensure its citizens access to quality education. The child-centred approach to learning is key to these reforms. The goal is to establish at least five demonstration sites in each of Thailand's 12 education districts before the end of the year 2000.

Prepared to teach

For many teachers, the child-friendly approach can be a radical departure from traditional teaching methods. Nevertheless, there is a broad awareness that such change is needed to engage children as partners in their education and keep them coming to school.

UNICEF/Iran

Schoolgirls in class in Iran.

James Hopkins, Director of Save the Children's programme in Thailand, says that the cultural norms of how adults and children interact in school need to be understood so that teachers can take child-friendly teaching fully to heart. "When we listen closely," explains Mr. Hopkins, "we hear the fears of teachers who ask: 'In the future, will we have to bow to children? Will children stop bowing down when they pass us? How will we maintain discipline if we can no longer spank children?'"

Mobilizing community and parent support becomes critical, because with such support the child-friendly school truly becomes a place where children, teachers and parents work together, using a holistic approach to address the health, education, protection and participation needs of children as part of the full spectrum of child rights.

for all children and to attract and retain girls in school. Children are being educated in multigrade classrooms, in cluster schools and by radio. Two of the dozens of countries that are closing the enrolment gap between girls and boys are Chad and Yemen. In Chad, women are being trained as teachers to serve as role models for girls. In Yemen during 1998-1999, as many as 2,000 women teachers were trained in rural areas, and the Community Schools Project – which began in 1994 with approximately 1,000 girls in 120 villages – now reaches more than 11,000 girls who would not otherwise have received primary education. While communities provide classroom space in most of the villages, in some cases the classes meet under trees. More than 50 new classrooms have been constructed and another 25 classrooms repaired for the girls' schooling.

In addition to similar 'girl-friendly' activities, communities in Chad are attacking the economic hardship at the heart of families' decisions to keep their daughters at home to work. Families receive dry grain rations to compensate for their lost labour, and women have gained more time for gardening and sewing since labour-saving changes were introduced, such as grain mills, a village water tank and wagons to haul the water.

Adolescents

At once vulnerable and worldly, adolescents are a particularly heterogeneous group: in some societies, married or parents themselves; in others, alienated and isolated from the adult world or in need of special protection from sexual exploitation, child labour or recruitment into armed conflict. In still other societies, they head households because their parents have died from AIDS or as a result of war or violence. In many, they are the primary wage earners.

In all cases, the rights of adolescents to development and participation are ensured by the Convention on the Rights of the Child. Protecting their rights is an effective 'immunization' that helps prevent sexually transmitted infections, including HIV/AIDS, and reduces school drop-out rates, drug abuse and violent behaviour. Young people themselves have proven their ability to best reach and move other adolescents. Youth-friendly health services, already in place in Indonesia, Latvia, Namibia, Nigeria, Uganda, Ukraine and Zambia, are a case in point.

In Indonesia, for example, peer educators in health, together with local NGOs, target street and out-of-school youth. In Java, the activities combine relevant information on HIV/AIDS prevention and the teaching of life skills for vulnerable groups, addressing real-life situations of violence and risk among adolescents. In Sulawesi, 150 students in Islamic boarding schools have been trained as peer educators to reach 2,000 fellow students.

In every region of the world, countries are moving forward with a diverse range of programmes focusing on topics that illustrate the range of an adolescent's world: the age of marriage and child-bearing, girls' school enrolment, the nutritional status of girls, child labour, HIV/AIDS, armed conflict and family separation, child soldiers, sexual abuse and exploitation and female genital mutilation.

Because an estimated 250 million children living today will be killed by tobacco, UNICEF has joined WHO in efforts to put a stop to the gross violation of children's rights that tobacco use poses. The WHO/UNICEF collaboration, funded by the United Nations Fund for International Partnerships, seeks to accelerate national action to fight the targeting of youths by tobacco companies and will involve young people in all aspects of the planning and programme work.

Adolescents, like all children, have the right to be heard and to participate in matters affecting them and in which they have an interest, in accordance with their age and maturity. For adolescents, involvement in programmes specifically designed for them and in more general community activities is a way of developing their talents and bolstering their confidence and sense of self, as well as contributing to the wider world. One intercountry project on adolescents' rights to participation and development is now under way in 13 countries – Bangladesh, China, Côte d'Ivoire, Democratic Republic of Congo, Egypt, Ghana, Jamaica, Jordan, Malawi, Mali, Mongolia, the Russian Federation and Zambia.

Youth from each of the countries have met to discuss and plan initiatives that are designed to address the particular needs of the young people they represent. Programme planning will focus on a number of key issues, such as Youth-Friendly Health Services, access to education, peer counselling, freedom from exploitation and abuse, and safe spaces for meeting, recreation and sports.

Working to promote and protect the rights of adolescents is admittedly a relatively recent phenomenon for UNICEF but one which is gaining momentum as the new century begins.

Measures of humanity

When challenges are great, determining success is never simple. But certain benchmarks exist that help define universal standards of basic moral decency and against which the world can gauge the depth of its commitments and the success of its efforts. Grounded in the principles and articles of the Convention on the Rights of the Child, they are goals around which a global alliance can come together on behalf of children – that infants start life healthy and young children are nurtured in a caring environment; that all children including the poorest and most disadvantaged complete a basic education of good quality; and that adolescents have the opportunities to develop fully and participate in their societies.

Each of these in its own right is worthy of a global movement. Taken together, they set down the basic structure of a humane society.

The world has more children living in poverty than it did 10 years ago. It is more unstable and more violent than it was in 1990 when leaders at the World Summit pledged to reach 27 goals for children and women by the year 2000.

What were not easy promises to keep in the last 10 years are even more difficult today, and so the leadership that is called for now is qualitatively different than before. It is a leadership not only of governments but one broad enough to include all those in every country of every region who have embraced the cause of children as their own. As part of one of the more phenomenal movements in history, this 21st century leadership will be tested often and tested severely in the coming years.

It will need to be far-sighted enough to ensure that all pregnant women are adequately nourished and immediate enough to protect children from being deliberately slaughtered in conflict.

It will need to be as specifically focused as the monks who serve as HIV/AIDS community counsellors in the Mekong Delta region of East Asia and as broad as changing the world's mindset about the rights of women and children.

It will need to be on as grand a scale as the 1992 constitutional amendment in India – home to 1 billion people – that set aside a third of all governmental seats for women and a percentage of those for women of the lowest castes. And as personal as sending a young girl to school rather than keeping her at home.

No less will do.

We start the 21st century . . .

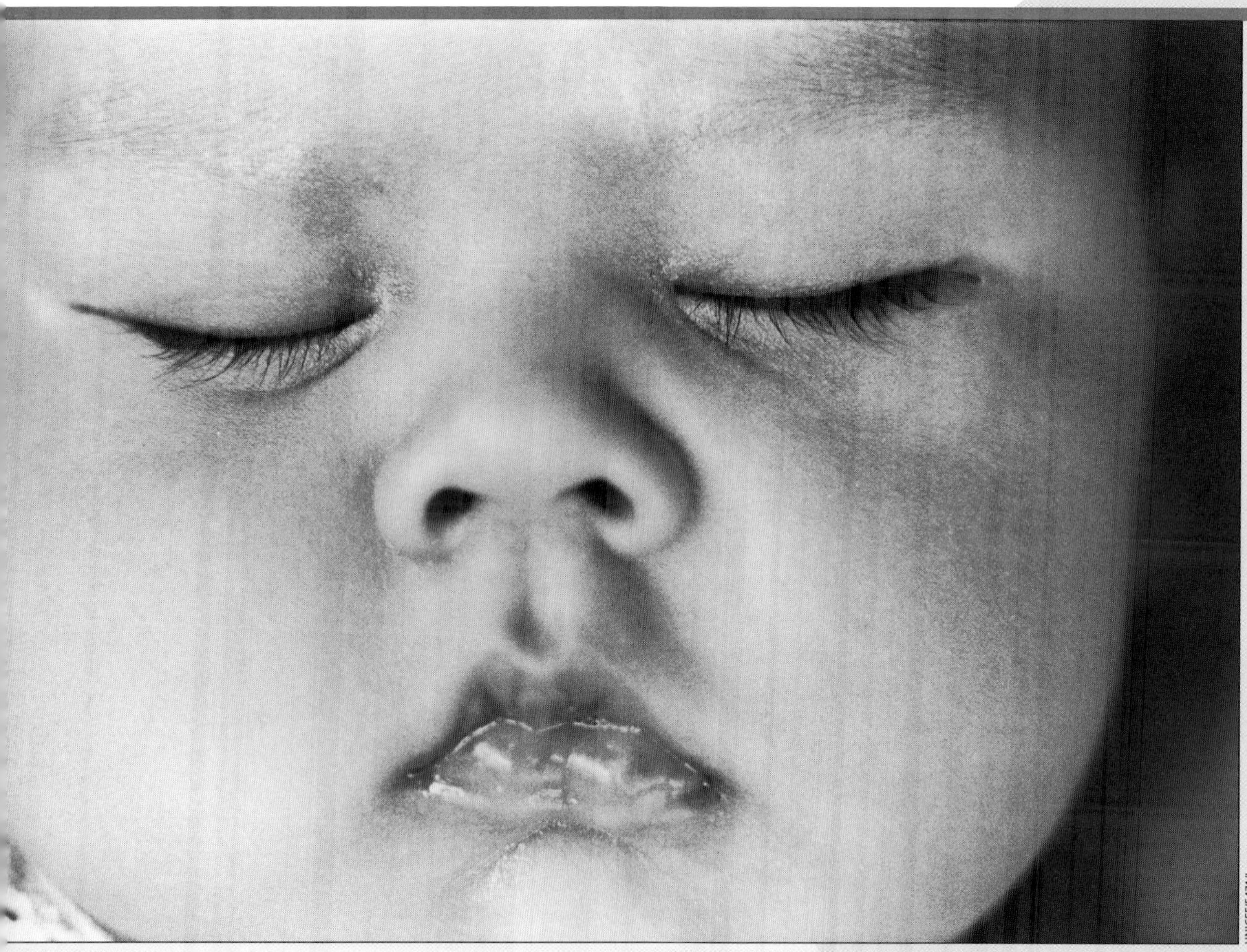

THAILAND

. . . with a vision

for the children of the world: that every one of them – without exception – lives a full and healthy life, with rights secured and protected, freed from poverty, violence and discrimination.

. . . with a commitment

to spare no effort in making certain that all infants start life healthy, all young children are nurtured in caring environments, all children, including the poorest and most disadvantaged, complete a basic education of good quality and that all adolescents have the opportunities to develop fully and to participate in their societies.

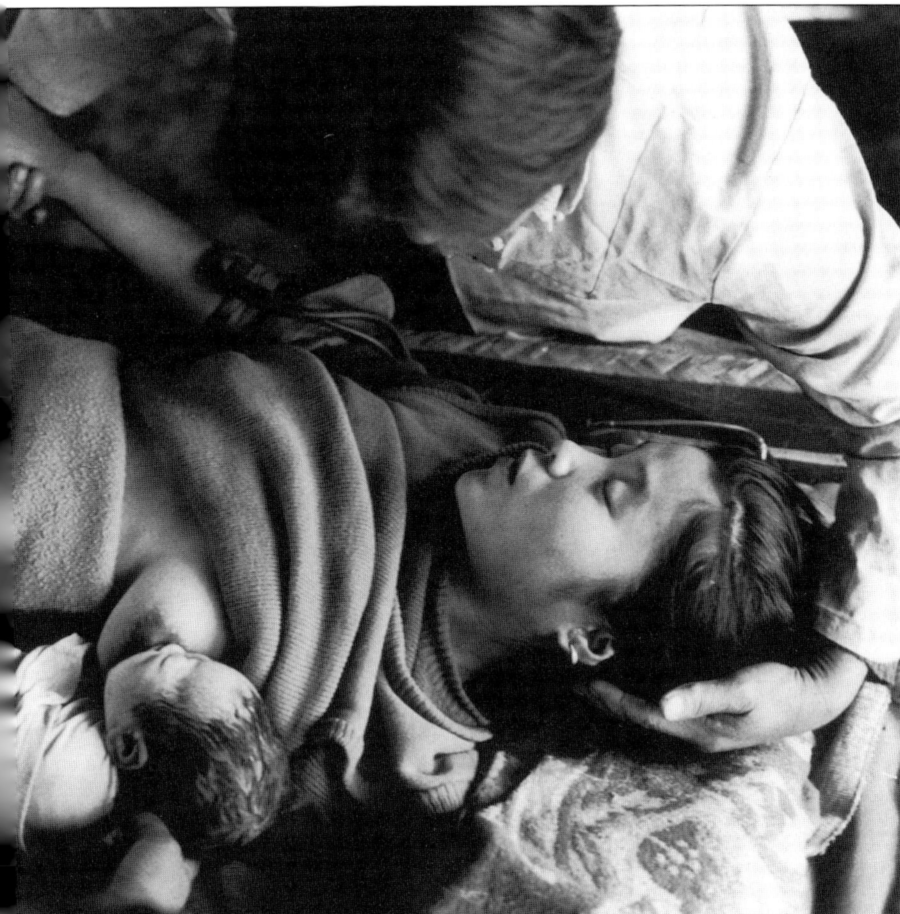

UNICEF/93-1721/Lemoyne

CHINA

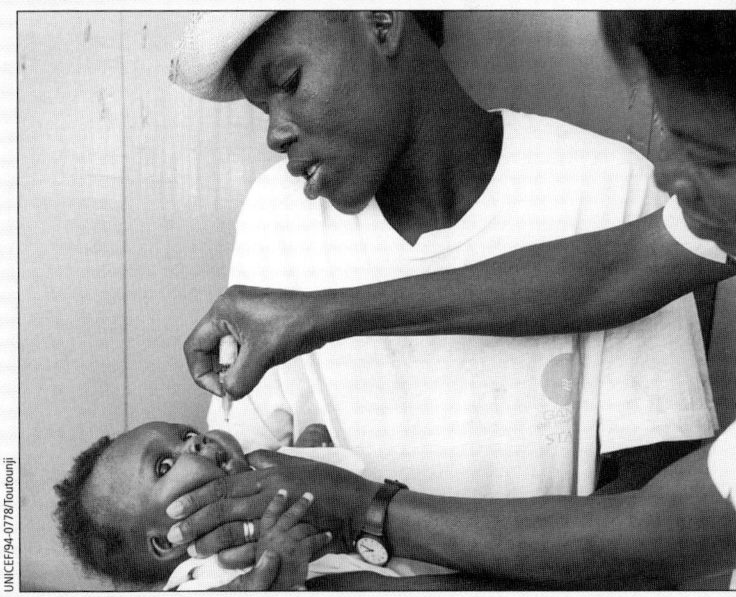

UNICEF/94-0778/Toutounji

HAITI

Early childhood care. There is an urgency to working with children and their families during the very early childhood years – a time with the greatest possibilities for breaking through intergenerational cycles of chronic poor health and suboptimal human development. This is when the foundation can best be set to ensure that children are physically healthy, mentally

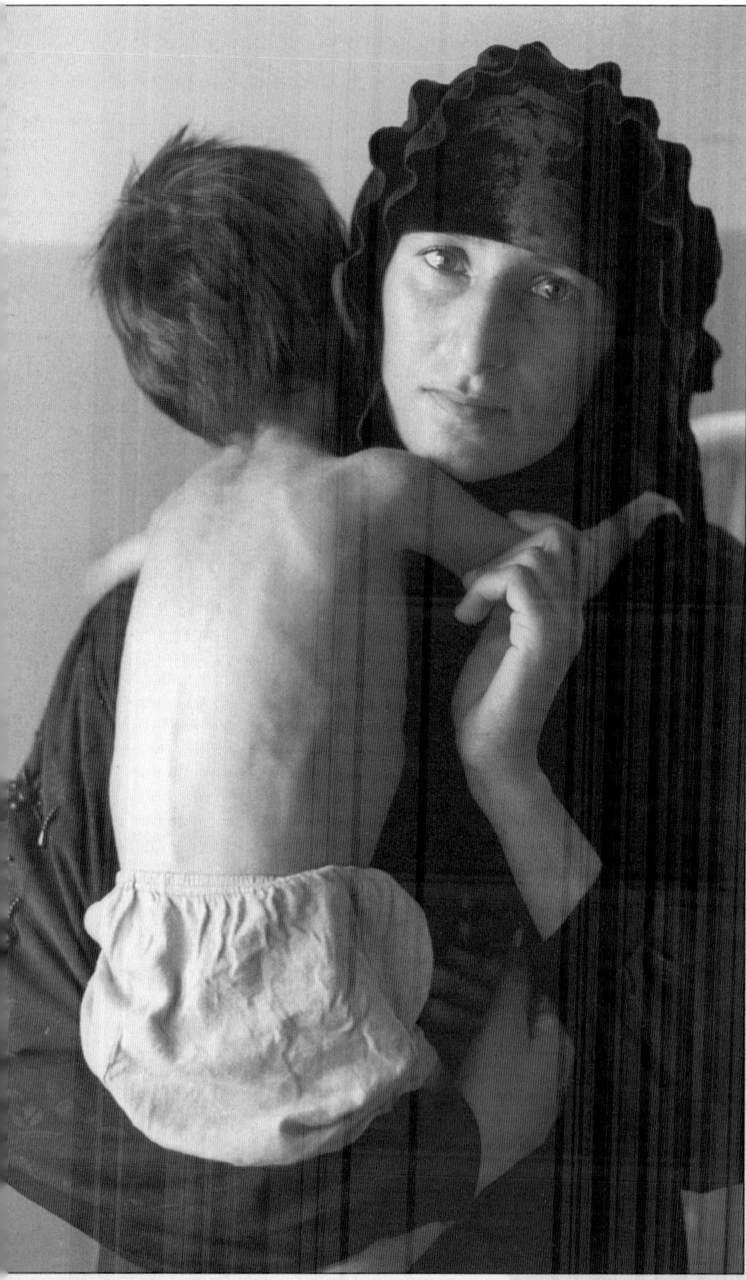

UNICEF/99-0580/Pirozzi

IRAQ

UNICEF/98-0219/Lemoyne

YUGOSLAVIA

Early childhood care

UNICEF/90-0005/Tolmie

COLOMBIA

alert, emotionally secure, socially competent and intellectually able to learn by the time they reach primary school age.

This foundation depends on care and nurturing for the child, good nutrition, including breastfeeding for up to six months, access to safe water and sanitation, and immunization against vaccine-preventable diseases. It also depends on a protective atmosphere that encourages early socialization, stimulation and positive interaction with family and community.

And it requires that mothers are well cared for during pregnancy, delivery and lactation as a way to assure children the healthiest beginnings and to prevent the needless deaths of the 585,000 women who die each year of complications during pregnancy and childbirth.

UNICEF/93-1743/Lemoyne

CHINA

UNICEF/93-2146/Pirozzi

MALI

Education. Education does not begin when the child sets foot in primary school, nor does it end when the school bell rings and class lets out. Learning begins at birth; it occurs in the family, in neighbourhoods, in communities, during play. Life's teachers are parents, siblings, peers, workplaces, the mass media.

A basic, quality education is a human right, yet more than 130 million primary-school-age children in developing countries are out of school. Nearly

Education

VIET NAM

60 per cent of them are girls, many saddled with domestic obligations and household chores; many others limited by traditions in which families consider school costs too high to pay when it comes to their daughters; and still others living such long distances from school that travel is a risk to their health and well-being.

Too often, girls and boys must abandon their education when they are forced to work despite their young age or the hazards of their labour, when armed conflict

UNICEF/98-0021/Freedman

ANGOLA

UNICEF/98-0660/Balaguer

NICARAGUA

and other emergencies disrupt their lives, when poverty surrounds them or when adults exploit them sexually or buy and sell them like commodities.

Despite these deterrents, children embrace the opportunity to learn about the world around them and develop their abilities to succeed – critical thinking, self-confidence, problem-solving and working with others. As children grow and develop, these skills will serve them not only to function in their daily lives but also to transform their futures.

Adolescents

UNICEF/96-1233/Pirozzi

ZAMBIA

Adolescents. The Convention on the Rights of the Child recognizes the rights of children up to the age of 18; but adolescents are no longer children in the traditional sense and not yet adults. Working to support their families, fighting their countries' wars and heading households, adolescents often find that they must fend for themselves, lacking a political voice and without the base of family and community support they had when they were younger.

It is a human tragedy, not to mention a gross violation of human rights, to bring adolescents to the brink of adulthood – and then deny them the opportunity to

INDIA

SIERRA LEONE

realize their full potential. Adolescents need and deserve a chance to finish school and to participate in activities with their peers. They need and deserve 'safe' places such as schools, vocational settings and youth centres in which to develop the skills to deal

UNICEF/99-0247/Horner

COLOMBIA

with life situations. And they need and deserve services that enlist the support of caring adults and offer a connection with family and community.

A resource of enormous potential – as peers, older siblings or heads of households, as parents or future parents – adolescents contribute to their societies in myriad ways. As partners in advancing a global agenda, adolescents are uniquely poised to change the course of human development.

Leadership in the best interests of the child

At the heart of the Convention on the Rights of the Child is the core value that policies be made, structures and processes be established and actions be taken that are, always and invariably, in the best interests of the child. There are many thousands of people around the world who have worked to support that principle. The names that follow are but a few of those people. Identified by UNICEF offices, the list includes a broad cross-section of advocates for children – community workers, medical personnel, grass-roots organizations, non-governmental organizations (NGOs), religious leaders, writers, journalists, educators, lawyers, government officials and others. We print their names to acknowledge their contributions and also to indirectly acknowledge the many, many thousands more whose names we may never know but whose work on behalf of children continues to move us all towards a more just world.

AFGHANISTAN
Co-operation Centre for Afghanistan
NGO that promotes human rights and reports on human rights abuses.

ARGENTINA
Estela B. de Carlotto
President, Asociación de Abuelas de Plaza de Mayo

AUSTRALIA
Justice Marcus Einfeld
Special Representative for UNICEF Australia

AUSTRIA
Prof. Clemens von Pirquet, M.D. (1874-1929)
Secretary-General, International Union for Youth Welfare to the League of Nations

AZERBAIJAN
Hadi Recebli
Head, Social Legislation Department, National Assembly

BENIN
Monsignor Isidore de Souza (1934-1999)
Archbishop of Cotonou, founding member and honorary President, Institute of Human Rights and Promotion of Democracy of Benin

BOLIVIA
Ana María Romero de Campero
Journalist and Bolivia's current People's Defender

BRAZIL
Herbert de Souza (Betinho) (1935-1997)
Involved in the design and launch of the coalition, Pact for Children

BULGARIA
Elena Kostova
President, Future of Bulgaria Foundation

CAMBODIA
Mom Thany
Affiliated with the NGO Redd Barna, built an NGO network in Cambodia

CANADA
Denise Avard
Former Executive Director, Canadian Institute of Child Health

COLOMBIA
Children's Movement for Peace
Nominated for Nobel Peace Prize

CONGO
Thérèse Françoise Engambé
Chief, Projet Plaidoyer pour l'application de la Convention relative aux droits de l'enfant

DEMOCRATIC REPUBLIC OF CONGO
Emery Mpwate Munfe
President, Union de la Jeunesse protestante, National Director, Church of Christ Youth

DENMARK
Peter Sabroe (1867-1913)
Member of Parliament, journalist and editor

EGYPT
Justice Mohamed Abdel Aziz ElGuindy
Former Attorney-General of Egypt, Co-organizer, Alexandria International Conference on the CRC, 1988

FIJI
Justice Nazhat Shameem
Former Chair of Fiji's Children's Coordinating Committee

GAMBIA
Amie Joof Cole
Secretary-General, West African Women's Association

GERMANY
Reinald Eichholz
First ombudsperson for children for the state of North Rhine-Westphalia

GREECE
Antonis Samarakis
Writer, UNICEF National Goodwill Ambassador

GUINEA
Hadja Mariama Diabate
The 'national mother' for orphaned, abandoned and underprivileged children

INDIA
Tara Ali Baig (1916-1989)
Social reformer, writer, first Asian woman President of the International Union for Child Welfare in Geneva

INDONESIA
Nafsiah Mboi, M.D.
Secretary-General, National Commission for the Protection of Children (NGO)

JAMAICA
Marjorie Taylor
Special Envoy for Children, former Minister of State for Children's Issues

JAPAN
Toyohiko Kagawa (1888-1960)
Member, National Council on Child Welfare, inspired government and social action to promote child rights

KENYA
Justice Effie Owuor
Chair, Task Force on child law reform, UNICEF National Goodwill Ambassador

LEBANON
Nayla Moawad
President, Parliamentary Committee on the Rights of the Child, and René Moawad Foundation

MALAYSIA
Raj Binte Abdul Karim
Director-General, National Population and Family Development Board

MALI
Général Amadou Toumani Touré
Founder, Fondation pour l'enfance

MEXICO
Libertad Hernandez (1947-1998)
Director, women's programme in Veracruz

MOZAMBIQUE
Graça Machel
United Nations Secretary-General's expert on children in armed conflict

NEPAL
Gauri Pradhan
Founder, Child Workers in Nepal

NIGERIA
Irene Thomas, M.D.
President, Inter-African Committee on Female Genital Mutilation

PAKISTAN
Hakim Mohammed Said (1920-1998)
Established various institutions for children

PANAMA
Dora Boyd de Pérez Balladares
Founder, Pacto por la Niñez Panameña

PHILIPPINES
Feny de los Angeles-Bautista
Executive Director, Philippine Children's Television Foundation

POLAND
Prof. Adam Lopatka
President, Working Group on the Convention on the Rights of the Child

ROMANIA
Dragos Serafim, M.D.
President, Romanian Association for Child Rights

SENEGAL
Doudou Camara (1941-1998)
Author of *Approche culturelle pour la promotion des droits de l'enfant* and *Droits de l'enfant: Contes et légendes du Sénégal*

SINGAPORE
Lim Eng Seng
Director, Rehabilitation and Protection Division, Ministry of Community Development

SOMALIA
Elman Ali Ahmed (1954-1996)
Founder, Elman School in Mogadishu

SOUTH AFRICA
Nelson Mandela
Nobel Peace Prize laureate, Founder, Nelson Mandela Children's Fund

SRI LANKA
Prof. Savitri Goonesekere
Vice Chancellor, University of Colombo

SWEDEN
Thomas Hammarberg
United Nations Secretary-General's Special Representative for Human Rights in Cambodia

SYRIA
Hussein Hassun
Minister of Justice, active in juvenile law and justice

THAILAND
Anand Panyarachun
UNICEF National Goodwill Ambassador

UKRAINE
Natalia Petrova
Head, All-Ukrainian Committee on Children's Rights Protection (NGO)

UNITED KINGDOM
Nigel Cantwell
Coordinator of the NGOs that participated in drafting the CRC

UNITED STATES
James P. Grant (1922-1995)
Executive Director, UNICEF

VENEZUELA
Comité Juntos por una Nueva Ley
Coalition of NGOs that promote child rights

YEMEN
Nageeba M. Haddad
'Director-General of children's culture', Ministry of Culture, writer

ZIMBABWE
Jarios Jiri (1921-1982)
Founder, Jarios Jiri Association for Disabled Children

References

An urgent call to leadership

1. World Bank, 'World Bank warns global poverty fight failing, unveils enhanced poverty strategy', population table in News Release No. 2000/059/S, 30 September 1999, p. 4.
2. The Convention on the Rights of the Child, articles 3 and 4.
3. The Vienna Declaration and Programme of Action, adopted in 1993 at the World Conference on Human Rights, highlights the need to protect children in a range of harmful circumstances and devotes a section to the rights of the child. The Report of the Fourth World Conference on Women (1995) calls for promotion and protection of all human rights of women and girls and devotes a section to 'the girl child'. Perhaps the World Summit for Social Development (1995) made the most extensive links with the articles and spirit of the Convention on the Rights of the Child, reaffirming rights to health, education, nutrition, sanitation and literacy.
4. United Nations Development Programme, *Human Development Report 1994*, UNDP, New York, Oxford University Press, 1994.
5. Organisation for Economic Co-operation and Development, *Shaping the 21st Century: The contribution of development co-operation*, October 1998.
6. United Nations, ECOSOC, E/ICEF/1996/15.
7. United Nations, Press release GA/SM/94, 14 September 1999.
8. Joint United Nations Programme on HIV/AIDS and the World Health Organization, *AIDS epidemic update: December 1998*, UNAIDS/WHO, Geneva, December 1998, p. 1.
9. Office of the United Nations High Commissioner for Refugees, *Refugees and Others of Concern to UNHCR: 1998 statistical overview,* UNHCR Statistical Unit, Geneva, July 1999, table 1.4, Indicative number of refugees, 1989-1998, pp. 20-23; and 'Principal Sources of Internationally Displaced Persons', *World Refugee Survey 1999*, US Committee for Refugees, table 5, Internally displaced persons, p. 6.

Box 1

1. Black, Maggie, *Children First: The story of UNICEF past and present,* UNICEF/Oxford University Press, New York, 1996, p. 21.
2. Save the Children Fund archive reference: SC/SF/17.

Undeclared war

1. United Nations Population Division, Too young to die: Genes or gender?, ESA/P/WP.126 unedited version, December 1996.
2. Jain, Sharda, 'Save before they perish', and Vaid, Sudershan and Sharda Jain, 'Nipped in the bud', both in *Family Medicine, India*, Vol. 3, No. 4, July-September 1999, pp. 7 and 9, respectively.
3. Human Rights Watch, *Broken People: Caste violence against India's 'Untouchables',* Human Rights Watch, New York, March 1999.
4. Ibid., p. 1.
5. Human Rights Watch, *The Small Hands of Slavery: Bonded child labour in India,* Human Rights Watch, New York, September 1996, pp. 2 and 17.
6. Ibid., p. 17.
7. International Labour Organization, 'ILO concludes 87th Conference with adoption of new instruments against child labour', *World of Work,* No. 30, July 1999, p. 6.
8. Ibid., p. 2.
9. United Nations Children's Fund, 'Women in Transition', *Regional Monitoring Report*, No. 6, Florence: UNICEF International Child Development Centre, 1999, p. 10.
10. World Bank, 'World Bank Poverty Update', table 4, in News Release No. 99/2214/S of 2 June 1999: 'Latest World Bank Poverty Update Shows Urgent Need to Better Shield Poor in Crisis'.
11. Mehrotra, Santosh, 'Health and Education Policies in High-Achieving Countries: Some lessons', *Development with a Human Face*, Santosh Mehrotra and Richard Jolly (eds.), Clarendon Press, Oxford, 1997, pp. 68-75; and Watkins, Kevin, *Economic Growth with Equity: Lessons from East Asia*, Oxfam, Oxford, 1998, pp. 57-67.
12. Citizens' Committee for Children of New York, Inc., *Keeping Track of New York City's Children*, New York, 1999, pp. 6 and 18.
13. Stockholm International Peace Research Institute, *SIPRI Yearbook 1999*, SIPRI, Oxford University Press, 1999, p. 2.
14. International Committee of the Red Cross, *Landmines Must Be Stopped: ICRC overview 1998*, Geneva, May 1998, p. 16.
15. United Nations Children's Fund, *The State of the World's Children 1996*, UNICEF, New York, 1995, p. 13.

16. United Nations, 'The Causes of Conflict and the Promotion of Durable Peace and Sustainable Development in Africa', Secretary-General's Report to the United Nations Security Council, 16 April 1998, paragraph 4.

17. Human Rights Watch, *Sudan: Global Trade, Local Impact; Arms transfers to all sides of the civil war in Sudan,* Human Rights Watch, New York, Vol. 10, No. 4 (A), August 1998, p. 20.

18. Joint United Nations Programme on HIV/AIDS, *Facts and Figures 1999*, UNAIDS, Geneva, February 1999, p. 1.

19. Joint United Nations Programme on HIV/AIDS and the World Health Organization, *AIDS epidemic update: December 1998*, UNAIDS/WHO, Geneva, December, 1998, p. 1.

20. Sivard, Ruth Leger, *World Military and Social Expenditures, 1996*, World Priorities Inc., Washington, D.C., 1996, p. 18.

21. Joint United Nations Programme on HIV/AIDS and the World Health Organization, *AIDS epidemic update: December 1998,* UNAIDS/WHO, Geneva, December, 1998, p. 3.

22. Vandemoortele, Jan, 'AIDS conspires against the poor: An analysis of 35 DHS surveys', UNICEF, New York, 1999.

23. United Nations Children's Fund, 'Report of the ESAR HIV/AIDS Task Force held in Nairobi, 11-12 March 1999', UNICEF, April 1999.

24. United Nations Children's Fund, *The Progress of Nations 1999*, UNICEF, New York, July 1999, p. 20.

25. Joint United Nations Programme on HIV/AIDS, *The Demographic Impact of HIV/AIDS*, New York, November 1998, p. 42.

26. Ibid., p. 43.

27. Ahmed, Sadia, 'HIV/AIDS and Children: A South Asian perspective', Save the Children (UK), Office for South and Central Asia Region, Kathmandu, March 1998, p. 10.

28. Joint United Nations Programme on HIV/AIDS and the World Health Organization, *AIDS epidemic update: December 1998*, UNAIDS/WHO, Geneva, December, 1998, p. 5.

In a single generation

1. Shropshire, Steve and Alexandra MacKenzie, *Arms Trade Bulletin No. 10*, Saferworld, 5 November 1998, p. 8.

2. United Nations Children's Fund, *Children in Jeopardy: The challenge of freeing poor nations from the shackles of debt*, New York, UNICEF, 1999, p. 2.

3. United Nations Development Programme, *Human Development Report 1999*, Oxford University Press, New York, 1999, p. 2.

4. United Nations Children's Fund, 'Child impact assessment', *Making Children Count: Implementing the Convention on the Rights of the Child*, UNICEF, New York, January 1999, p. 8.

5. "All wars, just or unjust, disastrous or victorious, are waged against the child." This longer quote is attributed to Eglantyne Jebb, founder of Save the Children Fund.

6. United Nations Children's Fund, *The State of the World's Children 1996*, UNICEF, New York, 1995, p. 41.

7. Machel, Graça, Statement to the Third Committee of the General Assembly, 8 November 1996, p. 2.

8. International Campaign to Ban Landmines, 'Ratification Updates', 20 September 1999.

9. United Nations, 'The Causes of Conflict and the Promotion of Durable Peace and Sustainable Development in Africa', Secretary-General's Report to the United Nations Security Council, 16 April 1998, Humanitarian Imperatives, paragraph 52.

10. Joint United Nations Programme on HIV/AIDS and the Harvard School of Public Health, 'Level and flow of national and international resources for the response to HIV/AIDS, 1996-1997', Geneva, April 1999, pp. 9-11.

11. Sesit, Michael R., 'Cost of Kosovo War could hit $40 billion – biggest economic impact could turn out to be end of peace dividend', *The Wall Street Journal*, New York, 29 June 1999, p. A-11.

Glossary

AIDS
acquired immune deficiency syndrome

CEDAW
Convention on the Elimination of All Forms of Discrimination against Women

CIS
Commonwealth of Independent States

CRC
Convention on the Rights of the Child

DAC
Development Assistance Committee of the Organisation for Economic Co-operation and Development

DHS
Demographic and Health Surveys coordinated by the United States National Institutes of Health

ECOSOC
Economic and Social Council of the United Nations General Assembly

ESAR
Eastern and Southern Africa Region

FGM
female genital mutilation

GA
General Assembly of the United Nations

GNP
gross national product

HIV
human immunodeficiency virus

ICCIDD
International Council for the Control of Iodine Deficiency Disorders

ICRC
International Committee of the Red Cross

ILO
International Labour Organization

IMF
International Monetary Fund

NATO
North Atlantic Treaty Organization

NGO
non-governmental organization

OCHA
United Nations Office for the Coordination of Humanitarian Affairs

ODA
official development assistance

OECD
Organisation for Economic Co-operation and Development

ORT
oral rehydration therapy

SIPRI
Stockholm International Peace Research Institute

U5MR
under-five mortality rate

UN
United Nations

UNAIDS
Joint United Nations Programme on HIV/AIDS

UNDP
United Nations Development Programme

UNESCO
United Nations Educational, Scientific and Cultural Organization

UNHCR
Office of the United Nations High Commissioner for Refugees

UNICEF
United Nations Children's Fund

USSR
Union of Soviet Socialist Republics

WHO
World Health Organization

Note: All dollars are US dollars.
In all instances, 1 billion is 1,000 million.

Maps

Pictorial representations of indices of the well-being of children around the world

Maps

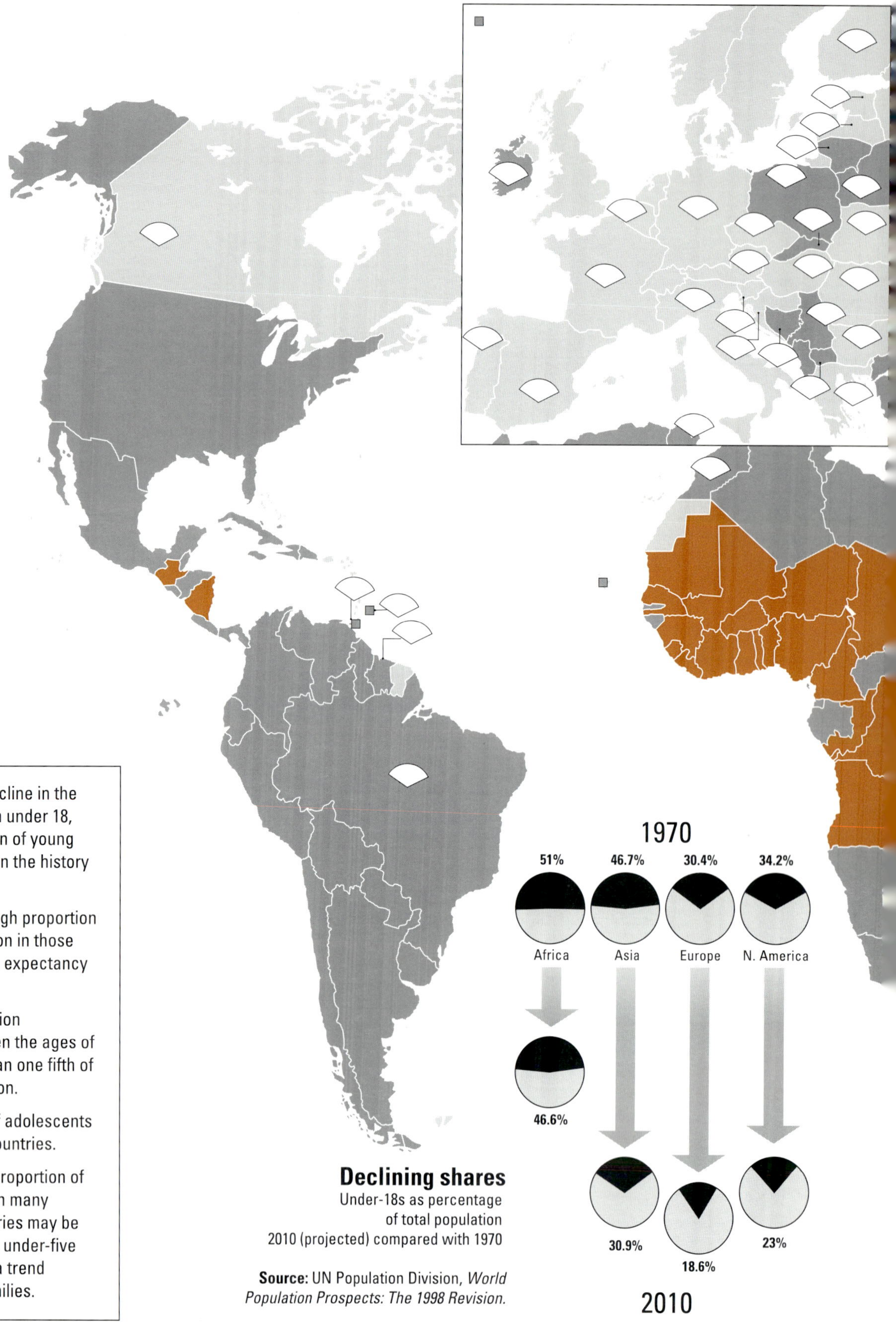

Despite an overall decline in the proportion of children under 18, the current generation of young people is the largest in the history of the world.

- Children remain a high proportion of the total population in those countries where life expectancy is low.
- There are over 1 billion adolescents between the ages of 10 and 19 – more than one fifth of the world's population.
- About 85 per cent of adolescents live in developing countries.
- The relatively high proportion of 12- to 17-year-olds in many industrialized countries may be associated with low under-five mortality rates and a trend towards smaller families.

Declining shares

Under-18s as percentage of total population 2010 (projected) compared with 1970

Source: UN Population Division, *World Population Prospects: The 1998 Revision.*

Child and adolescent populations

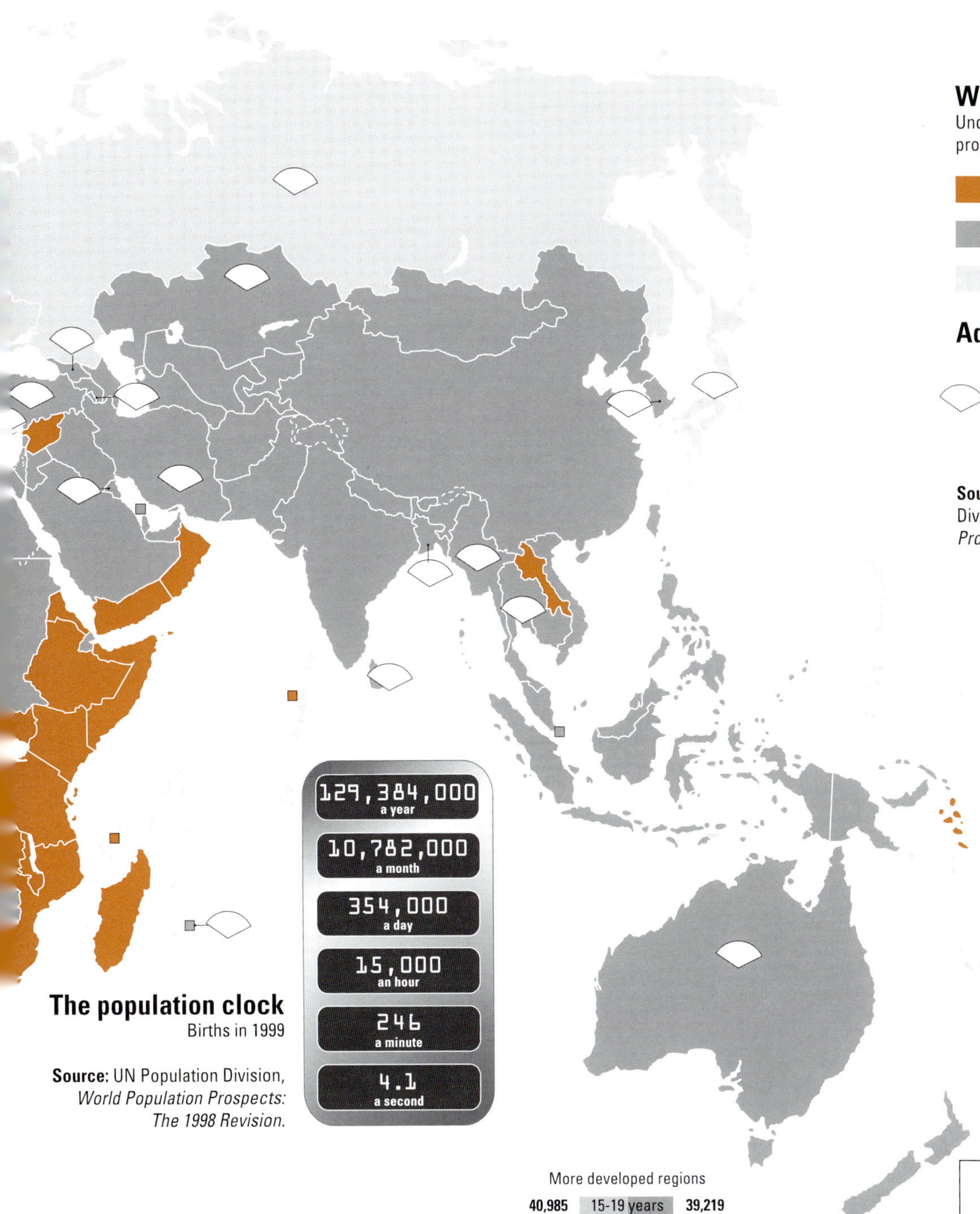

Where the children are

Under-18-year-olds as a proportion of total population

- 50% and over
- 25%-49%
- Under 25%

Adolescents

12- to 17-year-olds are more than one third of the under-18 population

Source: UN Population Division, *World Population Prospects: The 1998 Revision.*

The population clock

Births in 1999

129,384,000	a year
10,782,000	a month
354,000	a day
15,000	an hour
246	a minute
4.1	a second

Source: UN Population Division, *World Population Prospects: The 1998 Revision.*

opulation pyramids

nder-19-year-old populations
y age group and gender
n thousands)

ource: UN Population Division, *Vorld Population Prospects: he 1998 Revision.*

More developed regions

Males	Age	Females
40,985	15-19 years	39,219
41,011	10-14 years	39,158
38,220	5-9 years	36,404
34,536	0-4 years	32,830

Less developed regions

Males	Age	Females
233,070	15-19 years	221,730
260,612	10-14 years	246,914
270,292	5-9 years	255,615
276,095	0-4 years	261,378

This map does not reflect a position by UNICEF on the legal status of any country or territory or the delimitation of any frontiers. Dotted line represents approximately the Line of Control in Jammu and Kashmir agreed upon by India and Pakistan. The final status of Jammu and Kashmir has not yet been agreed upon by the parties.

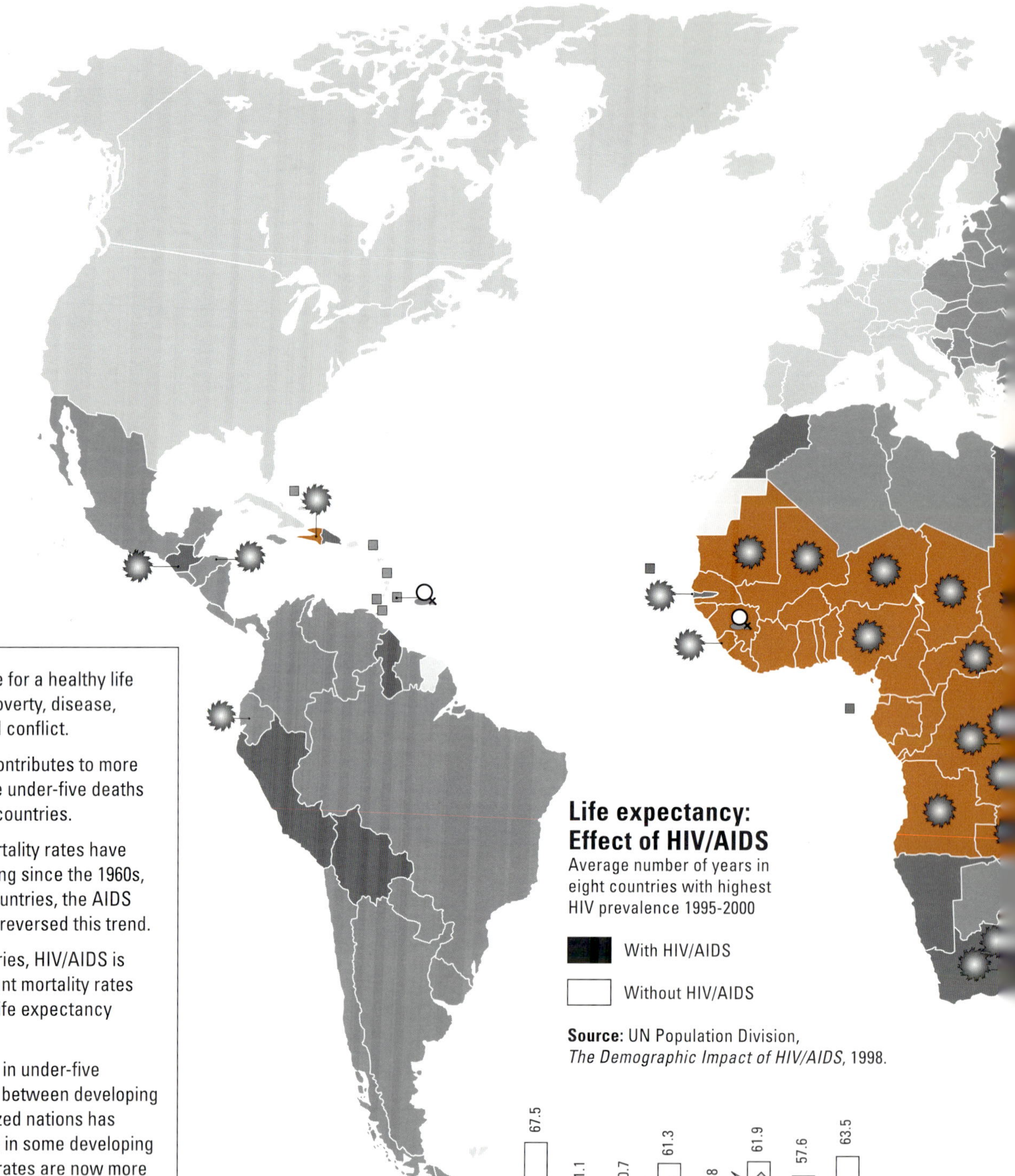

A child's chance for a healthy life is affected by poverty, disease, malnutrition and conflict.

- Malnutrition contributes to more than half of the under-five deaths in developing countries.
- Under-five mortality rates have been decreasing since the 1960s, but in many countries, the AIDS pandemic has reversed this trend.
- In many countries, HIV/AIDS is increasing infant mortality rates and reducing life expectancy dramatically.
- The difference in under-five mortality rates between developing and industrialized nations has increased, and in some developing countries, the rates are now more than 50 times higher than in the industrialized world.
- In countries where the under-five mortality rate for girls exceeds that for boys, gender discrimination is thought to be a factor.

Life expectancy: Effect of HIV/AIDS

Average number of years in eight countries with highest HIV prevalence 1995-2000

With HIV/AIDS

Without HIV/AIDS

Source: UN Population Division, *The Demographic Impact of HIV/AIDS*, 1998.

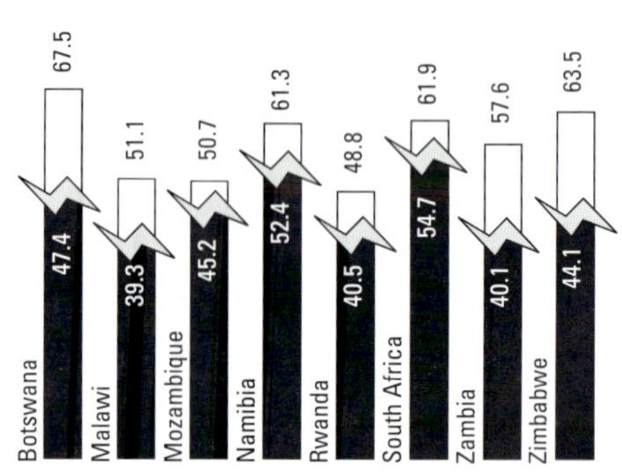

Life expectancy

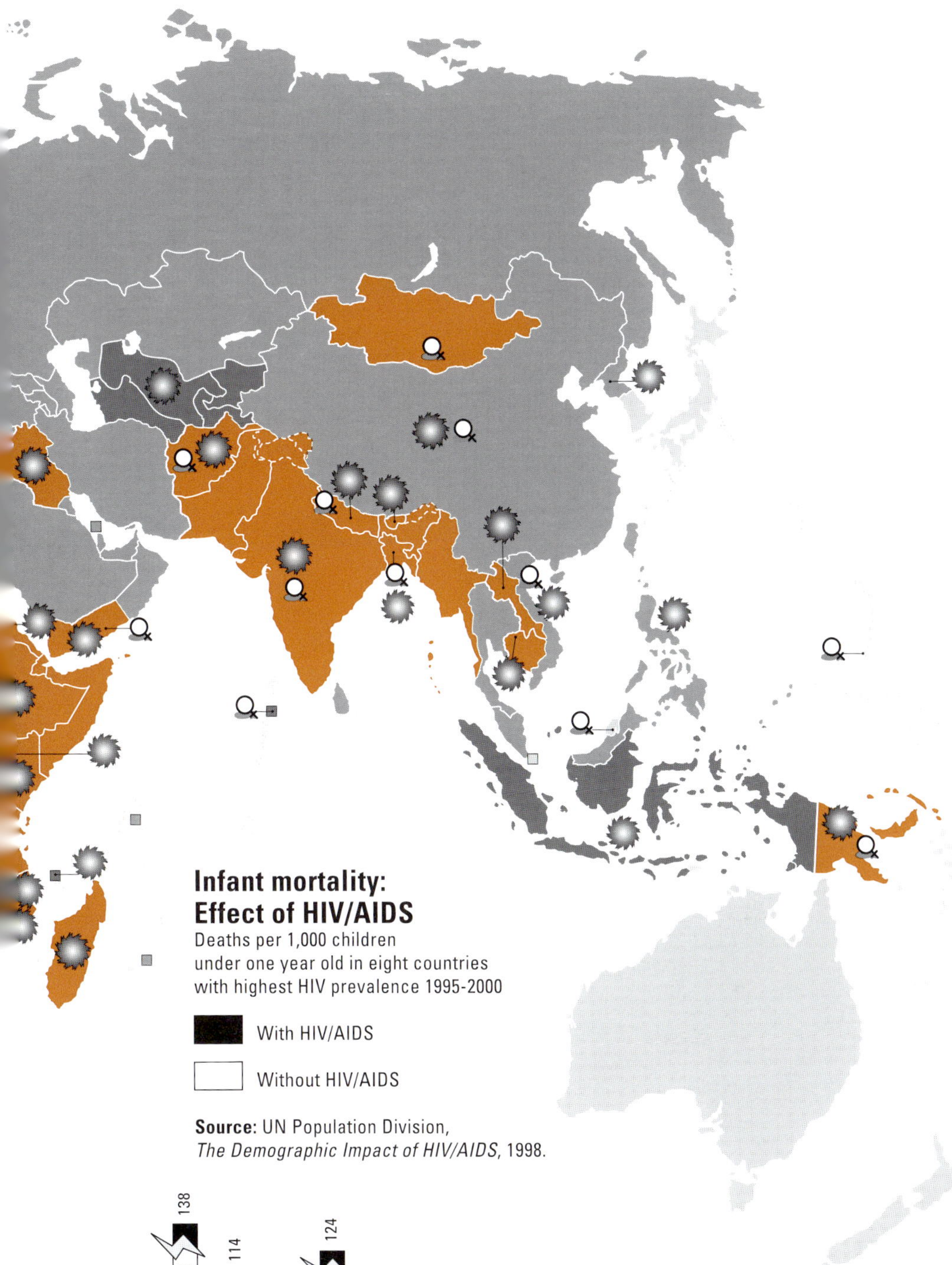

Under-5 mortality

Number of deaths
per 1,000 children 1998

- Under 10
- 10–49
- 50–99
- 100 and over
- No data

Girl children

Under-5 mortality rate for girls is disproportionately high

Malnutrition

30% or more under-5-year-olds suffering from severe or moderate stunting

Source: UNICEF, *The State of the World's Children 2000*, tables 1 and 2.

Infant mortality: Effect of HIV/AIDS

Deaths per 1,000 children
under one year old in eight countries
with highest HIV prevalence 1995-2000

- With HIV/AIDS
- Without HIV/AIDS

Source: UN Population Division, *The Demographic Impact of HIV/AIDS*, 1998.

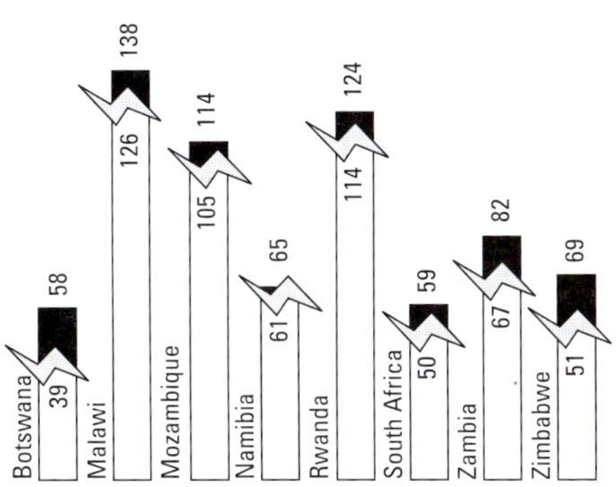

This map does not reflect a position by UNICEF on the legal status of any country or territory or the delimitation of any frontiers. Dotted line represents approximately the Line of Control in Jammu and Kashmir agreed upon by India and Pakistan. The final status of Jammu and Kashmir has not yet been agreed upon by the parties.

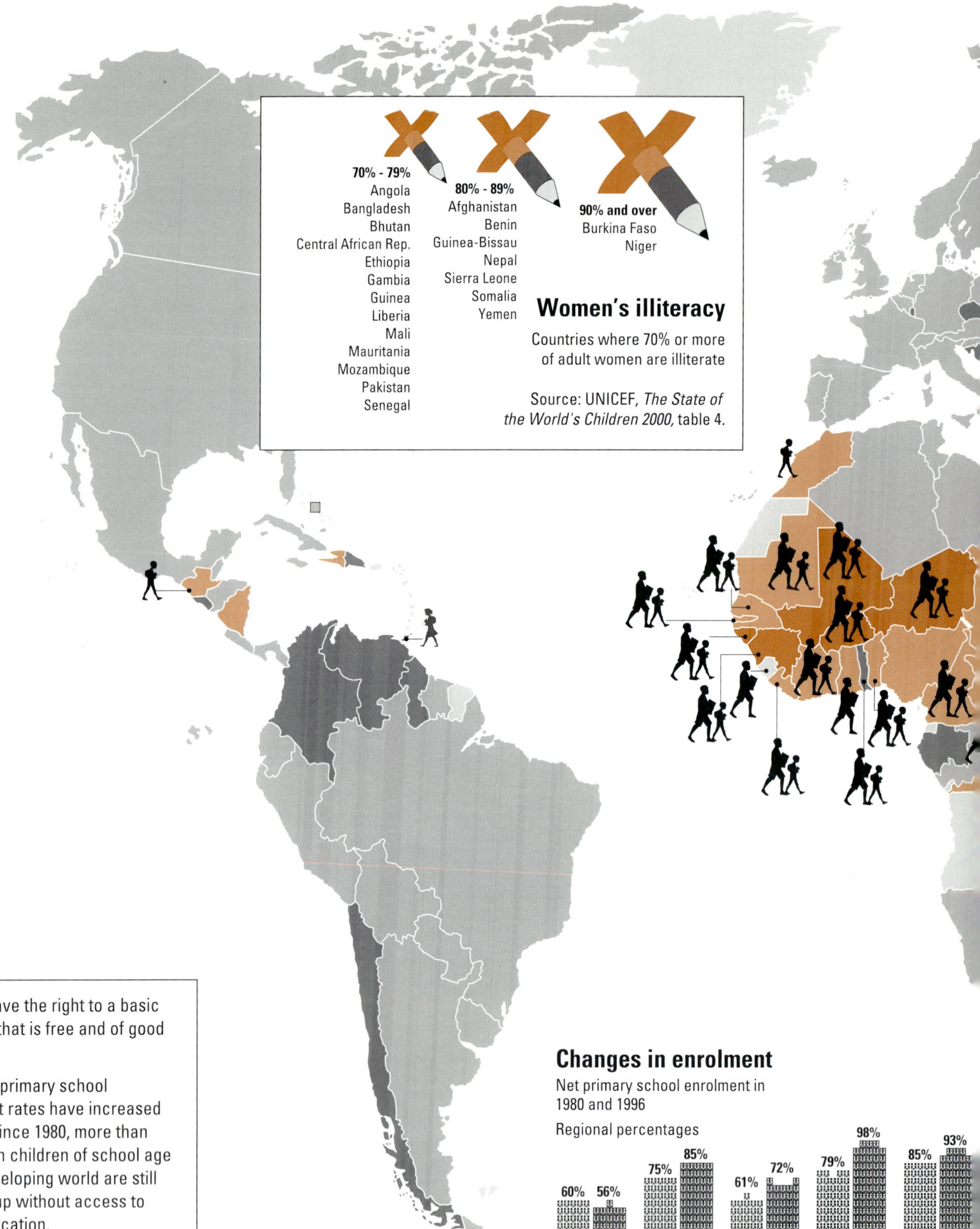

Children have the right to a basic education that is free and of good quality.

- Although primary school enrolment rates have increased globally since 1980, more than 130 million children of school age in the developing world are still growing up without access to basic education.
- Girls represent nearly 60% of the children out of school.
- In many countries, this gender gap widens even further at the secondary level.

Changes in enrolment

Net primary school enrolment in 1980 and 1996

Regional percentages

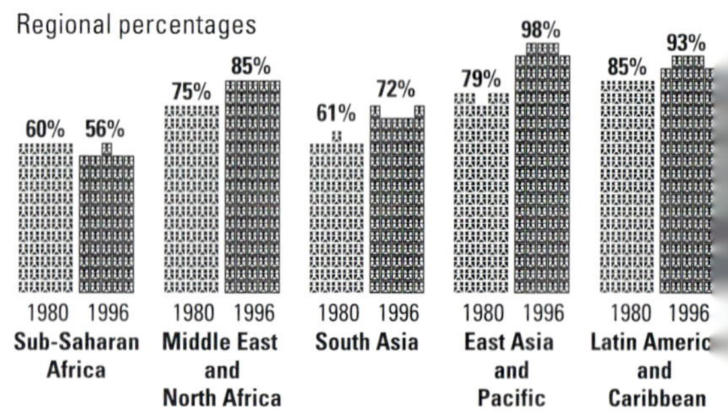

Source: UNICEF.

Learning and education

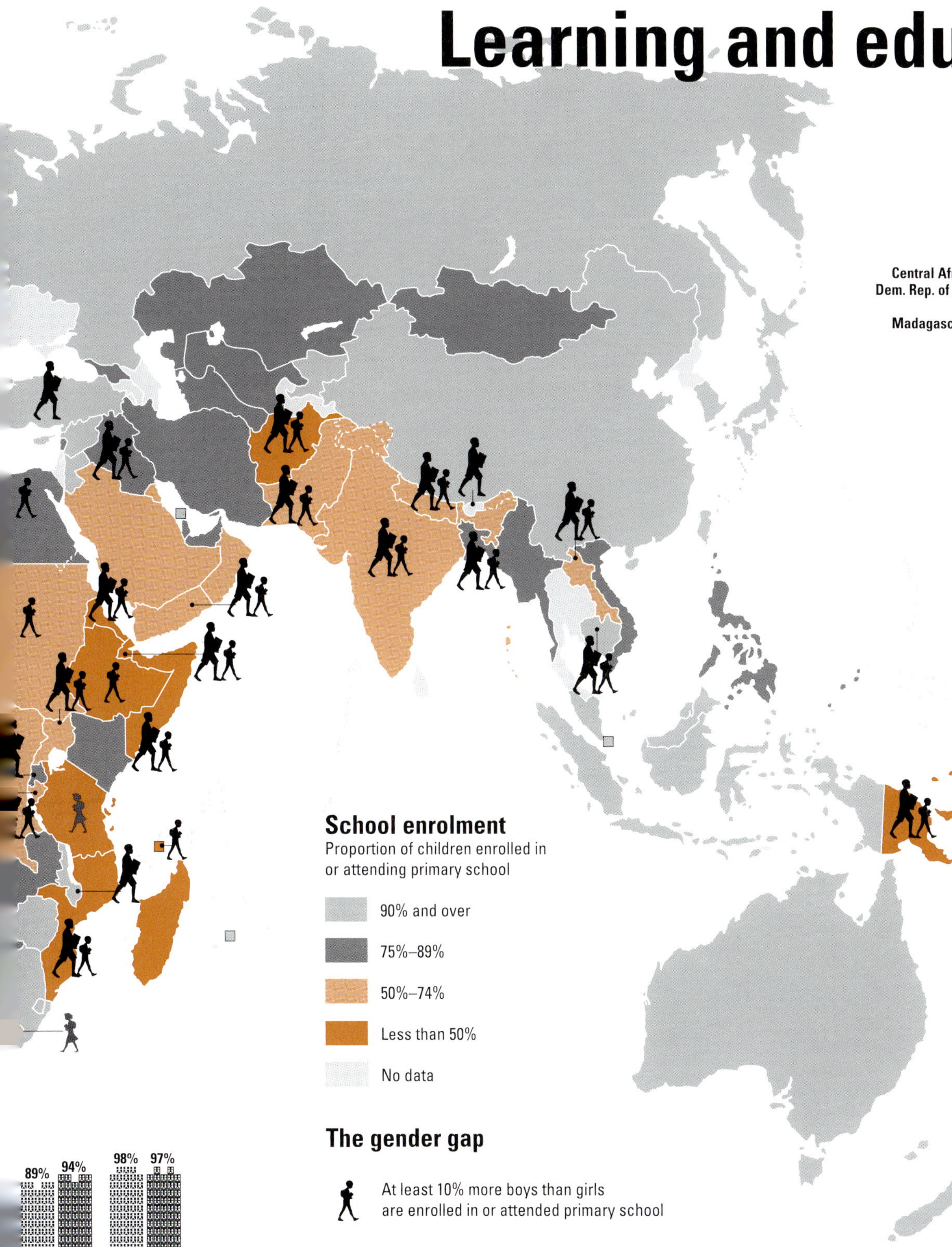

Egypt, Pakistan	15%
Uganda	16%
Cameroon, Rwanda	17%
Ghana	19%
Guinea, India	20%
Côte d'Ivoire	21%
Guatemala	22%
Central African Rep., Haiti	26%
Dem. Rep. of Congo, Yemen	28%
Zambia	29%
Madagascar, Nigeria	30%
Senegal	33%
Mali	34%
Morocco	38%
Niger	42%
Burkina Faso	49%

The rural gap

Countries where primary school attendance in rural areas is lower than in urban areas by 15% or more 1990-95

Source: UNICEF, *The Progress of Nations 1997.*

School enrolment

Proportion of children enrolled in or attending primary school

- 90% and over
- 75%–89%
- 50%–74%
- Less than 50%
- No data

The gender gap

- At least 10% more boys than girls are enrolled in or attended primary school
- At least 10% more girls than boys are enrolled in or attended primary school
- At least 30% more boys than girls are enrolled in secondary school

Sources: UNESCO and household survey data; UNICEF, *The State of the World's Children 2000,* table 4.

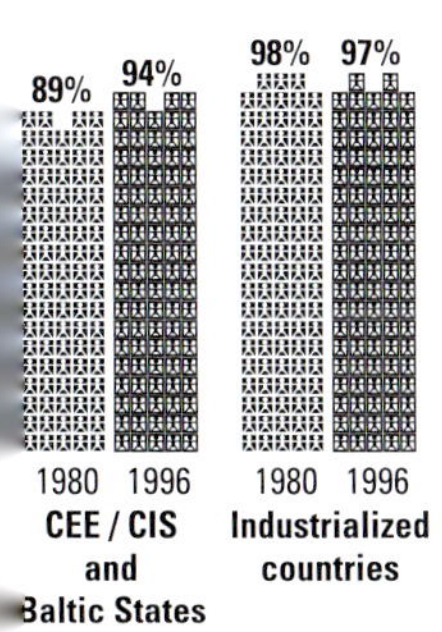

This map does not reflect a position by UNICEF on the legal status of any country or territory or the delimitation of any frontiers. Dotted line represents approximately the Line of Control in Jammu and Kashmir agreed upon by India and Pakistan. The final status of Jammu and Kashmir has not yet been agreed upon by the parties.

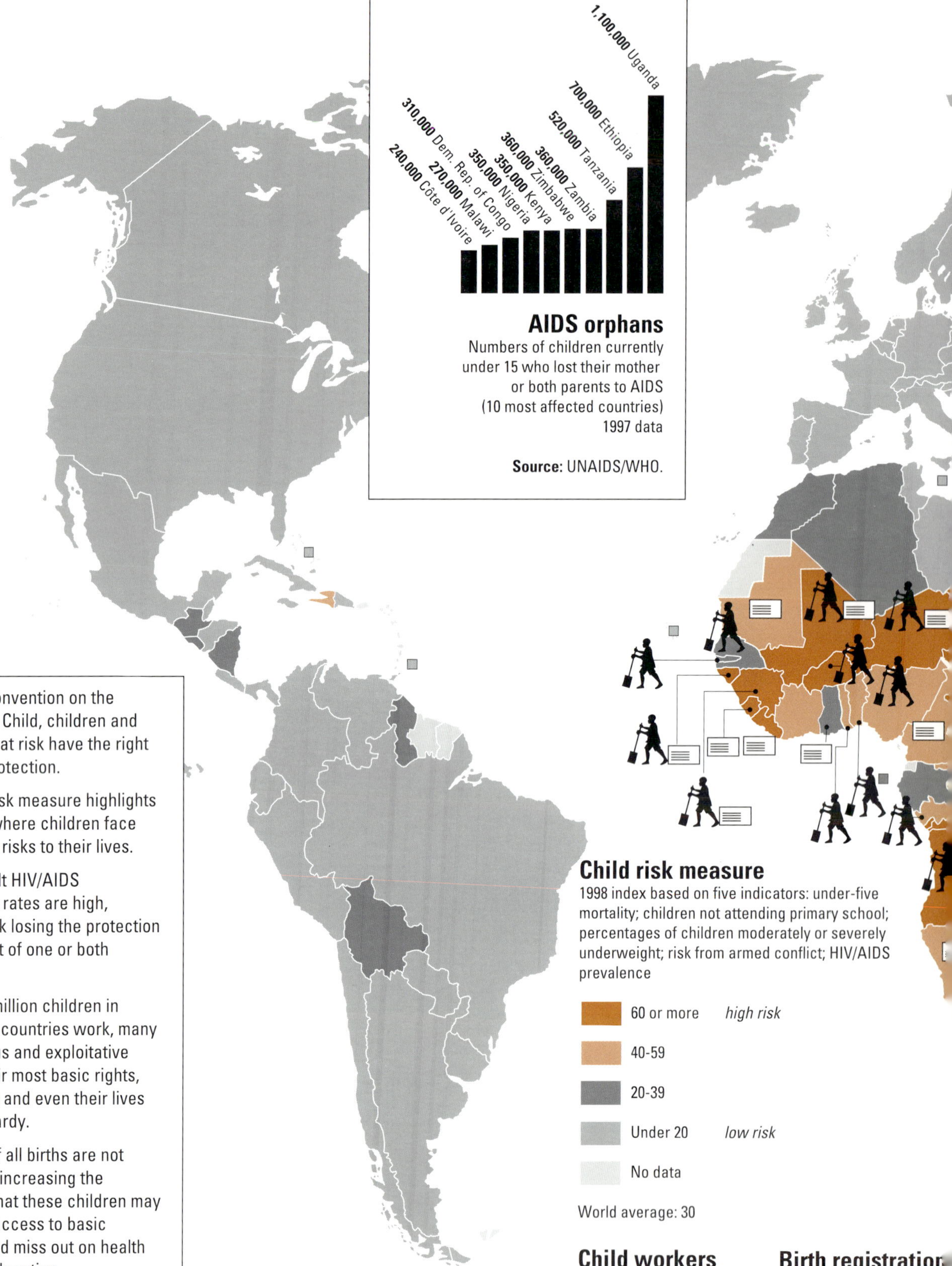

AIDS orphans

Numbers of children currently under 15 who lost their mother or both parents to AIDS (10 most affected countries) 1997 data

Source: UNAIDS/WHO.

Under the Convention on the Rights of the Child, children and adolescents at risk have the right to special protection.

- The child risk measure highlights countries where children face the highest risks to their lives.
- Where adult HIV/AIDS prevalence rates are high, children risk losing the protection and support of one or both parents.
- Some 250 million children in developing countries work, many in hazardous and exploitative labour. Their most basic rights, their health and even their lives are in jeopardy.
- One third of all births are not registered, increasing the likelihood that these children may be denied access to basic services and miss out on health care and education.
- Many children still die from diseases that could be prevented by vaccines.

Child risk measure

1998 index based on five indicators: under-five mortality; children not attending primary school; percentages of children moderately or severely underweight; risk from armed conflict; HIV/AIDS prevalence

- 60 or more *high risk*
- 40-59
- 20-39
- Under 20 *low risk*
- No data

World average: 30

Child workers

25% or more children are working

Birth registration

Fewer than 50% c children are registered

Sources: UNICEF, *The Progress of Nations 1999*; ILO; UNICEF, *The Progress of Nations 1998.*

Children and adolescents at special risk

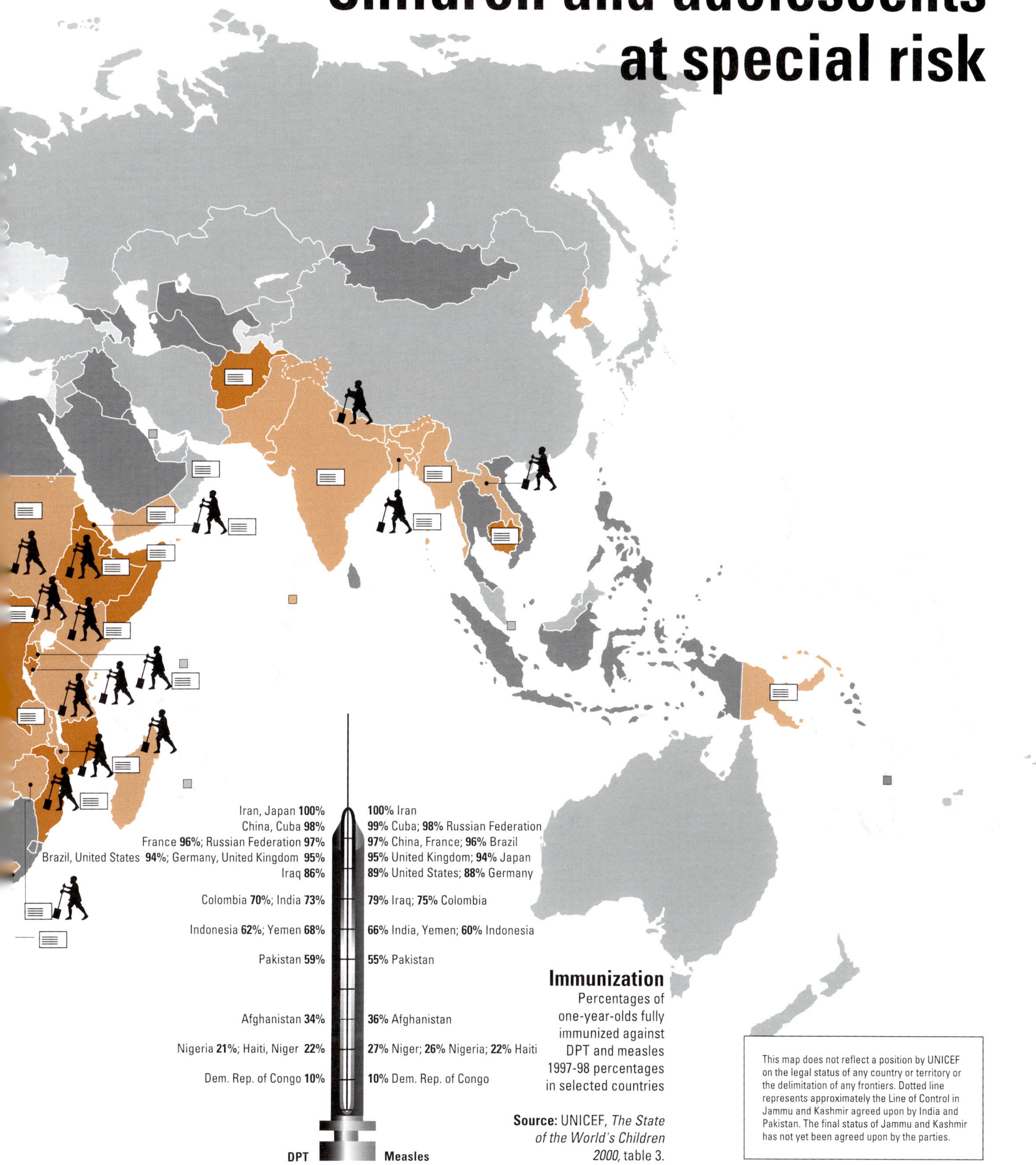

Immunization

Percentages of one-year-olds fully immunized against DPT and measles 1997-98 percentages in selected countries

Source: UNICEF, *The State of the World's Children 2000*, table 3.

This map does not reflect a position by UNICEF on the legal status of any country or territory or the delimitation of any frontiers. Dotted line represents approximately the Line of Control in Jammu and Kashmir agreed upon by India and Pakistan. The final status of Jammu and Kashmir has not yet been agreed upon by the parties.

Child poverty in industrialized countries

Percentages of children who are likely to be living in a poor family (defined by a household disposable income less than half of the country's overall median income)

Source: B. Bradbury and M. Jäntti, *Child Poverty Across Industrialized Nations*, Innocenti Occasional Papers, Economic and Social Policy Series, No. 71, UNICEF International Child Development Centre, September 1999.

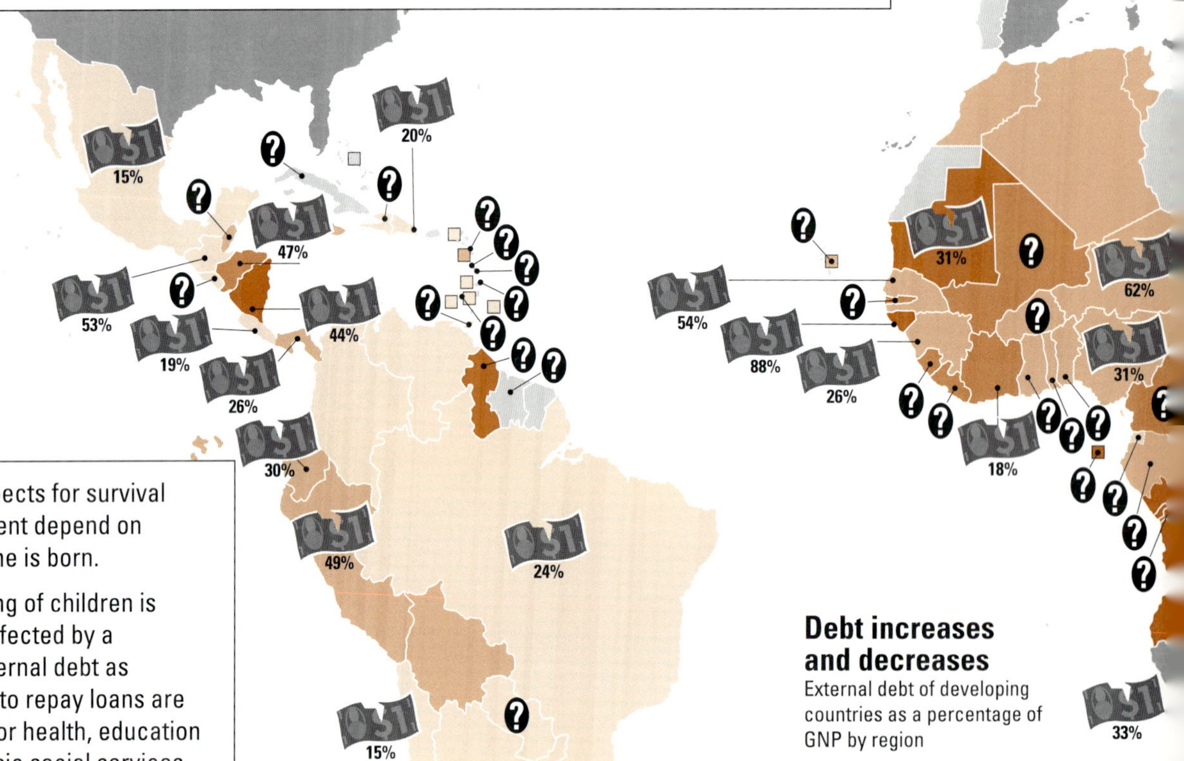

A child's prospects for survival and development depend on where she or he is born.

- The well-being of children is profoundly affected by a country's external debt as monies used to repay loans are unavailable for health, education and other basic social services.
- Almost 30% of the population in poor countries live on less than $1 a day – the majority of the poor are women and children.
- But child poverty is not confined to developing countries. Although poverty is measured on a different scale in the industrialized world, more than 1 in every 10 children in some of the richest nations are raised in families living below the established poverty line.

Debt increases and decreases

External debt of developing countries as a percentage of GNP by region

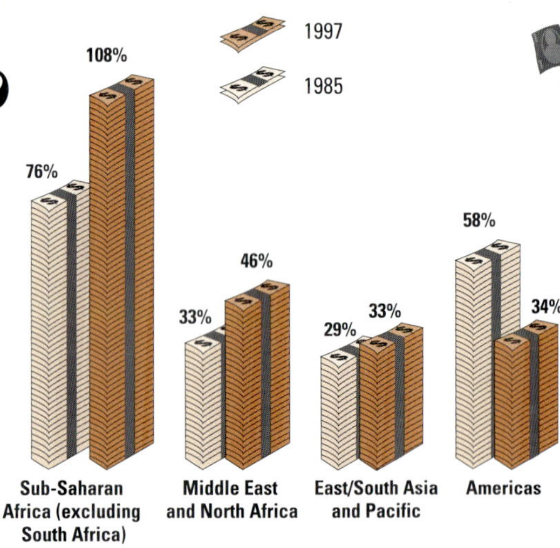

Source: UNICEF, *The Progress of Nations 1999.*

Rich world, poor world

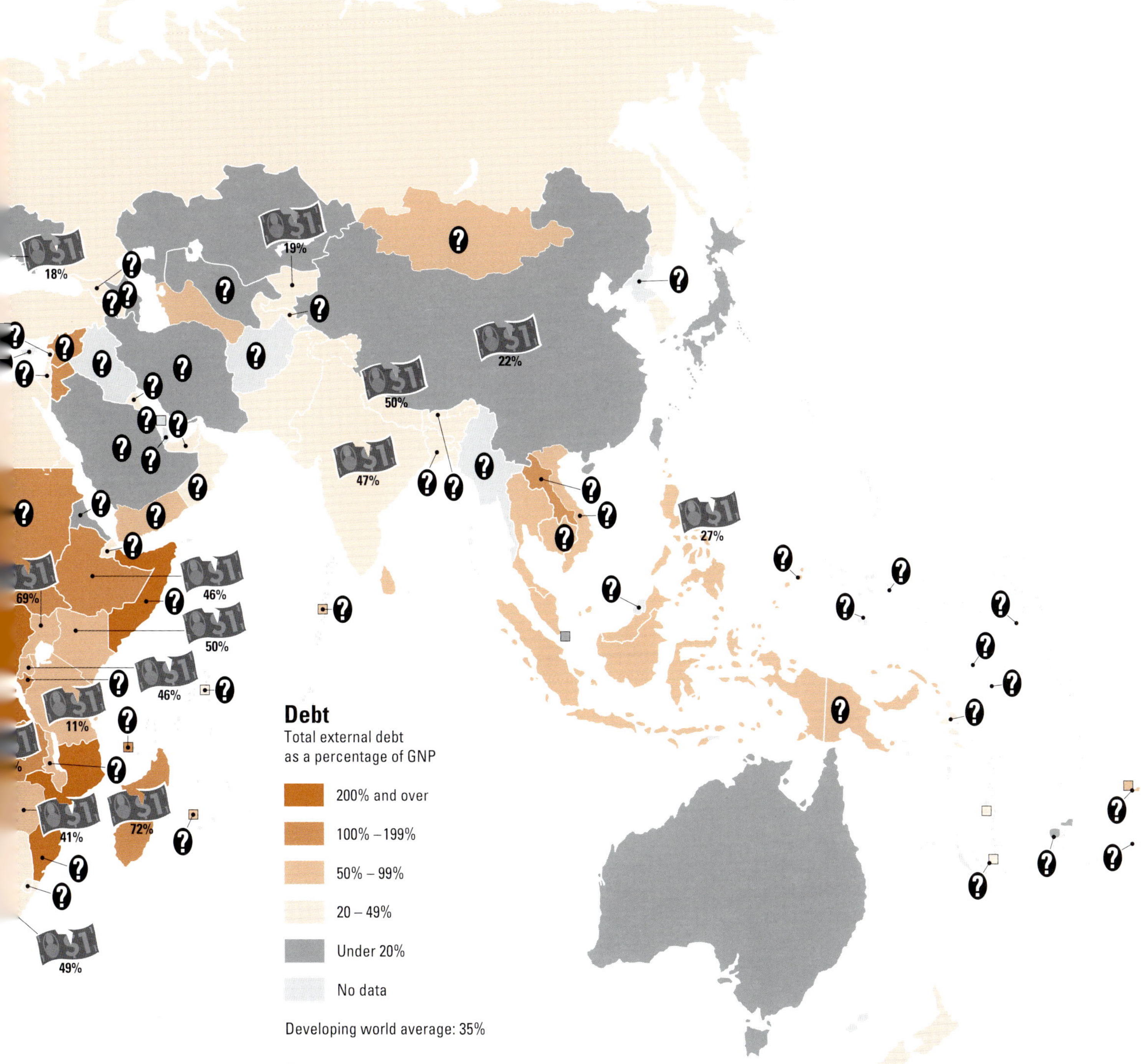

Debt

Total external debt as a percentage of GNP

- 200% and over
- 100% – 199%
- 50% – 99%
- 20 – 49%
- Under 20%
- No data

Developing world average: 35%

Poverty

- More than 10% of the population live on less than $1 a day (percentages given)
- No data available

Sources: UNICEF, *The Progress of Nations 1999;* UNICEF, *The State of the World's Children 2000,* table 6; World Bank.

This map does not reflect a position by UNICEF on the legal status of any country or territory or the delimitation of any frontiers. Dotted line represents approximately the Line of Control in Jammu and Kashmir agreed upon by India and Pakistan. The final status of Jammu and Kashmir has not yet been agreed upon by the parties.

Anti-personnel landmine producers

China, Cuba, Dem. People's Rep. of Korea, Egypt, India, Iran, Iraq, Myanmar, Pakistan, Rep. of Korea, Russian Federation, Singapore, Turkey, United States, Viet Nam, Yugoslavia.

Source: International Campaign to Ban Landmines, 1999.

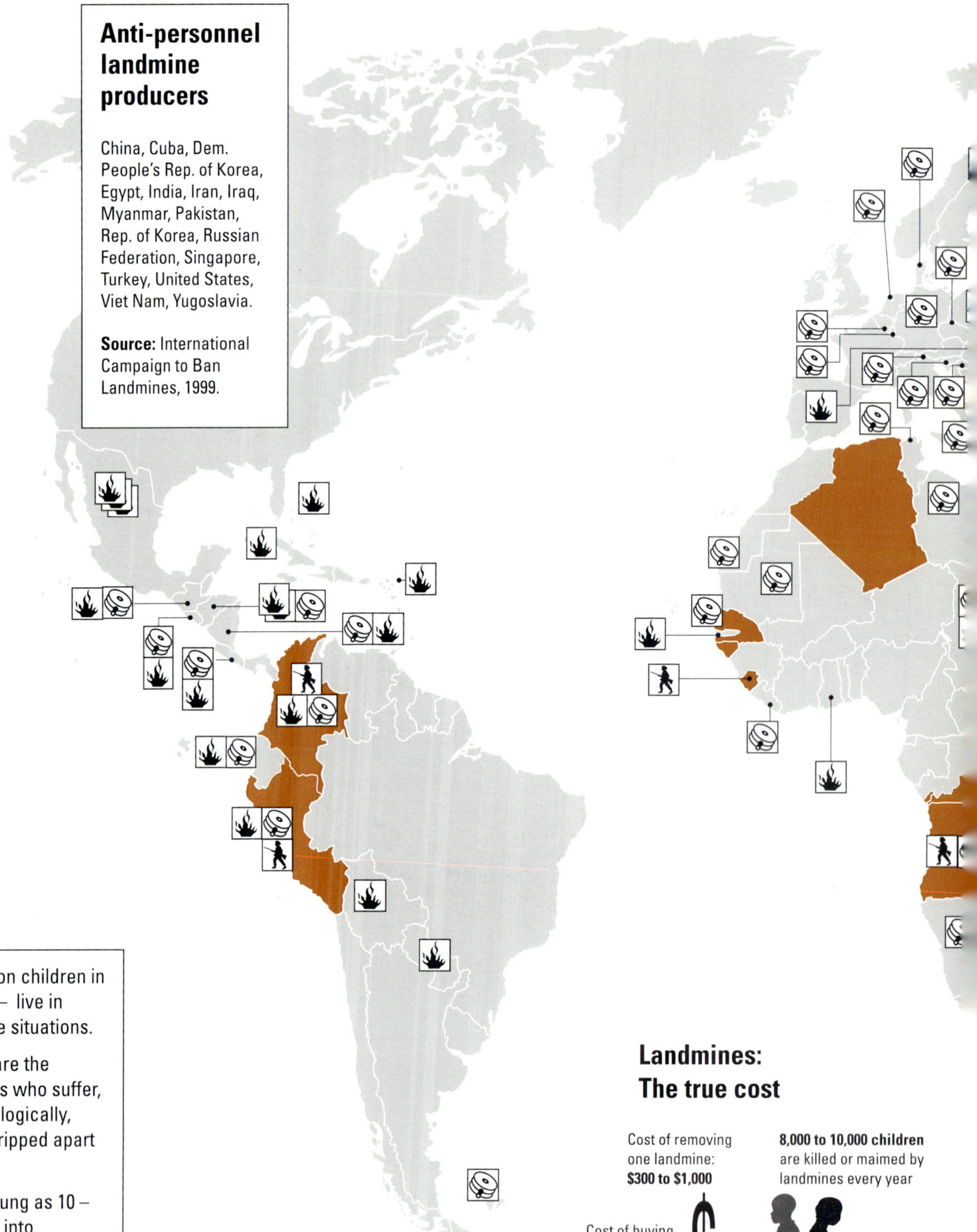

Approximately 540 million children in the world – one in four – live in dangerous and unstable situations.

- Children and women are the majority of the civilians who suffer, physically and psychologically, when their country is ripped apart by war and conflict.
- Children – some as young as 10 – are forced or coerced into services by governments and armed opposition groups.
- Environmental catastrophes, such as floods, hurricanes and earthquakes, also have grave effects on children.

Landmines: The true cost

Cost of removing one landmine: **$300 to $1,000**

8,000 to 10,000 children are killed or maimed by landmines every year

Cost of buying one landmine: **$3 to $10**

Sources: International Campaign to Ban Landmines, 1999; UNICEF.

Unstable environments

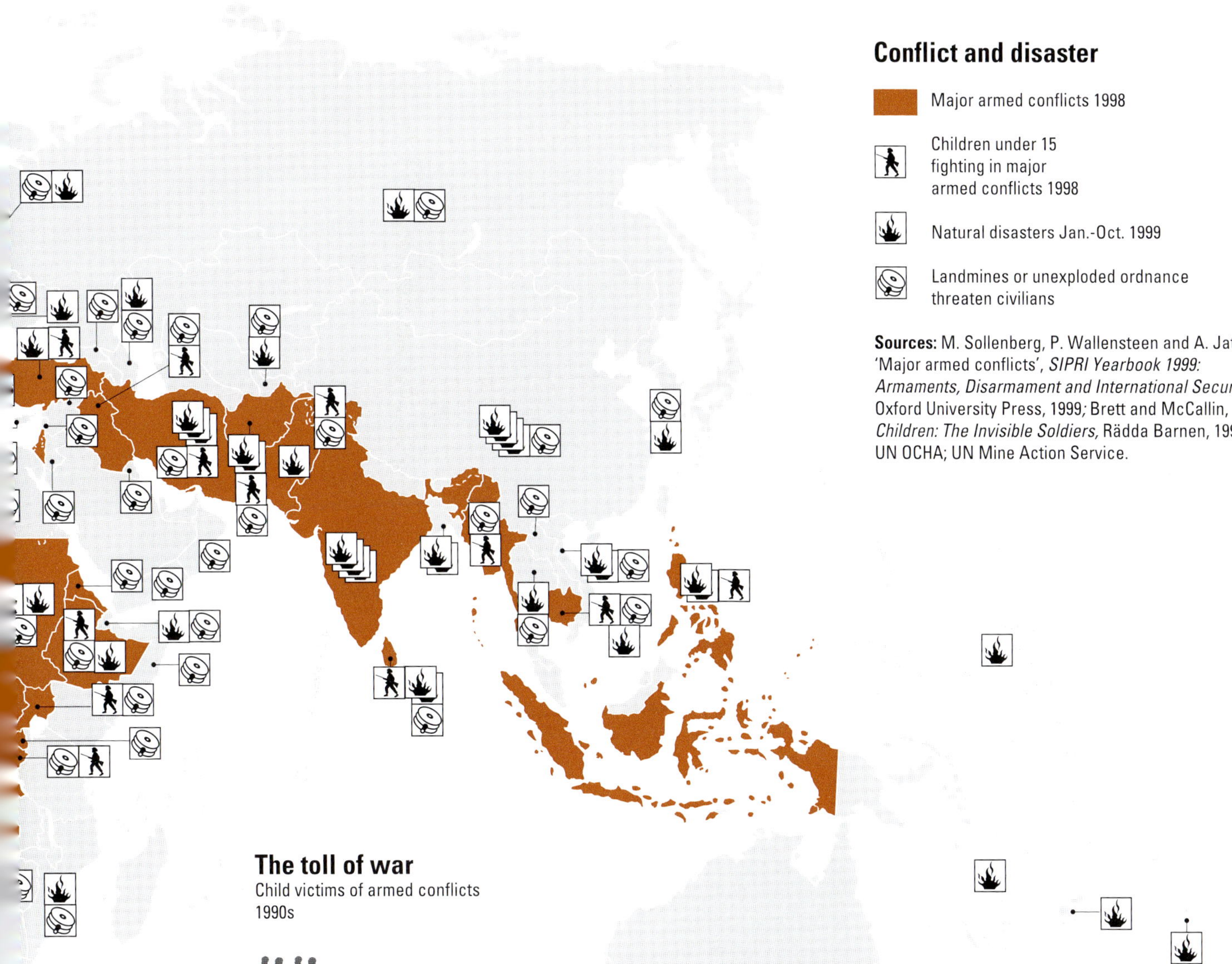

Conflict and disaster

- Major armed conflicts 1998
- Children under 15 fighting in major armed conflicts 1998
- Natural disasters Jan.-Oct. 1999
- Landmines or unexploded ordnance threaten civilians

Sources: M. Sollenberg, P. Wallensteen and A. Jato, 'Major armed conflicts', *SIPRI Yearbook 1999: Armaments, Disarmament and International Security,* Oxford University Press, 1999; Brett and McCallin, *Children: The Invisible Soldiers,* Rädda Barnen, 1998; UN OCHA; UN Mine Action Service.

The toll of war

Child victims of armed conflicts 1990s

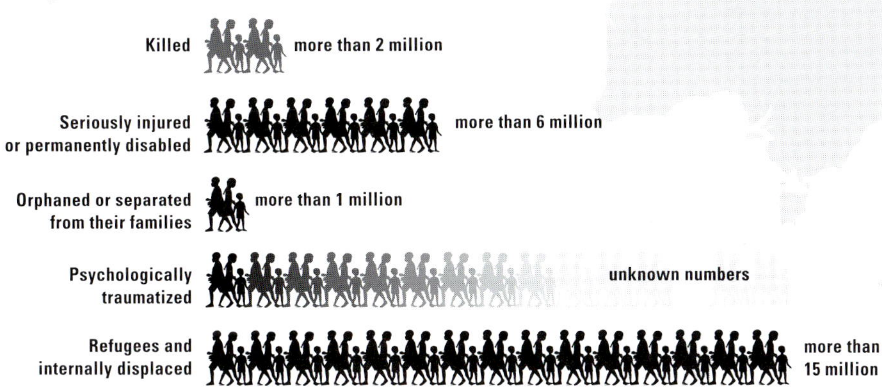

Sources: UNICEF; UNHCR; US Committee for Refugees.

This map does not reflect a position by UNICEF on the legal status of any country or territory or the delimitation of any frontiers. Dotted line represents approximately the Line of Control in Jammu and Kashmir agreed upon by India and Pakistan. The final status of Jammu and Kashmir has not yet been agreed upon by the parties.

General notes on maps

These maps are included to illustrate various aspects of the lives of children around the world. The selected indices capture some important but not all elements that affect children's well-being. Data sources for illustrations are given on each map. For illustrations based on data from tables in *The State of the World's Children 2000*, see 'General note on the data' on page 82 and the relevant table for further explanation of the data. As many countries as space allows have been included. Some island nations are surrounded by a box if an indicator may not otherwise be seen easily. Together, these maps present a snapshot of the well-being of children today. When the data on these maps are correlated, they show that negative conditions do not occur in isolation but, instead, clump together with the same children being affected by multiple and simultaneous events. These maps are graphic reminders of the effect of the absence, collapse or destruction of social service networks. However, the maps are ultimately positive as they also demonstrate the long-term benefits of social investment and stable environments on the welfare of women and children.

Map 1. Child and adolescent populations: The child and adolescent populations map focuses on demographic indicators that demonstrate the declining proportion of children and adolescents in the aggregate global population. These indicators are the child-specific pieces of a global demographic shift. The shift is the result of a global decline in birth and death rates with a corresponding increase in life expectancy at birth. As the map demonstrates, the demographic reversal is most visible in northern industrialized countries and is less pronounced in developing countries. While the deceleration has occurred in all regions of the world, it began earlier and has been more pronounced in industrially developed countries. This has exacerbated the existing differences in population and has helped to create the difference in under-19 populations between the more developed and less developed regions.

Map 2. Learning and education: The map demonstrates the progress made towards the World Summit for Children goal of universal primary education for at least 80% of school-age children with a special emphasis on reducing the inequality between boys and girls. It shows primary school enrolment and attendance around the world, with a particular emphasis on the countries where the education of girls is significantly behind that of boys. Primary school under-enrolment and inequality are concentrated in two bands, one across the centre of Africa and the other in South Asia. The largest differences between urban and rural attendance occur mostly within the bands. These are also the countries where female illiteracy exceeds 70%.

Map 3. Life expectancy: No special note.

Map 4. Children and adolescents at special risk: The child risk measure (CRM) is a new indicator used for the first time in *The Progress of Nations 1999*, in an attempt to capture in numbers some of the risks a child faces until the age of 18. Higher numbers represent greater risk. The CRM was designed as a composite of five factors which have great impact on a child's well-being: under-five mortality rate, per cent of children moderately or severely underweight, per cent of primary-school-age children not attending school, likelihood of risk from armed conflict and from HIV/AIDS.

Map 5. Rich world, poor world: Poverty is measured differently in developing and industrialized nations. In developing countries, the international poverty line is less than $1 a day and the lack of access to basic social services is assumed. In industrialized countries, different criteria apply.

Map 6. Unstable environments: Using the *SIPRI Yearbook 1999*, a 'major armed conflict' is defined as prolonged use of armed force between the military of two or more governments, or of one government and at least one organized armed group, incurring the battle-related deaths of at least 1,000 people during the entire conflict and in which the incompatibility concerns government and/or territory. Countries using child soldiers are shown only when children under 15 fought in major armed conflicts in 1998. In some of the European countries shown, landmines or unexploded ordnance date back to the Second World War and may be less of a threat to civilians than in other countries. Using information from the UN Office for the Coordination of Humanitarian Affairs, the map shows many of the natural disasters of concern to the humanitarian community, although not all countries where a natural disaster took place are shown.

Statistical tables

Economic and social statistics on the nations of the world, with particular reference to children's well-being.

Tables

General note on the data

The data presented in the following statistical tables are accompanied by definitions, sources and explanations of symbols. The tables are derived from many sources and thus will inevitably cover a wide range of data quality. Official government data received by the responsible United Nations agency have been used whenever possible. In the many cases where there are no reliable official figures, estimates made by the responsible United Nations agency have been used. Where such internationally standardized estimates do not exist, the tables draw on other sources, particularly data received from the appropriate UNICEF field office. Where possible, only comprehensive or representative national data have been used.

Data quality is likely to be adversely affected for countries that have recently suffered from man-made or natural disasters. This is particularly so where basic country infrastructure has been fragmented or major population movements have occurred.

Data for life expectancy, total fertility rates, crude birth and death rates, etc. are part of the regular work on estimates and projections undertaken by the United Nations Population Division. These and other internationally produced estimates are revised periodically, which explains why some of the data will differ from those found in earlier UNICEF publications.

Several changes have been made to the statistical tables in this issue of the report. In table 2, the 'total goitre rate' is no longer included alongside the 'percentage of households using adequately iodized salt' as an indicator of progress made in eliminating iodine deficiency, based on a 1999 decision of WHO, UNICEF and ICCIDD. Also in table 2, 'vitamin A supplementation coverage rate' has been added as an indicator of progress made in eliminating vitamin A deficiency.

The second major change concerns the data on maternal mortality in table 7. Last year, two columns of data were published on maternal mortality – the 'reported' and 'adjusted' rates. The first column included the most recent estimates reported by national authorities, and the second column included these rates adjusted for misclassification and underreporting of maternal deaths. This was done to better account for the undercoverage of maternal mortality common in most countries. New estimates for the adjusted rates are not yet available, and therefore this column has not been included.

Finally, in table 3 some changes were made to previously published 'ORT use rates' in order to make the data more comparable among countries.

Explanation of symbols

Since the aim of this statistics chapter is to provide a broad picture of the situation of children and women worldwide, detailed data qualifications and footnotes are seen as more appropriate for inclusion elsewhere. Only three symbols are used to classify the table data.

- Indicates data are not available.

x Indicates data that refer to years or periods other than those specified in the column heading, differ from the standard definition, or refer to only part of a country.

* Data refer to the most recent year available during the period specified in the column heading.

Under-five mortality rankings

The following list ranks countries in descending order of their estimated 1998 under-five mortality rate (U5MR), a critical indicator of the well-being of children. Countries are listed alphabetically in the tables that follow.

Country	Under-5 mortality rate Value	Rank
Sierra Leone	316	**1**
Angola	292	**2**
Niger	280	**3**
Afghanistan	257	**4**
Mali	237	**5**
Liberia	235	**6**
Malawi	213	**7**
Somalia	211	**8**
Congo, Dem. Rep.	207	**9**
Mozambique	206	**10**
Guinea-Bissau	205	**11**
Zambia	202	**12**
Chad	198	**13**
Guinea	197	**14**
Nigeria	187	**15**
Mauritania	183	**16**
Burundi	176	**17**
Central African Rep.	173	**18**
Ethiopia	173	**18**
Equatorial Guinea	171	**20**
Rwanda	170	**21**
Benin	165	**22**
Burkina Faso	165	**22**
Cambodia	163	**24**
Madagascar	157	**25**
Djibouti	156	**26**
Cameroon	153	**27**
Côte d'Ivoire	150	**28**
Mongolia	150	**28**
Gabon	144	**30**
Togo	144	**30**
Tanzania	142	**32**
Lesotho	136	**33**
Pakistan	136	**33**
Uganda	134	**35**
Haiti	130	**36**
Iraq	125	**37**
Senegal	121	**38**
Yemen	121	**38**
Kenya	117	**40**
Bhutan	116	**41**
Lao People's Dem. Rep.	116	**41**
Sudan	115	**43**
Myanmar	113	**44**
Eritrea	112	**45**
Papua New Guinea	112	**45**
Congo	108	**47**
Bangladesh	106	**48**
Ghana	105	**49**
India	105	**49**
Nepal	100	**51**
Marshall Islands	92	**52**
Comoros	90	**53**
Swaziland	90	**53**
Zimbabwe	89	**55**
Maldives	87	**56**
Bolivia	85	**57**
South Africa	83	**58**
Gambia	82	**59**
Guyana	79	**60**
Sao Tome and Principe	77	**61**
Kiribati	74	**62**
Namibia	74	**62**
Tajikistan	74	**62**
Cape Verde	73	**65**
Turkmenistan	72	**66**
Morocco	70	**67**
Egypt	69	**68**
Kyrgyzstan	66	**69**
Uzbekistan	58	**70**
Indonesia	56	**71**
Tuvalu	56	**71**
Peru	54	**73**
Guatemala	52	**74**
Dominican Rep.	51	**75**
Vanuatu	49	**76**
Botswana	48	**77**
Nicaragua	48	**77**
China	47	**79**
Azerbaijan	46	**80**
Honduras	44	**81**
Philippines	44	**81**
Belize	43	**83**
Kazakhstan	43	**83**
Brazil	42	**85**
Turkey	42	**85**
Viet Nam	42	**85**
Algeria	40	**88**
Ecuador	39	**89**
Albania	37	**90**
Saint Kitts and Nevis	37	**90**
Thailand	37	**90**
Jordan	36	**93**
Lebanon	35	**94**
Moldova, Rep. of	35	**94**
Suriname	35	**94**
El Salvador	34	**97**
Mexico	34	**97**
Palau	34	**97**
Iran	33	**100**
Paraguay	33	**100**
Syria	32	**102**
Tunisia	32	**102**
Armenia	30	**104**
Colombia	30	**104**
Cook Islands	30	**104**
Korea, Dem. People's Rep.	30	**104**
Nauru	30	**104**
Grenada	28	**109**
Belarus	27	**110**
Samoa	27	**110**
TFYR Macedonia†	27	**110**
Saudi Arabia	26	**113**
Solomon Islands	26	**113**
Russian Federation	25	**115**
Venezuela	25	**115**
Libya	24	**117**
Micronesia, Fed. States of	24	**117**
Romania	24	**117**
Fiji	23	**120**
Georgia	23	**120**
Lithuania	23	**120**
Mauritius	23	**120**
Saint Vincent/Grenadines	23	**120**
Tonga	23	**120**
Argentina	22	**126**
Estonia	22	**126**
Latvia	22	**126**
Ukraine	22	**126**
Bahamas	21	**130**
Saint Lucia	21	**130**
Yugoslavia	21	**130**
Antigua and Barbuda	20	**133**
Bahrain	20	**133**
Dominica	20	**133**
Panama	20	**133**
Bosnia and Herzegovina	19	**137**
Sri Lanka	19	**137**
Uruguay	19	**137**
Oman	18	**140**
Qatar	18	**140**
Seychelles	18	**140**
Trinidad and Tobago	18	**140**
Bulgaria	17	**144**
Costa Rica	16	**145**
Barbados	15	**146**
Kuwait	13	**147**
Chile	12	**148**
Hungary	11	**149**
Jamaica	11	**149**
Liechtenstein	11	**149**
Poland	11	**149**
Malaysia	10	**153**
Slovakia	10	**153**
United Arab Emirates	10	**153**
Brunei Darussalam	9	**156**
Croatia	9	**156**
Cyprus	9	**156**
Portugal	9	**156**
Cuba	8	**160**
United States	8	**160**
Greece	7	**162**
Ireland	7	**162**
Malta	7	**162**
Andorra	6	**165**
Belgium	6	**165**
Canada	6	**165**
Czech Rep.	6	**165**
Israel	6	**165**
Italy	6	**165**
New Zealand	6	**165**
San Marino	6	**165**
Spain	6	**165**
United Kingdom	6	**165**
Australia	5	**175**
Austria	5	**175**
Denmark	5	**175**
Finland	5	**175**
France	5	**175**
Germany	5	**175**
Iceland	5	**175**
Korea, Rep. of	5	**175**
Luxembourg	5	**175**
Monaco	5	**175**
Netherlands	5	**175**
Singapore	5	**175**
Slovenia	5	**175**
Switzerland	5	**175**
Japan	4	**189**
Norway	4	**189**
Sweden	4	**189**
Holy See	no data	-
Niue	no data	-

† The former Yugoslav Republic of Macedonia, referred to in the following tables as TFYR Macedonia.

Table 1: Basic indicators

	Under-5 mortality rank	Under-5 mortality rate 1960	Under-5 mortality rate 1998	Infant mortality rate (under 1) 1960	Infant mortality rate (under 1) 1998	Total population (thousands) 1998	Annual no. of births (thousands) 1998	Annual no. of under-5 deaths (thousands) 1998	GNP per capita (US$) 1997	Life expectancy at birth (years) 1998	Total adult literacy rate 1995	Primary school enrolment ratio (gross) 1990-96*	% share of household income 1990-96* lowest 40%	% share of household income 1990-96* highest 20%
Afghanistan	**4**	360	257	215	165	21354	1113	286	250x	46	32	49	-	-
Albania	**90**	151	37	112	30	3119	63	2	760	73	-	101	-	-
Algeria	**88**	255	40	152	35	30081	875	35	1500	69	58	107	19	43
Andorra	**165**	-	6	-	5	72	1	0	d	-	-	-	-	-
Angola	**2**	345	292	208	170	12092	583	170	260	47	42x	88	-	-
Antigua and Barbuda	**133**	-	20	-	17	67	1	0	7380	76	95x	100x	-	-
Argentina	**126**	72	22	60	19	36123	715	16	8950	73	96	113	-	-
Armenia	**104**	48	30	38	25	3536	45	1	560	71	100	86	-	-
Australia	**175**	24	5	20	5	18520	246	1	20650	78	-	103	19x	41x
Austria	**175**	43	5	37	5	8140	82	0	27920	77	-	100	25x	33x
Azerbaijan	**80**	74	46	55	36	7669	122	6	510	70	100	107	-	-
Bahamas	**130**	68	21	51	18	296	6	0	11830x	74	96	100	-	-
Bahrain	**133**	203	20	130	16	595	11	0	8640x	73	85	106	-	-
Bangladesh	**48**	247	106	151	79	124774	3468	368	360	58	38	69	23	38
Barbados	**146**	90	15	74	13	268	3	0	6590x	76	97	90	-	-
Belarus	**110**	47	27	37	22	10315	98	3	2150	68	99	98	26	33
Belgium	**165**	35	6	31	6	10141	106	1	26730	77	-	103	24	35
Belize	**83**	104	43	74	35	230	7	0	2670	75	70x	121	-	-
Benin	**22**	300	165	176	101	5781	238	39	380	53	32	76	-	-
Bhutan	**41**	300	116	175	84	2004	75	9	430	61	42	25x	-	-
Bolivia	**57**	255	85	152	66	7957	262	22	970	62	82	95	15	48
Bosnia and Herzegovina	**137**	160	19	105	16	3675	37	1	a	73	-	-	-	-
Botswana	**77**	170	48	117	38	1570	52	3	3310	47	73	112	11x	59x
Brazil	**85**	177	42	115	36	165851	3340	140	4790	67	83	123	8	64
Brunei Darussalam	**156**	87	9	63	8	315	6	0	25160x	76	89	107	-	-
Bulgaria	**144**	70	17	49	14	8336	71	1	1170	71	98	99	21	39
Burkina Faso	**22**	315	165	181	109	11305	519	86	250	45	19	40	-	-
Burundi	**17**	255	176	151	106	6457	271	48	140	43	42	51	-	-
Cambodia	**24**	217	163	146	104	10716	364	59	300	53	65x	131	-	-
Cameroon	**27**	255	153	151	94	14305	562	86	620	55	63	88	-	-
Canada	**165**	33	6	28	6	30563	344	2	19640	79	97x	102	20	39
Cape Verde	**65**	164	73	110	54	408	13	1	1090	69	69	131	-	-
Central African Rep.	**18**	327	173	187	113	3485	130	22	320	45	40	58	-	-
Chad	**13**	325	198	195	118	7270	318	63	230	47	48	65	-	-
Chile	**148**	138	12	107	11	14824	291	3	4820	75	95	101	10	61
China	**79**	209	47	140	38	1255698	20134	946	860	70	80	120	15	48
Colombia	**104**	130	30	82	25	40803	988	30	2180	71	90	118	10	62
Comoros	**53**	265	90	200	67	658	23	2	400	59	57	74	-	-
Congo	**47**	220	108	143	81	2785	121	13	670	49	74	114	-	-
Congo, Dem. Rep.	**9**	302	207	175	128	49139	2264	469	110	51	77	72	-	-
Cook Islands	**104**	-	30	-	26	19	0	0	-	-	99x	98	-	-
Costa Rica	**145**	112	16	80	14	3841	89	1	2680	76	95	107	13	52
Côte d'Ivoire	**28**	300	150	195	90	14292	533	80	710	47	40	71	18x	44x
Croatia	**156**	98	9	70	8	4481	47	0	4060	73	97	87	-	-
Cuba	**160**	54	8	39	7	11116	143	1	1170x	76	96	106	-	-
Cyprus	**156**	36	9	30	8	771	10	0	10260x	78	95	100	-	-
Czech Rep.	**165**	25	6	22	5	10282	88	1	5240	74	-	104	24	37
Denmark	**175**	25	5	22	5	5270	63	0	34890	76	-	100	25	35
Djibouti	**26**	289	156	186	111	623	23	4	b	51	46	38	-	-
Dominica	**133**	-	20	-	17	71	1	0	3040	76	-	-	-	-
Dominican Rep.	**75**	149	51	102	43	8232	196	10	1750	71	82	103	12x	56x
Ecuador	**89**	180	39	115	30	12175	309	12	1570	70	89	127	14	53
Egypt	**68**	282	69	189	51	65978	1726	119	1200	67	51	102	21	41
El Salvador	**97**	210	34	130	30	6032	166	6	1810	69	76	94	12	54
Equatorial Guinea	**20**	316	171	188	108	431	17	3	1060	50	78	149x	-	-
Eritrea	**45**	250	112	170	70	3577	144	16	230	51	-	54	-	-
Estonia	**126**	52	22	40	18	1429	12	0	3360	69	98	94	17	46

	Under-5 mortality rank	Under-5 mortality rate		Infant mortality rate (under 1)		Total population (thousands) 1998	Annual no. of births (thousands) 1998	Annual no. of under-5 deaths (thousands) 1998	GNP per capita (US$) 1997	Life expectancy at birth (years) 1998	Total adult literacy rate 1995	Primary school enrolment ratio (gross) 1990-96*	% share of household income 1990-96*	
		1960	1998	1960	1998								lowest 40%	highest 20%
Ethiopia	**18**	280	173	175	110	59649	2652	459	110	43	33	37	21x	41x
Fiji	**120**	97	23	71	19	796	17	0	2460	73	91	128	-	-
Finland	**175**	28	5	22	4	5154	57	0	24790	77	-	100	24	36
France	**175**	34	5	29	5	58683	713	4	26300	78	-	106	20x	40x
Gabon	**30**	287	144	171	85	1167	43	6	4120	52	63	-	-	-
Gambia	**59**	364	82	207	64	1229	49	4	340	47	39	77	-	-
Georgia	**120**	70	23	52	19	5059	69	2	860	73	99	84	-	-
Germany	**175**	40	5	34	5	82133	749	4	28280	77	-	103	23x	37x
Ghana	**49**	215	105	127	67	19162	711	75	390	60	64	76	20	42
Greece	**162**	64	7	53	6	10600	97	1	11640	78	96	94	-	-
Grenada	**109**	-	28	-	23	93	2	0	3140	72	96x	88x	-	-
Guatemala	**74**	202	52	136	41	10801	393	20	1580	64	65	84	8x	63x
Guinea	**14**	380	197	215	124	7337	309	61	550	47	36	48	11	50
Guinea-Bissau	**11**	336	205	200	130	1161	48	10	230	45	31	64	9	59
Guyana	**60**	126	79	100	58	850	18	1	800	65	98	95	-	-
Haiti	**36**	253	130	169	91	7952	253	33	380	54	44	56	-	-
Holy See	**-**	-	-	-	-	-	-	-	-	-	-	-	-	-
Honduras	**81**	204	44	137	33	6147	203	9	740	70	70	111	11	58
Hungary	**149**	57	11	51	10	10116	97	1	4510	71	99	104	24	38
Iceland	**175**	22	5	17	5	276	4	0	26470x	79	-	98	-	-
India	**49**	236	105	144	69	982223	24671	2590	370	63	50	101	22	39
Indonesia	**71**	216	56	128	40	206338	4662	261	1110	65	84	114	20	43
Iran	**100**	233	33	145	29	65758	1389	46	1780	69	71	90	-	-
Iraq	**37**	171	125	117	103	21800	792	99	b	63	58	85	-	-
Ireland	**162**	36	7	31	6	3681	52	0	17790	76	-	103	18x	43x
Israel	**165**	39	6	32	6	5984	117	1	16180	78	95	99	18	43
Italy	**165**	50	6	44	6	57369	512	3	20170	78	98	99	21	39
Jamaica	**149**	76	11	58	10	2538	54	1	1550	75	85	107	16	48
Japan	**189**	40	4	31	4	126281	1261	5	38160	80	-	102	22x	38x
Jordan	**93**	139	36	97	30	6304	218	8	1520	70	86	94	16	50
Kazakhstan	**83**	74	43	55	36	16319	298	13	1350	68	100	96	20	40
Kenya	**40**	205	117	122	75	29008	987	115	340	52	77	85	10	62
Kiribati	**62**	-	74	-	54	81	3	0	910	60	93x	91	-	-
Korea, Dem. People's Rep.	**104**	120	30	85	23	23348	485	15	970x	72	-	104x	-	-
Korea, Rep. of	**175**	127	5	90	5	46109	682	3	10550	73	97	94	20x	42x
Kuwait	**147**	128	13	89	12	1811	39	1	20190x	76	79	75	-	-
Kyrgyzstan	**69**	180	66	135	56	4643	117	8	480	68	97	107	18	42
Lao People's Dem. Rep.	**41**	235	116	155	96	5163	202	23	400	53	57	111	23	40
Latvia	**126**	44	22	35	18	2424	20	0	2430	69	100	96	23	37
Lebanon	**94**	85	35	65	29	3191	74	3	3350	70	83	111	-	-
Lesotho	**33**	203	136	137	94	2062	72	10	680	56	81	97	9x	60x
Liberia	**6**	288	235	190	157	2666	117	28	490x	48	45	35x	-	-
Libya	**117**	270	24	159	20	5339	156	4	5540x	70	74	110	-	-
Liechtenstein	**149**	-	11	-	10	32	0	0	d	-	100x	-	-	-
Lithuania	**120**	70	23	52	19	3694	36	1	2260	70	99	98	20	42
Luxembourg	**175**	41	5	33	5	422	5	0	44690x	77	-	99	-	-
Madagascar	**25**	364	157	219	95	15057	600	94	250	58	46	73	16	50
Malawi	**7**	361	213	205	134	10346	489	104	210	39	56	135	-	-
Malaysia	**153**	105	10	73	9	21410	525	5	4530	72	84	91	13x	54x
Maldives	**56**	300	87	180	62	271	9	1	1180	65	95	125	-	-
Mali	**5**	517	237	293	144	10694	499	118	260	54	32	37	-	-
Malta	**162**	42	7	37	6	384	4	0	9330	77	91	110	-	-
Marshall Islands	**52**	-	92	-	63	60	2	0	1610	-	91x	95	-	-
Mauritania	**16**	310	183	180	120	2529	102	19	440	54	37	83	14x	47x
Mauritius	**120**	92	23	67	19	1141	17	0	3870	72	82	107	-	-
Mexico	**97**	134	34	94	28	95831	2335	79	3700	72	89	115	12	55
Micronesia, Fed. States of	**117**	-	24	-	20	114	4	0	1920	67	81x	100	-	-

Table 1: Basic indicators

	Under-5 mortality rank	Under-5 mortality rate		Infant mortality rate (under 1)		Total population (thousands) 1998	Annual no. of births (thousands) 1998	Annual no. of under-5 deaths (thousands) 1998	GNP per capita (US$) 1997	Life expectancy at birth (years) 1998	Total adult literacy rate 1995	Primary school enrolment ratio (gross) 1990-96*	% share of household income 1990-96*	
		1960	1998	1960	1998								lowest 40%	highest 20%
Moldova, Rep. of	**94**	88	35	64	28	4378	56	2	460	68	98	96	19	42
Monaco	**175**	-	5	-	5	33	0	0	d	-	-	-	-	-
Mongolia	**28**	185	150	128	105	2579	58	9	390	66	83	89	20	41
Morocco	**67**	220	70	135	57	27377	706	49	1260	67	44	84	17	46
Mozambique	**10**	313	206	180	129	18880	817	168	140	44	38	60	-	-
Myanmar	**44**	252	113	169	80	44497	943	107	220x	60	83	100	-	-
Namibia	**62**	206	74	129	57	1660	59	4	2110	51	78	131	-	-
Nauru	**104**	-	30	-	25	11	0	0	-	-	-	-	-	-
Nepal	**51**	297	100	199	72	22847	779	78	220	58	36	110	19	45
Netherlands	**175**	22	5	18	5	15678	179	1	25830	78	-	107	21	40
New Zealand	**165**	26	6	22	5	3796	57	0	15830	77	-	103	16x	45x
Nicaragua	**77**	193	48	130	39	4807	172	8	410	68	66	110	12	55
Niger	**3**	354	280	211	166	10078	488	137	200	49	13	29	19	44
Nigeria	**15**	207	187	123	112	106409	4114	769	280	50	57	89	13	49
Niue	**-**	-	-	-	-	2	0	-	-	-	99x	-	-	-
Norway	**189**	23	4	19	4	4419	57	0	36100	78	-	99	24	35
Oman	**140**	280	18	164	15	2382	83	1	4940x	71	64	77	-	-
Pakistan	**33**	226	136	139	95	148166	5306	722	500	64	39	74	21	40
Palau	**97**	-	34	-	28	19	1	0	c	-	98x	103	-	-
Panama	**133**	104	20	67	18	2767	61	1	3080	74	91	104	8	60
Papua New Guinea	**45**	204	112	137	79	4600	146	16	930	58	72	80	12	57
Paraguay	**100**	90	33	66	27	5222	162	5	2000	70	92	112	8	62
Peru	**73**	234	54	142	43	24797	611	33	2610	68	88	122	14	50
Philippines	**81**	110	44	80	32	72944	2064	91	1200	68	94	117	16	50
Poland	**149**	70	11	62	10	38718	418	5	3590	73	100	96	23	37
Portugal	**156**	112	9	81	8	9869	103	1	11010	75	90	128	-	-
Qatar	**140**	239	18	145	15	579	10	0	11340x	72	79	86	-	-
Romania	**117**	82	24	69	21	22474	202	5	1410	70	98	104	24	35
Russian Federation	**115**	64	25	48	21	147434	1420	36	2680	67	99	108	20	38
Rwanda	**21**	210	170	124	105	6604	282	48	210	41	60	82	23x	39x
Saint Kitts and Nevis	**90**	-	37	-	30	39	1	0	6260	70	90x	-	-	-
Saint Lucia	**130**	-	21	-	18	150	3	0	3510	70	-	95x	-	-
Saint Vincent/Grenadines	**120**	-	23	-	20	112	2	0	2420	73	82x	95x	-	-
Samoa	**110**	210	27	134	22	174	4	0	1140	71	98x	107	-	-
San Marino	**165**	-	6	-	6	26	0	0	-	-	-	-	-	-
Sao Tome and Principe	**61**	-	77	-	60	141	6	0	290	64	57x	-	-	-
Saudi Arabia	**113**	292	26	170	22	20181	680	18	7150	72	71	76	-	-
Senegal	**38**	300	121	173	70	9003	358	43	540	53	33	69	11	59
Seychelles	**140**	-	18	-	14	76	3	0	6910	71	84x	102x	-	-
Sierra Leone	**1**	390	316	220	182	4568	211	67	160	38	31	50	3x	63x
Singapore	**175**	40	5	31	4	3476	50	0	32810	77	91	94	15x	49x
Slovakia	**153**	40	10	33	9	5377	56	1	3680	73	-	102	28	31
Slovenia	**175**	45	5	37	5	1993	18	0	9840	74	100	105	23	39
Solomon Islands	**113**	185	26	120	22	417	14	0	870	72	62x	97	-	-
Somalia	**8**	294	211	175	125	9237	484	102	110x	47	24x	11x	-	-
South Africa	**58**	130	83	89	60	39357	1056	88	3210	54	83	116	9	63
Spain	**165**	57	6	46	6	39628	360	2	14490	78	97	105	20	40
Sri Lanka	**137**	133	19	83	17	18455	327	6	800	73	90	109	22	39
Sudan	**43**	210	115	125	73	28292	932	107	290	55	51	53	-	-
Suriname	**94**	98	35	70	28	414	8	0	1320	70	93	127x	-	-
Swaziland	**53**	233	90	157	64	952	36	3	1520	60	76	129	-	-
Sweden	**189**	20	4	16	4	8875	86	0	26210	79	-	105	24	35
Switzerland	**175**	27	5	22	5	7299	80	0	43060	79	-	107	19x	44x
Syria	**102**	201	32	136	26	15333	464	15	1120	69	70	101	-	-
Tajikistan	**62**	140	74	95	55	6015	190	14	330	67	99	93	-	-
Tanzania	**32**	240	142	142	91	32102	1314	187	210	48	69	66	18	45
TFYR Macedonia	**110**	177	27	120	23	1999	31	1	1100	73	-	88	-	-

	Under-5 mortality rank	Under-5 mortality rate 1960	Under-5 mortality rate 1998	Infant mortality rate (under 1) 1960	Infant mortality rate (under 1) 1998	Total population (thousands) 1998	Annual no. of births (thousands) 1998	Annual no. of under-5 deaths (thousands) 1998	GNP per capita (US$) 1997	Life expectancy at birth (years) 1998	Total adult literacy rate 1995	Primary school enrolment ratio (gross) 1990-96*	% share of household income 1990-96* lowest 40%	% share of household income 1990-96* highest 20%
Thailand	**90**	148	37	103	30	60300	1000	37	2740	69	94	88	14	53
Togo	**30**	267	144	158	81	4397	181	26	340	49	51	119	-	-
Tonga	**120**	-	23	-	19	98	2	0	1810	71	99x	98x	-	-
Trinidad and Tobago	**140**	73	18	61	16	1283	17	0	4250	74	98	96	-	-
Tunisia	**102**	254	32	170	25	9335	189	6	2110	70	65	114	16	46
Turkey	**85**	219	42	163	37	64479	1425	60	3130	69	82	105	-	-
Turkmenistan	**66**	150	72	100	53	4309	121	9	640	66	98x	-	18	43
Tuvalu	**71**	-	56	-	40	11	0	0	-	-	99x	101	-	-
Uganda	**35**	224	134	133	84	20554	1054	141	330	40	62	73	17	48
Ukraine	**126**	53	22	41	18	50861	486	11	1040	69	99	87	24	35
United Arab Emirates	**153**	223	10	149	9	2353	43	0	18240x	75	79	89	-	-
United Kingdom	**165**	27	6	23	6	58649	689	4	20870	77	-	116	20x	40x
United States	**160**	30	8	26	7	274028	3788	30	29080	77	99x	102	15	45
Uruguay	**137**	56	19	48	16	3289	57	1	6130	74	97	113	-	-
Uzbekistan	**70**	120	58	84	45	23574	652	38	1020	68	100	77	-	-
Vanuatu	**76**	225	49	141	38	182	5	0	1340	68	64x	106	-	-
Venezuela	**115**	75	25	56	21	23242	572	14	3480	72	91	91	13	52
Viet Nam	**85**	219	42	147	31	77562	1681	71	310	68	91	114	19	44
Yemen	**38**	340	121	220	87	16887	807	98	270	58	40	70	17	46
Yugoslavia	**130**	120	21	87	18	10635	136	3	b	73	98	71	-	-
Zambia	**12**	213	202	126	112	8781	372	75	370	40	78	89	12	50
Zimbabwe	**55**	159	89	97	59	11377	353	31	720	44	85	113	10	62

Regional summaries

	Under-5 mortality rate 1960	Under-5 mortality rate 1998	Infant mortality rate 1960	Infant mortality rate 1998	Total population (thousands) 1998	Annual no. of births (thousands) 1998	Annual no. of under-5 deaths (thousands) 1998	GNP per capita (US$) 1997	Life expectancy at birth (years) 1998	Total adult literacy rate 1995	Primary school enrolment ratio (gross) 1990-96*	lowest 40%	highest 20%
Sub-Saharan Africa	261	173	156	107	580939	23671	4093	513	48	56	74	12	57
Middle East and North Africa	241	66	153	51	324970	9227	613	2078	66	60	89	-	-
South Asia	239	114	146	76	1320094	35748	4060	385	62	48	94	22	39
East Asia and Pacific	201	50	133	38	1837039	33054	1643	1273	69	82	116	17	47
Latin America and Caribbean	154	39	102	32	498220	11441	446	3894	69	86	113	10	60
CEE/CIS and Baltic States	101	35	76	29	475350	6413	225	2339	69	97	99	22	37
Industrialized countries	37	6	31	6	847998	9830	60	27146	78	98	104	19	41
Developing countries	216	95	138	64	4702849	116297	11007	1299	62	70	100	15	51
Least developed countries	282	167	172	107	614920	23660	3950	256	50	49	68	20	42
World	193	86	124	59	5884610	129384	11140	5132	64	74	100	19	42

Countries in each region are listed on page 112.

Definitions of the indicators

Under-five mortality rate – Probability of dying between birth and exactly five years of age expressed per 1,000 live births.

Infant mortality rate – Probability of dying between birth and exactly one year of age expressed per 1,000 live births.

GNP per capita – Gross national product (GNP) is the sum of gross value added by all resident producers, plus any taxes that are not included in the valuation of output, plus net receipts of primary income from non-resident sources. GNP per capita is the gross national product, converted to United States dollars using the World Bank Atlas method, divided by the mid-year population.

Life expectancy at birth – The number of years newborn children would live if subject to the mortality risks prevailing for the cross-section of population at the time of their birth.

Adult literacy rate – Percentage of persons aged 15 and over who can read and write.

Gross primary school enrolment ratio – The number of children enrolled in primary school, regardless of age, divided by the population of the age group that officially corresponds to primary schooling.

Income share – Percentage of income received by the 20 per cent of households with the highest income and by the 40 per cent of households with the lowest income.

Main data sources

Under-five and infant mortality rates – UNICEF, United Nations Population Division and United Nations Statistics Division.

Total population – United Nations Population Division.

Births – United Nations Population Division.

Under-five deaths – UNICEF.

GNP per capita – World Bank.

Life expectancy – United Nations Population Division.

Adult literacy – United Nations Educational, Scientific and Cultural Organization (UNESCO).

School enrolment – United Nations Educational, Scientific and Cultural Organization (UNESCO).

Household income – World Bank.

Notes

a: Range $785 or less.
b: Range $786 to $3125.
c: Range $3126 to $9655.
d: Range $9656 or more.

\- Data not available.
x Indicates data that refer to years or periods other than those specified in the column heading, differ from the standard definition, or refer to only part of a country.
* Data refer to the most recent year available during the period specified in the column heading.

Table 2: Nutrition

	Under-5 mortality rank	% of infants with low birthweight 1990-97*	% of children (1990-99*) who are: exclusively breastfed (0-3 months)	breastfed with complementary food (6-9 months)	still breastfeeding (20-23 months)	% of under-fives (1990-98*) suffering from: underweight moderate & severe	underweight severe	wasting moderate & severe	stunting moderate & severe	Vitamin A supplementation coverage rate (6-59 months) 1998	% of households consuming iodized salt 1992-98*
Afghanistan	**4**	20	25	-	-	48	-	25	52	-	-
Albania	**90**	7	-	-	-	-	-	-	-	-	-
Algeria	**88**	9	48	29	21	13	3	9	18	-	92
Andorra	**165**	-	-	-	-	-	-	-	-	-	-
Angola	**2**	19	12	70	49	42	14	6	53	-	10
Antigua and Barbuda	**133**	8	-	-	-	10x	4x	10x	7x	-	-
Argentina	**126**	7	-	-	-	-	-	-	-	-	90
Armenia	**104**	7	21	34	-	-	-	-	-	-	-
Australia	**175**	6	-	-	-	-	-	-	-	-	-
Austria	**175**	6	-	-	-	-	-	-	-	-	-
Azerbaijan	**80**	6	53	75	-	10	2	3	22	-	-
Bahamas	**130**	-	-	-	-	-	-	-	-	-	-
Bahrain	**133**	6	-	69	-	9	2	5	10	-	-
Bangladesh	**48**	50	52	69	90	56	21	18	55	95	78
Barbados	**146**	10	-	-	-	5x	1x	4x	7x	-	-
Belarus	**110**	-	-	-	-	-	-	-	-	-	37
Belgium	**165**	6	-	-	-	-	-	-	-	-	-
Belize	**83**	4	24	49	-	6	1	-	-	-	90
Benin	**22**	-	15	97	65	29	7	14	25	100	79
Bhutan	**41**	-	-	-	-	38x	-	4x	56x	87	82
Bolivia	**57**	5	61	80	32	10	2	2	26	73	90
Bosnia and Herzegovina	**137**	-	-	-	-	-	-	-	-	-	-
Botswana	**77**	11	39	-	-	17	5	11	29	-	27
Brazil	**85**	8	42	30	17	6	1	2	11	20	95
Brunei Darussalam	**156**	-	-	-	-	-	-	-	-	-	-
Bulgaria	**144**	6	-	-	-	-	-	-	-	-	-
Burkina Faso	**22**	21	5	56	-	30	8	13	29	97	23
Burundi	**17**	-	89x	66x	73x	37	11	9	43	15	80
Cambodia	**24**	-	60	-	48	52	18	13	56	80	7
Cameroon	**27**	13	16	-	29	22	5	6	29	-	82
Canada	**165**	6	-	-	-	-	-	-	-	-	-
Cape Verde	**65**	9	18	-	-	14	2	6	16	-	99
Central African Rep.	**18**	15	23	-	-	27	8	7	34	-	65
Chad	**13**	-	2	81	62	39	14	14	40	0	55
Chile	**148**	5	77	17	-	1	-	0	2	-	97
China	**79**	9	64	-	-	16	-	-	34	-	83
Colombia	**104**	9	16	61	17	8	1	1	15	-	92
Comoros	**53**	8	5	87	45	26	8	8	34	-	-
Congo	**47**	16	43x	95x	27x	17x	3x	4x	21x	93	-
Congo, Dem. Rep.	**9**	15	32	40	64	34	10	10	45	46	90
Cook Islands	**104**	1	-	-	-	-	-	-	-	-	-
Costa Rica	**145**	7	35	47	12	2	-	-	-	-	89
Côte d'Ivoire	**28**	12	4	77	-	24	6	8	24	-	-
Croatia	**156**	-	24	-	-	1	-	1	1	-	70
Cuba	**160**	7	76	66	-	9	-	3	-	-	45
Cyprus	**156**	-	-	-	-	-	-	-	-	-	-
Czech Rep.	**165**	6	-	-	-	1	0	2	2	-	-
Denmark	**175**	6	-	-	-	-	-	-	-	-	-
Djibouti	**26**	11	-	-	-	18	6	13	26	41	-
Dominica	**133**	10	-	-	-	5x	0x	2x	6x	-	-
Dominican Rep.	**75**	13	25	47	7	6	1	1	11	16	13
Ecuador	**89**	13	29	52	34	17x	0x	2x	34x	69	97
Egypt	**68**	10	53	37	-	12	3	6	25	-	0
El Salvador	**97**	11	16	76	68	11	1	1	23	-	91
Equatorial Guinea	**20**	-	-	-	-	-	-	-	-	-	20
Eritrea	**45**	13	66	45	60	44	17	16	38	86	80
Estonia	**126**	-	-	-	-	-	-	-	-	-	-

	Under-5 mortality rank	% of infants with low birthweight 1990-97*	% of children (1990-99*) who are: exclusively breastfed (0-3 months)	breastfed with complementary food (6-9 months)	still breastfeeding (20-23 months)	% of under-fives (1990-98*) suffering from: underweight moderate & severe	underweight severe	wasting moderate & severe	stunting moderate & severe	Vitamin A supplementation coverage rate (6-59 months) 1998	% of households consuming iodized salt 1992-98*
Ethiopia	**18**	16	74	-	35	48	16	8	64	83	0
Fiji	**120**	12	-	-	-	8	1	8	3	-	31
Finland	**175**	4	-	-	-	-	-	-	-	-	-
France	**175**	5	-	-	-	-	-	-	-	-	-
Gabon	**30**	-	32	-	-	-	-	-	-	-	-
Gambia	**59**	-	-	8	58	26	5	-	30	-	0
Georgia	**120**	-	-	-	-	-	-	-	-	-	-
Germany	**175**	-	-	-	-	-	-	-	-	-	-
Ghana	**49**	8	37	-	66	27	8	11	26	90	10
Greece	**162**	6	-	-	-	-	-	-	-	-	-
Grenada	**109**	9	-	-	-	-	-	-	-	-	-
Guatemala	**74**	15	50	56	43	27	6	3	50	57	64
Guinea	**14**	13	52	-	15	-	-	12	29	97	37
Guinea-Bissau	**11**	20	-	-	-	23x	-	-	-	-	-
Guyana	**60**	15	-	-	-	12	-	12	10	-	-
Haiti	**36**	15	3	83	25	28	8	8	32	60	10
Holy See	**-**	-	-	-	-	-	-	-	-	-	-
Honduras	**81**	9	42	69	45	18	3	2	40	58	85
Hungary	**149**	9	-	-	-	2x	0x	2x	3x	-	-
Iceland	**175**	-	-	-	-	-	-	-	-	-	-
India	**49**	33	51	31	67	53	21	18	52	25	70
Indonesia	**71**	8	52	-	65	34	8	13	42	66	62
Iran	**100**	10	66	-	41	16	3	7	19	35	94
Iraq	**37**	15	-	-	25	23	6	10	31	89	10
Ireland	**162**	4	-	-	-	-	-	-	-	-	-
Israel	**165**	7	-	-	-	-	-	-	-	-	-
Italy	**165**	5	-	-	-	-	-	-	-	-	-
Jamaica	**149**	10	-	-	-	10	1	4	6	-	100
Japan	**189**	7	-	-	-	-	-	-	-	-	-
Jordan	**93**	10	15	68	12	5	1	2	8	-	95
Kazakhstan	**83**	9	12	61	21	8	2	3	16	-	53
Kenya	**40**	16	17	94	54	22	5	6	33	10	100
Kiribati	**62**	3	-	-	-	13x	-	11x	28x	-	-
Korea, Dem. People's Rep.	**104**	-	-	-	-	60	-	19	60	-	5
Korea, Rep. of	**175**	9	-	-	-	-	-	-	-	-	-
Kuwait	**147**	7	-	-	-	6x	-	3x	12x	-	-
Kyrgyzstan	**69**	6	31	-	79	11	2	3	25	-	27
Lao People's Dem. Rep.	**41**	18	36	-	31	40	12	11	47	39	93
Latvia	**126**	-	-	-	-	-	-	-	-	-	-
Lebanon	**94**	10	-	-	-	3	-	3	12	-	92
Lesotho	**33**	11	54	47	52	16	4	5	44	-	73
Liberia	**6**	-	-	17	25	-	-	-	-	-	-
Libya	**117**	7	-	-	39	5	-	3	15	-	90
Liechtenstein	**149**	-	-	-	-	-	-	-	-	-	-
Lithuania	**120**	-	-	-	-	-	-	-	-	-	-
Luxembourg	**175**	-	-	-	-	-	-	-	-	-	-
Madagascar	**25**	5	61	93	49	40	13	7	48	100	73
Malawi	**7**	20	11	78	68	30	9	7	48	34	58
Malaysia	**153**	8	-	-	-	19	1	-	-	-	-
Maldives	**56**	13	8	-	-	43	10	17	27	-	-
Mali	**5**	16	13	33	60	40	17	23	30	93	9
Malta	**162**	-	-	-	-	-	-	-	-	-	-
Marshall Islands	**52**	14	-	-	-	-	-	-	-	35	-
Mauritania	**16**	11	60	64	59	23	9	7	44	80	3
Mauritius	**120**	13	16	29	-	16	2	15	10	0	0
Mexico	**97**	7	38x	36x	21x	14x	-	6x	22x	93	99
Micronesia, Fed. States of	**117**	9	-	-	-	-	-	-	-	50	-

Table 2: Nutrition

	Under-5 mortality rank	% of infants with low birthweight 1990-97*	% of children (1990-99*) who are: exclusively breastfed (0-3 months)	breastfed with complementary food (6-9 months)	still breastfeeding (20-23 months)	% of under-fives (1990-98*) suffering from: underweight moderate & severe	underweight severe	wasting moderate & severe	stunting moderate & severe	Vitamin A supplementation coverage rate (6-59 months) 1998	% of households consuming iodized salt 1992-98*
Moldova, Rep. of	**94**	4	-	-	-	-	-	-	-	-	-
Monaco	**175**	-	-	-	-	-	-	-	-	-	-
Mongolia	**28**	7	93	84	74	10	-	2	22	87	68
Morocco	**67**	9	31	33	20	9	2	2	23	75	-
Mozambique	**10**	20	38	87	58	26	9	8	36	-	62
Myanmar	**44**	24	-	78	75	39	13	-	-	91	65
Namibia	**62**	16	22	65	23	26	6	9	28	83	59
Nauru	**104**	-	-	-	-	-	-	-	-	-	-
Nepal	**51**	-	83	63	88	47	16	11	48	90	93
Netherlands	**175**	-	-	-	-	-	-	-	-	-	-
New Zealand	**165**	6	-	-	-	-	-	-	-	-	-
Nicaragua	**77**	9	29	65	29	12	2	2	25	63	86
Niger	**3**	15	1	-	47	50	20	21	41	82	64
Nigeria	**15**	16	2	52	43	36	12	9	43	-	98
Niue	**-**	-	-	-	-	-	-	-	-	-	-
Norway	**189**	4	-	-	-	-	-	-	-	-	-
Oman	**140**	8	28	85	64	23	3	13	23	98	65
Pakistan	**33**	25	16	31	56	38	13	-	-	1	19
Palau	**97**	8	-	-	-	-	-	-	-	-	-
Panama	**133**	8	32	38	21	7	1	1	9	-	92
Papua New Guinea	**45**	23	75	74	66	30x	6x	6x	43x	-	-
Paraguay	**100**	5	7	59	15	4	1	0	17	-	79
Peru	**73**	11	63	83	43	8	1	1	26	-	93
Philippines	**81**	9	47	-	23	28	-	6	30	80	15
Poland	**149**	-	-	-	-	-	-	-	-	-	-
Portugal	**156**	5	-	-	-	-	-	-	-	-	-
Qatar	**140**	-	-	-	-	6	-	2	8	-	-
Romania	**117**	7	-	-	-	6	1	3	8	-	-
Russian Federation	**115**	6	-	-	-	3	1	4	13	-	30
Rwanda	**21**	17	90	68	85	27	11	9	42	75	95
Saint Kitts and Nevis	**90**	9	-	-	-	-	-	-	-	-	-
Saint Lucia	**130**	8	-	-	-	-	-	-	-	-	-
Saint Vincent/Grenadines	**120**	8	-	-	-	-	-	-	-	-	-
Samoa	**110**	6	-	-	-	-	-	-	-	-	-
San Marino	**165**	-	-	-	-	-	-	-	-	-	-
Sao Tome and Principe	**61**	7	-	-	-	16	5	5	26	-	-
Saudi Arabia	**113**	7	-	-	-	-	-	-	-	-	-
Senegal	**38**	4	16	69	50	22	-	7	23	0	9
Seychelles	**140**	10	-	-	-	6x	0x	2x	5x	-	-
Sierra Leone	**1**	11	-	94	41	29	-	9	35	-	75
Singapore	**175**	7	-	-	-	-	-	-	-	-	-
Slovakia	**153**	-	-	-	-	-	-	-	-	-	-
Slovenia	**175**	-	-	-	-	-	-	-	-	-	-
Solomon Islands	**113**	20	-	-	-	21x	4x	7x	27x	-	-
Somalia	**8**	16	-	-	-	-	-	-	-	90	-
South Africa	**58**	-	-	-	-	9	1	3	23	-	40
Spain	**165**	4	-	-	-	-	-	-	-	-	-
Sri Lanka	**137**	25	24	60	66	34	-	14	18	-	47
Sudan	**43**	15	14x	45x	44x	34	11	13	33	80	0
Suriname	**94**	13	-	-	-	-	-	-	-	-	-
Swaziland	**53**	10	37	51	20	10x	-	1x	30x	-	26
Sweden	**189**	5	-	-	-	-	-	-	-	-	-
Switzerland	**175**	5	-	-	-	-	-	-	-	-	-
Syria	**102**	7	-	50	-	13	4	9	21	-	40
Tajikistan	**62**	-	-	-	-	-	-	-	-	-	20
Tanzania	**32**	14	41	93	53	27	8	6	42	80	74
TFYR Macedonia	**110**	-	8	-	-	-	-	-	-	-	100

	Under-5 mortality rank	% of infants with low birthweight 1990-97*	% of children (1990-99*) who are: exclusively breastfed (0-3 months)	breastfed with complementary food (6-9 months)	still breastfeeding (20-23 months)	% of under-fives (1990-98*) suffering from: underweight moderate & severe	underweight severe	wasting moderate & severe	stunting moderate & severe	Vitamin A supplementation coverage rate (6-59 months) 1998	% of households consuming iodized salt 1992-98*
Thailand	**90**	6	4	71	27	19	-	6	16	4	50
Togo	**30**	20	15	-	77	25	7	12	22	-	73
Tonga	**120**	2	-	-	-	-	-	-	-	-	-
Trinidad and Tobago	**140**	10	-	-	-	7x	0x	4x	5x	-	-
Tunisia	**102**	8	12	-	16	9	-	4	23	-	98
Turkey	**85**	8	9	38	-	10	3	-	-	-	18
Turkmenistan	**66**	5	54	-	-	-	-	-	-	-	0
Tuvalu	**71**	3	-	-	-	-	-	-	-	-	-
Uganda	**35**	13	70	64	40	26	7	5	38	95	69
Ukraine	**126**	-	-	-	-	-	-	-	-	-	4
United Arab Emirates	**153**	6	-	52	-	14	3	15	17	-	-
United Kingdom	**165**	7	-	-	-	-	-	-	-	-	-
United States	**160**	7	-	-	-	1	0	1	2	-	-
Uruguay	**137**	8	-	-	-	5	1	1	8	-	-
Uzbekistan	**70**	-	4	-	35	19	5	12	31	-	0
Vanuatu	**76**	7	-	-	-	20x	-	-	19x	-	-
Venezuela	**115**	9	-	-	-	5	1	3	13	-	65
Viet Nam	**85**	17	-	-	-	41	9	14	44	98	65
Yemen	**38**	19	25	79	41	46	15	13	52	100	39
Yugoslavia	**130**	-	6	35	13	2	0	2	7	25	70
Zambia	**12**	13	26	95	43	24	5	4	42	91	78
Zimbabwe	**55**	10	16	93	26	15	3	6	32	-	80

Regional summaries

	Under-5 mortality rank	% of infants with low birthweight 1990-97*	exclusively breastfed (0-3 months)	breastfed with complementary food (6-9 months)	still breastfeeding (20-23 months)	underweight moderate & severe	underweight severe	wasting moderate & severe	stunting moderate & severe	Vitamin A supplementation coverage rate (6-59 months) 1998	% of households consuming iodized salt 1992-98*
Sub-Saharan Africa		15	31	66	49	32	10	9	41	68	62
Middle East and North Africa		11	41	45	33	18	5	8	25	69	48
South Asia		33	45	36	68	51	19	18	52	30	65
East Asia and Pacific		10	59	74	-	22	-	-	36	70	74
Latin America and Caribbean		9	39	45	23	10	1	3	18	52	89
CEE/CIS and Baltic States		7	-	-	-	8	2	5	16	25	25
Industrialized countries		6	-	-	-	-	-	-	-	-	-
Developing countries		18	44	47	53	31	12	11	39	48	68
Least developed countries		22	43	67	59	40	13	12	47	80	57
World		17	44	47	53	30	11	11	37	48	66

Countries in each region are listed on page 112.

Definitions of the indicators

Low birthweight – Less than 2,500 grams.

Underweight – Moderate and severe – below minus two standard deviations from median weight for age of reference population; severe – below minus three standard deviations from median weight for age of reference population.

Wasting – Moderate and severe – below minus two standard deviations from median weight for height of reference population.

Stunting – Moderate and severe – below minus two standard deviations from median height for age of reference population.

Vitamin A – Percentage of children aged 6-59 months who have received a high dose of vitamin A capsules within the last six months.

Main data sources

Low birthweight – World Health Organization (WHO) and UNICEF.

Breastfeeding – Demographic and Health Surveys (DHS), Multiple Indicator Cluster Surveys (MICS), World Health Organization (WHO) and UNICEF.

Underweight, wasting and stunting – Demographic and Health Surveys (DHS), Multiple Indicator Cluster Surveys (MICS), World Health Organization (WHO) and UNICEF.

Salt iodization – Multiple Indicator Cluster Surveys (MICS) and UNICEF.

Vitamin A – UNICEF field offices.

Notes

- \- Data not available.
- x Indicates data that refer to years or periods other than those specified in the column heading, differ from the standard definition, or refer to only part of a country.
- * Data refer to the most recent year available during the period specified in the column heading.

Table 3: Health

	Under-5 mortality rank	% of population with access to safe water 1990-98* total	urban	rural	% of population with access to adequate sanitation 1990-98* total	urban	rural	% of routine EPI vaccines financed by government 1995-98* total	% fully immunized 1995-98* 1-year-old children TB	DPT	polio	measles	pregnant women tetanus	ORT use rate (%) 1990-98*
Afghanistan	**4**	6	16	3	10	23	7	0	33	34	35	36	19	36
Albania	**90**	-	-	-	-	-	-	0	87	96	97	89	65	-
Algeria	**88**	90	98	79	91	98	62	100	95	80	80	75	52	98x
Andorra	**165**	-	-	-	-	-	-	-	-	90	90	90	-	-
Angola	**2**	31	46	22	40	62	27	0	71	36	36	65	24	-
Antigua and Barbuda	**133**	-	-	-	96	-	-	100	-	100	100	100	-	-
Argentina	**126**	71	77	29	68	73	37	100	99	83	88	99	-	-
Armenia	**104**	-	-	-	-	-	-	7	95	82	96	94	-	30
Australia	**175**	-	-	-	-	-	-	-	-	86	86	86	-	-
Austria	**175**	-	-	-	-	-	-	-	-	90	95	90	-	-
Azerbaijan	**80**	-	-	-	-	-	-	0	96	97	98	98	-	-
Bahamas	**130**	94	98	75	82	98	2	100	-	89	88	93	-	-
Bahrain	**133**	94	94	-	97	97	-	100	72	98	98	100	80	39
Bangladesh	**48**	95	99	95	43	83	38	100	91	68	68	62	86	61
Barbados	**146**	100	100	100	100	100	100	100	-	93	93	92	-	-
Belarus	**110**	-	-	-	-	-	-	78	98	97	98	98	-	-
Belgium	**165**	-	-	-	-	-	-	-	-	62	72	64	-	-
Belize	**83**	83	100	69	57	23	87	100	93	87	87	84	65	-
Benin	**22**	56	71	46	27	57	8	15	92	81	81	82	66	33
Bhutan	**41**	58	75	54	70	90	66	0	94	86	85	71	80	85
Bolivia	**57**	80	95	56	65	82	35	65x	85	42	33	51	27	48
Bosnia and Herzegovina	**137**	-	-	-	-	-	-	0	99	87	90	80	-	-
Botswana	**77**	90	100	88	55	91	41	100	66	82	73	80	54	43
Brazil	**85**	76	88	25	70	80	30	100	99	94	96	96	30	54
Brunei Darussalam	**156**	-	-	-	-	-	-	-	96	97	98	100	52	-
Bulgaria	**144**	-	-	-	-	-	-	-	98	96	97	95	-	-
Burkina Faso	**22**	42	66	37	37	41	33	100	72	37	42	46	54	18
Burundi	**17**	52	92	49	51	60	50	2	58	50	51	44	9	38
Cambodia	**24**	30	53	25	19	57	9	0	76	64	64	63	31	48
Cameroon	**27**	54	81	41	89	99	84	27	72	46	42	44	49	34
Canada	**165**	-	-	-	-	-	-	-	-	97	-	96	-	-
Cape Verde	**65**	65	84	44	27	42	14	100	84	80	79	66	51	83
Central African Rep.	**18**	38	55	21	27	38	16	4	53	46	47	39	37	34
Chad	**13**	54	48	56	27	79	11	100	43	24	24	30	27	29
Chile	**148**	91	99	41	-	90	-	100	96	93	93	93	-	-
China	**79**	67	97	56	24	74	7	100	96	98	98	97	13	85
Colombia	**104**	85	97	56	85	97	56	100	82	70	72	75	57x	53
Comoros	**53**	53	76	45	23	40	16	-	84	75	75	67	22	32
Congo	**47**	34	53	7	69	-	-	0x	29	23	21	18	30	41
Congo, Dem. Rep.	**9**	42	89	26	18	53	6	-	13	10	10	10	-	90x
Cook Islands	**104**	95	100	95	95	-	-	50	99	95	95	94	29	-
Costa Rica	**145**	96	100	92	84	95	70	100	87	85	85	86	-	31
Côte d'Ivoire	**28**	42	56	32	39	71	17	95	84	61	61	66	44	29
Croatia	**156**	-	-	-	-	-	-	100	93	93	93	91	-	5
Cuba	**160**	93	96	85	66	71	51	97	99	98	97	99	70	-
Cyprus	**156**	100	100	100	-	96	-	-	-	98	98	90	-	-
Czech Rep.	**165**	-	-	-	-	-	-	-	99	98	97	95	-	-
Denmark	**175**	-	-	-	-	-	-	-	-	89x	100x	84	-	-
Djibouti	**26**	90	77	100	55	64	24	-	35	23	23	21	16	-
Dominica	**133**	96	97	95	80	80	85	100	99	99	98	98	-	-
Dominican Rep.	**75**	79	95	54	85	93	73	96	86	74	73	95	77	39
Ecuador	**89**	68	80	49	76	95	49	100	98	85	83	88	3	64
Egypt	**68**	87	97	77	88	98	79	100	97	96	96	98	61	95
El Salvador	**97**	66	84	40	90	98	80	100	99	99	99	98	-	69
Equatorial Guinea	**20**	95	88	100	54	61	48	95	99	81	81	82	70	-
Eritrea	**45**	22	60	8	13	48	-	0	71	60	60	52	34	38
Estonia	**126**	-	-	-	-	-	-	-	100	94	94	89	-	-

	Under-5 mortality rank	% of population with access to safe water 1990-98*			% of population with access to adequate sanitation 1990-98*			% of routine EPI vaccines financed by government 1995-98*	% fully immunized 1995-98*					ORT use rate (%) 1990-98*
									1-year-old children				pregnant women	
		total	urban	rural	total	urban	rural	total	TB	DPT	polio	measles	tetanus	
Ethiopia	**18**	25	91	19	19	97	7	15	74	58	57	46	30	95x
Fiji	**120**	77	-	-	92	100	85	50	95	86	88	75	-	-
Finland	**175**	-	-	-	-	-	-	-	99	99	98	98	-	-
France	**175**	-	-	-	-	-	-	-	83	96	97	97	83	-
Gabon	**30**	67	80	30	-	72	-	-	72	54	54	32	4	39
Gambia	**59**	69	80	65	37	83	23	30	99	96	95	91	96	99x
Georgia	**120**	-	-	-	-	-	-	0	91	86	92	90	-	14
Germany	**175**	-	-	-	-	-	-	-	-	95	95	88	80	-
Ghana	**49**	65	88	52	32	75	25	100	86	68	68	62	45	36
Greece	**162**	-	-	-	-	-	-	-	70	85	95	90	-	-
Grenada	**109**	-	-	-	-	-	-	100	-	97	95	97	-	-
Guatemala	**74**	68	92	54	87	97	81	100	88	89	91	81	38	22
Guinea	**14**	46	69	36	31	54	19	25	69	56	56	58	48	80x
Guinea-Bissau	**11**	43	-	-	46	-	-	0	82	63	60	51	46	-
Guyana	**60**	91	96	85	88	90	85	100	93	90	90	93	88	-
Haiti	**36**	37	50	28	25	49	17	25	28	22	20	22	38	31
Holy See	**-**	-	-	-	-	-	-	-	-	-	-	-	-	-
Honduras	**81**	78	95	65	74	94	56	100	96	97	98	99	-	32
Hungary	**149**	-	-	-	-	-	-	-	100	100	100	100	-	-
Iceland	**175**	-	-	-	-	-	-	-	98x	98x	99x	98x	-	-
India	**49**	81	85	79	29	70	14	98	79	73	73	66	80	67x
Indonesia	**71**	74	92	67	53	71	46	100	83	62	70	60	53	70
Iran	**100**	95	99	86	64	79	37	100	98	100	100	100	75	48
Iraq	**37**	81	96	48	75	93	31	75	76	86	86	79	45	54x
Ireland	**162**	-	-	-	-	-	-	-	-	-	63x	-	-	-
Israel	**165**	-	-	-	-	-	-	-	-	93	92	94	-	-
Italy	**165**	-	-	-	-	-	-	-	-	95	96	55	-	-
Jamaica	**149**	86	-	-	89	100	80	100	90	88	88	88	52	-
Japan	**189**	97	100	85	-	85	-	-	91	100	98	94	-	-
Jordan	**93**	97	98	88	99	100	97	100	-	91	91	86	22	29
Kazakhstan	**83**	93	99	84	99	100	98	80	99	100	100	100	-	31
Kenya	**40**	44	87	30	85	96	81	3	94	76	78	71	51	69
Kiribati	**62**	-	70	80	-	45	54	100	97	88	83	77	74	-
Korea, Dem. People's Rep.	**104**	100	100	100	99	99	100	-	64	37	77	34	5	-
Korea, Rep. of	**175**	93	100	76	100	100	100	-	75	74	71	85	-	-
Kuwait	**147**	-	-	-	-	100x	-	100	-	93	94	100	8	-
Kyrgyzstan	**69**	79	98	66	100	100	100	-	94	97	97	98	-	98x
Lao People's Dem. Rep.	**41**	44	-	-	18	-	-	0	56	55	67	71	32	32
Latvia	**126**	-	-	-	-	-	-	-	100	94	94	97	-	-
Lebanon	**94**	94	96	88	63	81	8	75	-	96	96	91	-	82
Lesotho	**33**	62	91	57	38	56	35	25	46	50	48	43	-	84x
Liberia	**6**	46	79	13	30	56	4	0	28	19	19	31	14	94x
Libya	**117**	97	97	97	98	99	94	2	100	97	95	92	-	49
Liechtenstein	**149**	-	-	-	-	-	-	-	-	-	-	-	-	-
Lithuania	**120**	-	-	-	-	-	-	-	99	93	88	97	-	-
Luxembourg	**175**	-	-	-	-	-	-	-	58	94	98	91	-	-
Madagascar	**25**	40	71	30	40	68	30	10	80	68	68	65	30	23
Malawi	**7**	47	95	40	3	18	1	2	100	96	93	90	81	70
Malaysia	**153**	78	96	66	94	94	94	100	100	95	94	86	71	-
Maldives	**56**	60	98	50	44	98	26	30	99	97	97	98	91	18
Mali	**5**	66	87	55	6	12	3	100	84	52	52	57	62	29
Malta	**162**	-	-	-	-	-	-	-	96	92	92	60	-	-
Marshall Islands	**52**	82	82	-	-	88	57	100	81	86	86	93	-	-
Mauritania	**16**	37	34	40	57	73	41	0	69	28	28	20	63	51
Mauritius	**120**	98	95	100	100	100	100	100	87	90	90	85	78	-
Mexico	**97**	85	-	-	72	-	-	100	93	94	95	89	70	80
Micronesia, Fed. States of	**117**	22	-	-	39	-	-	5	52	80	79	82	-	-

Table 3: Health

	Under-5 mortality rank	% of population with access to safe water 1990-98*			% of population with access to adequate sanitation 1990-98*			% of routine EPI vaccines financed by government 1995-98*	% fully immunized 1995-98* 1-year-old children				% fully immunized 1995-98*	ORT use rate (%) 1990-98*
		total	urban	rural	total	urban	rural	total	TB	DPT	polio	measles	pregnant women tetanus	
Moldova, Rep. of	**94**	55	98	18	50	90	8	29	99	97	98	99	-	-
Monaco	**175**	-	-	-	-	-	-	-	90x	99x	99x	98x	-	-
Mongolia	**28**	45	67	22	87	99	74	40	95	94	94	93	-	80
Morocco	**67**	65	98	34	58	94	24	100	90	93	93	91	33	29
Mozambique	**10**	46	85	37	34	68	26	0	99	77	78	87	41	49
Myanmar	**44**	60	78	50	43	56	36	0	91	87	88	85	78	96x
Namibia	**62**	83	100	71	62	93	20	100	85	74	74	63	70	100x
Nauru	**104**	-	-	-	-	-	-	-	78	50	36	100	-	-
Nepal	**51**	71	93	68	16	28	14	53	86	76	70	73	65	29
Netherlands	**175**	-	-	-	-	-	-	-	-	97	97	96	-	-
New Zealand	**165**	97	100	82	-	-	-	-	-	81	82	81	-	-
Nicaragua	**77**	78	94	52	85	96	68	100	96	69	73	71	42	58
Niger	**3**	61	70	59	19	78	5	80	46	22	21	27	19	21
Nigeria	**15**	49	58	40	41	50	32	100	27	21	22	26	29	86x
Niue	**-**	100	-	-	100	100	100	25	100	100	100	100	40	-
Norway	**189**	-	-	-	-	-	-	-	-	92x	92x	93x	-	-
Oman	**140**	85	-	-	78	90	57	100	96	100	100	98	96	61
Pakistan	**33**	79	89	73	56	93	39	100	66	59	59	55	58	97x
Palau	**97**	88	-	-	98	-	-	-	-	74	74	66	-	-
Panama	**133**	93	-	-	83	-	-	100	99	98	99	96	-	94x
Papua New Guinea	**45**	41	88	32	83	93	80	100	33	58	46	59	11	-
Paraguay	**100**	60	-	-	41	65	14	75	83	81	81	-	32	33
Peru	**73**	67	84	33	72	89	37	100	96	99	99	90	57	55
Philippines	**81**	85	92	79	87	95	80	100	91	79	81	71	38	64
Poland	**149**	-	-	-	-	-	-	-	94	95	95	91x	-	-
Portugal	**156**	-	-	-	-	-	-	-	88	97	96	96	-	-
Qatar	**140**	-	100	-	97	100	85	100	100	94	94	90	-	54
Romania	**117**	-	-	-	-	-	-	100	100	97	97	97	-	-
Russian Federation	**115**	-	-	-	-	-	-	100	95	97	99	98	-	-
Rwanda	**21**	-	-	79	-	-	85	0	79	77	77	66	43	47
Saint Kitts and Nevis	**90**	100	100	100	100	98	100	100	99	98	98	99	-	-
Saint Lucia	**130**	85	-	-	-	-	-	100	85	88	88	90	-	-
Saint Vincent/Grenadines	**120**	89	100	85	98	100	100	100	99	99	99	99	-	-
Samoa	**110**	68	-	-	-	100	95	100	100	100	100	100	99	-
San Marino	**165**	-	-	-	-	-	-	-	97x	98x	100x	96x	-	-
Sao Tome and Principe	**61**	82	-	-	35	-	-	-	80	73	72	59	31	74x
Saudi Arabia	**113**	95x	100x	74x	86x	100x	30x	100	92	94	94	93	66	53
Senegal	**38**	81	96	70	65	92	46	100	80	65	65	65	34	39
Seychelles	**140**	-	-	-	-	-	-	43	100	99	99	93	100	-
Sierra Leone	**1**	34	58	21	11	17	8	3	79	56	56	68	42	-
Singapore	**175**	100x	100x	-	-	-	-	-	98	96	96	96	-	-
Slovakia	**153**	-	-	-	-	-	-	-	92	99	99	99	-	-
Slovenia	**175**	-	-	-	-	-	-	-	98	91	90	93	-	-
Solomon Islands	**113**	-	80	62	-	60	9	60	72	69	69	64	55	-
Somalia	**8**	31	46	28	43	69	35	0	57	24	24	47	41	-
South Africa	**58**	87	99	70	87	92	80	100	95	73	73	76	26	-
Spain	**165**	-	-	-	-	-	-	-	-	88x	81x	78x	99x	-
Sri Lanka	**137**	57	88	52	63	68	62	100	90	94	94	91	78	34
Sudan	**43**	73	-	-	51	-	-	10	81	72	69	63	55	31
Suriname	**94**	-	-	-	-	-	43	100	-	90	90	82	-	-
Swaziland	**53**	50	-	-	59	-	-	100	85	76	76	62	79	99x
Sweden	**189**	-	-	-	-	-	-	-	12x	99x	99x	96x	-	-
Switzerland	**175**	-	-	-	-	-	-	-	-	-	-	-	-	-
Syria	**102**	86	95	77	67	96	31	100	75	97	97	97	53	61
Tajikistan	**62**	60	82	49	-	46	-	0	98	94	95	95	-	-
Tanzania	**32**	66	92	58	86	98	83	10	83	74	75	72	27	50
TFYR Macedonia	**110**	-	-	-	-	-	-	10	97	97	97	98	91x	-

	Under-5 mortality rank	% of population with access to safe water 1990-98*			% of population with access to adequate sanitation 1990-98*			% of routine EPI vaccines financed by government 1995-98*	% fully immunized 1995-98*					ORT use rate (%) 1990-98*
									1-year-old children				pregnant women	
		total	urban	rural	total	urban	rural	total	TB	DPT	polio	measles	tetanus	
Thailand	**90**	81	88	73	96	97	94	100	98	94	94	91	88	95
Togo	**30**	55	84	40	37	70	20	80	73	37	41	32	41	23
Tonga	**120**	95	-	-	95	-	-	50	100	97	97	96	93	-
Trinidad and Tobago	**140**	97	99	91	-	99	98	100	-	91	91	90	-	-
Tunisia	**102**	98	100	95	80	96	52	100	91	96	96	94	80	81
Turkey	**85**	49	66	25	80	95	56	100	73	79	79	76	32	27
Turkmenistan	**66**	74	-	-	91	-	-	36	98	99	100	99	-	98
Tuvalu	**71**	100	-	-	78	-	-	70	100	94	94	96	71	-
Uganda	**35**	46	77	41	57	75	55	50	69	46	47	30	38	49
Ukraine	**126**	-	-	-	-	-	-	1	97	98	98	96	-	-
United Arab Emirates	**153**	97	-	-	92	-	-	100	98	94	94	95	-	42
United Kingdom	**165**	-	-	-	-	-	-	-	99	95	96	95	-	-
United States	**160**	-	-	-	-	-	-	-	-	94x	84x	89x	-	-
Uruguay	**137**	-	95	-	-	98	-	100x	99	92	92	92	-	-
Uzbekistan	**70**	90	99	88	100	100	99	42	97	99	99	96	-	37
Vanuatu	**76**	77	96	67	28	72	18	90	99	93	87	94	78	-
Venezuela	**115**	79	80	75	59	64	30	100	80	38	64	94	-	-
Viet Nam	**85**	45	61	39	29	55	18	73	98	96	96	89	92	-
Yemen	**38**	61	72	57	66	96	57	38	77	68	68	66	26	35
Yugoslavia	**130**	76	98	57	69	92	49	100	87	94	95	94	-	99x
Zambia	**12**	38	84	10	71	94	57	10x	81	70	70	69	-	57
Zimbabwe	**55**	79	99	69	52	96	32	100	73	70	70	65	58	60

Regional summaries

Sub-Saharan Africa		50	77	39	45	70	35	51	63	48	48	48	37	64
Middle East and North Africa		85	97	72	74	92	53	83	89	89	89	87	54	60
South Asia		80	86	78	33	73	20	95	77	70	70	64	75	69
East Asia and Pacific		69	95	58	37	77	20	94	92	89	91	87	30	81
Latin America and Caribbean		78	88	42	71	82	44	97	92	85	87	89	46	58
CEE/CIS and Baltic States		-	-	-	-	-	-	-	91	93	94	92	-	-
Industrialized countries		-	-	-	-	-	-	-	-	94	90	89	-	-
Developing countries		72	89	62	44	79	25	85	81	75	76	72	50	69
Least developed countries		57	79	51	37	67	29	36	70	55	55	54	48	58
World		72	90	62	44	79	25	85	82	77	77	74	50	69

Countries in each region are listed on page 112.

Definitions of the indicators

Government funding of vaccines – Percentage of vaccines routinely administered in a country to protect children against TB, DPT, measles and polio that are financed by the national government.

EPI – Expanded Programme on Immunization: The immunizations in this programme include those against TB, DPT, polio and measles, as well as protecting babies against neonatal tetanus by vaccination of pregnant women. Other vaccines (e.g. against hepatitis B or yellow fever) may be included in the programme in some countries.

DPT – Diphtheria, pertussis (whooping cough) and tetanus.

ORT use – Percentage of all cases of diarrhoea in children under five years of age treated with oral rehydration salts and/or recommended home fluids.

Main data sources

Access to safe drinking water and adequate sanitation facilities – Demographic and Health Surveys (DHS), Multiple Indicator Cluster Surveys (MICS), World Health Organization (WHO) and UNICEF.

Government funding of vaccines – UNICEF.

Immunization – Demographic and Health Surveys (DHS), Multiple Indicator Cluster Surveys (MICS), World Health Organization (WHO) and UNICEF.

ORT use – Demographic and Health Surveys (DHS), Multiple Indicator Cluster Surveys (MICS), World Health Organization (WHO) and UNICEF.

Notes
- \- Data not available.
- x Indicates data that refer to years or periods other than those specified in the column heading, differ from the standard definition, or refer to only part of a country.
- * Data refer to the most recent year available during the period specified in the column heading.

Table 4: Education

	Under-5 mortality rank	Adult literacy rate 1980		Adult literacy rate 1995		No. of sets per 1000 population 1996		Primary school enrolment ratio 1990-97* (gross)		Primary school enrolment ratio 1990-96* (net)		Net primary school attendance (%) 1990-98*		% of primary school entrants reaching grade 5 1990-95*	Secondary school enrolment ratio 1990-96* (gross)	
		male	female	male	female	radio	television	male	female	male	female	male	female		male	female
Afghanistan	**4**	30	6	46	16	122	12	64	32	42	15	36	11	43x	32	11
Albania	**90**	-	-	-	-	235	118	100	102	95	97	-	-	82	35	35
Algeria	**88**	55	26	71	45	239	104	113	101	97	91	95	90	94	65	62
Andorra	**165**	-	-	-	-	217	370	-	-	-	-	-	-	-	-	-
Angola	**2**	16x	7x	56x	29x	54	27	95	88	-	-	-	-	34	-	-
Antigua and Barbuda	**133**	-	-	-	-	522	457	-	-	-	-	-	-	-	-	-
Argentina	**126**	94	94	96	96	677	221	114	113	95	95	-	-	-	73	81
Armenia	**104**	-	-	100	99	5	225	86	90	-	-	-	-	-	85	91
Australia	**175**	-	-	-	-	1385	554	103	103	97	97	-	-	99	153	153
Austria	**175**	-	-	-	-	740	518	100	101	100	100	-	-	99	105	101
Azerbaijan	**80**	-	-	100	99	20	22	109	106	-	-	-	-	-	73	81
Bahamas	**130**	93	94	95	96	739	232	95	94	92	96	-	-	78	88	91
Bahrain	**133**	79	59	89	79	579	470	105	107	97	100	-	-	95	91	98
Bangladesh	**48**	41	17	49	26	50	6	74	64	66	58	75	76	47	28	14
Barbados	**146**	97	94	98	97	904	287	90	91	78	78	-	-	-	90x	80x
Belarus	**110**	99	91	100	98	290	242	101	96	87	84	-	-	100	91	95
Belgium	**165**	99x	99x	-	-	792	463	103	102	98	98	-	-	-	141	151
Belize	**83**	-	-	70x	70x	589	183	124	118	100	98	-	-	70	47	52
Benin	**22**	26	10	45	19	108	18	96	56	78	46	52	34	61	23	10
Bhutan	**41**	41	15	56	28	19	6	31x	19x	-	-	-	-	82	7x	2x
Bolivia	**57**	80	59	90	75	672	115	99	90	95	87	95x	95x	60	40	34
Bosnia and Herzegovina	**137**	-	-	-	-	248	0	-	-	-	-	-	-	-	-	-
Botswana	**77**	56	59	70	75	155	20	111	112	82	86	-	-	90	63	69
Brazil	**85**	76	73	83	83	435	223	100x	96x	-	-	93x	94x	71	31x	36x
Brunei Darussalam	**156**	85	68	93	85	300	250	109	104	91	91	-	-	95	71	82
Bulgaria	**144**	97	93	99	97	531	390	100	98	93	91	-	-	95	77	76
Burkina Faso	**22**	18	4	29	10	32	8	48	31	37	24	38	28	75	11	6
Burundi	**17**	41	16	52	33	68	3	55	46	56	48	-	-	74	9	5
Cambodia	**24**	74x	23x	80x	53x	127	9	142	119	100	90	-	-	50	30	18
Cameroon	**27**	59	30	75	52	162	29	93	84	81x	71x	71x	70x	66	32	22
Canada	**165**	-	-	-	-	1078	714	103	101	96	94	-	-	99	107	106
Cape Verde	**65**	65	40	81	61	179	4	132	129	100	100	-	-	60x	28	26
Central African Rep.	**18**	36	12	54	27	84	5	71	46	65	43	70	55	24	15	6
Chad	**13**	47	19	62	35	249	1	85	44	66	37	44	29	59	16	4
Chile	**148**	92	91	95	95	354	215	103	100	89	87	-	-	100	72	78
China	**79**	78	51	89	71	195	319	121	120	100	100	95	94	94	74	67
Colombia	**104**	85	84	91	90	565	123	119	118	-	-	90	91	73	70	75
Comoros	**53**	56	41	64	50	138	2	85	71	58	48	45x	42x	80	21	17
Congo	**47**	64	38	83	67	124	11	119	109	99x	93x	-	-	55	62	45
Congo, Dem. Rep.	**9**	75	45	87	68	98	3	86	59	71	50	59	53	64	32	19
Cook Islands	**104**	-	-	-	99x	711	189	-	-	-	-	-	-	-	-	-
Costa Rica	**145**	92	92	95	95	271	143	108	107	87	88	-	-	88	48	52
Côte d'Ivoire	**28**	32	13	49	31	157	62	81	60	63	47	59x	46x	75	33	16
Croatia	**156**	97	88	99	96	333	267	87	86	83	82	-	-	98	81	83
Cuba	**160**	92	92	96	96	351	236	108	104	100	100	-	-	100	73	82
Cyprus	**156**	96	84	98	93	397	323	100	100	96	96	-	-	94	96	99
Czech Rep.	**165**	-	-	-	-	806	534	105	104	87	87	-	-	100	97	100
Denmark	**175**	-	-	-	-	1146	592	100	99	97	97	-	-	100	117	122
Djibouti	**26**	45	18	60	33	81	44	44	32	36	27	73x	62x	82	17	12
Dominica	**133**	-	-	-	-	634	77	-	-	-	-	-	-	84	-	-
Dominican Rep.	**75**	75	73	82	81	177	94	103	104	79	83	91x	93x	58	34	47
Ecuador	**89**	85	78	92	87	342	128	134	119	97	97	-	-	85	53	55
Egypt	**68**	54	25	64	38	316	119	109	94	86	74	83	72	98	80	70
El Salvador	**97**	71	62	79	73	461	675	94	94	78	80	-	-	77	30	35
Equatorial Guinea	**20**	76	44	89	67	427	10	-	-	-	-	-	-	-	-	-
Eritrea	**45**	-	-	-	-	101	0	59	49	32	29	39x	35x	70	24	17
Estonia	**126**	-	-	98	98	680	408	95	93	87	86	-	-	96	100	108

	Under-5 mortality rank	Adult literacy rate				No. of sets per 1000 population 1996		Primary school enrolment ratio				Net primary school attendance (%) 1990-98*		% of primary school entrants reaching grade 5 1990-95*	Secondary school enrolment ratio 1990-96* (gross)	
		1980		1995				1990-97* (gross)		1990-96* (net)						
		male	female	male	female	radio	television	male	female	male	female	male	female		male	female
Ethiopia	**18**	28	11	40	26	194	5	47	27	28	19	-	-	55	13	10
Fiji	**120**	87	78	94	89	615	25	128	127	99	100	-	-	87	64	65
Finland	**175**	-	-	-	-	1385	605	100	100	99	99	-	-	100	107	125
France	**175**	99x	98x	-	-	943	591	107	105	100	100	-	-	99	112	111
Gabon	**30**	54	28	74	53	182	54	-	-	-	-	87	86	59	-	-
Gambia	**59**	37	13	53	25	164	4	87	67	72	57	51	43	80	30	19
Georgia	**120**	-	-	100	99	553	470	85	84	83	83	-	-	98	74	72
Germany	**175**	-	-	-	-	946	564	104	103	100	100	-	-	100	103	101
Ghana	**49**	57	30	75	53	238	93	83	70	-	-	70	69	80	45	29
Greece	**162**	96	86	98	94	477	238	95	94	91	90	-	-	100	96	96
Grenada	**109**	-	-	-	-	652	351	-	-	-	-	-	-	-	-	-
Guatemala	**74**	62	46	73	58	73	57	90	79	-	-	61x	55x	50	26	24
Guinea	**14**	34	11	50	22	47	10	63	34	34x	17x	39	26	80	18	6
Guinea-Bissau	**11**	32	7	48	16	42x	-	81	47	58x	32x	-	-	20x	9x	4x
Guyana	**60**	96	93	99	97	495	54	95	94	87	87	-	-	91	73	78
Haiti	**36**	34	28	47	41	55	5	58	54	25	26	68x	69x	47	23	22
Holy See	**-**	-	-	-	-	-	-	-	-	-	-	-	-	-	-	-
Honduras	**81**	63	59	70	69	409	95	110	112	89	91	-	-	60	29	37
Hungary	**149**	99	99	99	99	697	438	105	103	98	97	-	-	98	97	100
Iceland	**175**	-	-	-	-	923	354	99	97	99	97	-	-	99	105	102
India	**49**	55	25	64	35	105	61	110	90	-	-	75	61	59	59	39
Indonesia	**71**	78	58	90	78	155	67	117	112	99	95	94	94	89	52	44
Iran	**100**	62	40	79	63	237	64	92	87	83	81	99	93	90	79	69
Iraq	**37**	55	25	71	45	228	82	92	78	81	71	88	80	72	51	32
Ireland	**162**	-	-	-	-	703	411	103	103	100	100	-	-	100	111	119
Israel	**165**	95	88	97	93	530	291	96	96	-	-	-	-	100	84	89
Italy	**165**	97	95	99	98	874	524	100	99	99	98	-	-	100	87	88
Jamaica	**149**	73	81	80	89	482	181	107	107	100	100	-	-	96	62	70
Japan	**189**	100x	99x	-	-	957	684	101	102	100	100	-	-	100	98	100
Jordan	**93**	82	54	91	80	287	86	94	95	89	89	91	91	98	52	54
Kazakhstan	**83**	-	-	100	99	384	230	95	96	-	-	87	83	-	80	89
Kenya	**40**	71	43	86	69	108	25	85	85	92x	89x	86x	85x	68	26	22
Kiribati	**62**	-	-	-	92x	213	13	-	-	-	-	-	-	89	-	-
Korea, Dem. People's Rep.	**104**	-	-	-	-	147	48	108x	101x	-	-	-	-	-	-	-
Korea, Rep. of	**175**	97	89	99	95	1037	337	94	94	92	93	-	-	100	102	102
Kuwait	**147**	73	59	82	76	688	510	76	74	65	65	-	-	99	65	65
Kyrgyzstan	**69**	-	-	99	95	115	45	108	105	99	95	89	90	92	76	85
Lao People's Dem. Rep.	**41**	56	28	69	44	139	10	125	97	77	66	70	67	53	36	23
Latvia	**126**	100	98	100	99	699	485	99	93	92	87	-	-	96	82	85
Lebanon	**94**	83	63	91	77	892	373	113	108	-	-	-	-	-	78	85
Lesotho	**33**	58	83	70	92	48	24	92	102	58	68	71x	79x	80	23	34
Liberia	**6**	42	14	62	28	318	27	51x	28x	-	-	59x	53x	-	31x	12x
Libya	**117**	71	31	87	60	232	122	110	110	98	96	-	-	-	95	95
Liechtenstein	**149**	-	-	100x	100x	668	342	-	-	-	-	-	-	-	-	-
Lithuania	**120**	98	95	100	99	292	451	99	96	-	-	-	-	98	85	88
Luxembourg	**175**	-	-	-	-	678	387	88	94	84x	86x	-	-	-	72	76
Madagascar	**25**	56x	43x	60	32	192	20	74	71	48	48	58	60	40	13	13
Malawi	**7**	64	27	72	41	256x	-	142	128	100	100	83	83	34	21	12
Malaysia	**153**	80	60	89	79	432	170	90	92	91	92	-	-	99	58	66
Maldives	**56**	92	91	95	95	122	27	127	123	-	-	-	-	93	49	49
Mali	**5**	19	8	40	25	49	4	41	27	32	21	45	36	82	12	6
Malta	**162**	83	84	90	91	678	751	111	109	100	100	-	-	100	93	86
Marshall Islands	**52**	-	-	-	90x	-	-	-	-	-	-	-	-	-	-	-
Mauritania	**16**	41	18	49	27	150	25	88	79	64	55	55	53	64	21	11
Mauritius	**120**	81	67	86	78	368	223	107	106	98	98	-	-	99	63	66
Mexico	**97**	86	80	92	87	324	270	116	113	-	-	-	-	84	61	61
Micronesia, Fed. States of	**117**	-	-	-	79x	-	-	-	-	-	-	-	-	-	-	-

Table 4: Education

	Under-5 mortality rank	Adult literacy rate				No. of sets per 1000 population 1996		Primary school enrolment ratio				Net primary school attendance (%) 1990-98*		% of primary school entrants reaching grade 5 1990-95*	Secondary school enrolment ratio 1990-96* (gross)	
		1980		1995				1990-97* (gross)		1990-96* (net)						
		male	female	male	female	radio	television	male	female	male	female	male	female		male	female
Moldova, Rep. of	**94**	96	88	99	97	720	281	96	95	-	-	-	-	93	78	81
Monaco	**175**	-	-	-	-	1021	727	-	-	-	-	-	-	98	-	-
Mongolia	**28**	82	63	89	77	139	46	86	91	80	84	-	-	-	48	65
Morocco	**67**	42	16	58	31	241	111	95	72	81	63	61x	45x	75	44	34
Mozambique	**10**	44	12	55	23	39	5	70	50	45	35	53	47	46	9	5
Myanmar	**44**	86	66	88	78	89	5	102	99	-	-	85	85	-	29	30
Namibia	**62**	71	61	80	77	143	48	130	132	86	93	74x	79x	79	56	66
Nauru	**104**	-	-	-	-	580x	-	-	-	-	-	-	-	-	-	-
Nepal	**51**	38	7	54	19	37	5	128	91	80x	41x	80	60	52	49	25
Netherlands	**175**	-	-	-	-	963	514	108	106	100	99	-	-	-	141	133
New Zealand	**165**	-	-	-	-	1027	521	103	103	100	100	-	-	96	117	123
Nicaragua	**77**	61	61	65	67	283	73	109	112	82	85	69x	74x	54	43	50
Niger	**3**	14	3	21	7	69	12	36	22	30	19	31x	21x	73	9	5
Nigeria	**15**	45	22	66	47	197	57	100	79	-	-	60	58	80	33	28
Niue	**-**	-	-	-	99x	564x	-	-	-	-	-	-	-	-	-	-
Norway	**189**	-	-	-	-	920	460	99	99	99	99	-	-	100	120	113
Oman	**140**	52	16	75	51	582	660	80	75	69	67	91	89	96	68	65
Pakistan	**33**	41	14	54	24	92	21	101	45	-	-	71	62	48	33	17
Palau	**97**	-	-	-	97x	-	-	-	-	-	-	-	-	-	-	-
Panama	**133**	86	85	91	90	299	187	108	104	91	92	-	-	82	60	65
Papua New Guinea	**45**	70	45	81	63	91	9	87	74	79x	67x	32x	31x	59	17	11
Paraguay	**100**	89	82	93	90	182	101	113	110	91	91	93x	93x	71	42	45
Peru	**73**	88	71	93	83	271	125	125	121	91	90	87x	87x	-	72	64
Philippines	**81**	90	88	94	94	159	51	110	112	100x	100x	81x	85x	70	71x	75x
Poland	**149**	99	99	100	100	518	337	97	95	95	94	-	-	98	98	97
Portugal	**156**	87	77	93	87	306	336	131	125	100	100	-	-	-	102	111
Qatar	**140**	72	65	79	80	448	403	87	85	81	80	-	-	99	81	79
Romania	**117**	98	92	99	96	317	231	105	103	96	95	-	-	99	78	78
Russian Federation	**115**	99	93	100	99	344	405	108	107	93	93	-	-	-	84	91
Rwanda	**21**	51	29	69	52	101x	-	83	81	76	76	61x	61x	60	12	9
Saint Kitts and Nevis	**90**	-	-	-	-	671	251	-	-	-	-	-	-	-	-	-
Saint Lucia	**130**	-	-	-	-	765	217	-	-	-	-	-	-	95	-	-
Saint Vincent/Grenadines	**120**	-	-	-	-	673	159	-	-	-	-	-	-	-	-	-
Samoa	**110**	-	-	-	98x	1054	60	111	103	97	97	-	-	85	59	66
San Marino	**165**	-	-	-	-	620	358	-	-	-	-	-	-	100	-	-
Sao Tome and Principe	**61**	-	-	-	-	272	166	-	-	-	-	-	-	-	-	-
Saudi Arabia	**113**	65	32	80	59	319	260	77	75	63	60	-	-	89	65	57
Senegal	**38**	31	12	43	23	141	41	76	62	64	53	48	42	85	20	12
Seychelles	**140**	-	-	83x	86x	541	145	-	-	-	-	-	-	100	-	-
Sierra Leone	**1**	30	9	45	18	251	12	59	41	-	-	-	-	-	22	13
Singapore	**175**	92	74	96	86	739	384	95	93	93	92	-	-	100	70	77
Slovakia	**153**	-	-	-	-	580	486	102	102	-	-	-	-	97	92	96
Slovenia	**175**	100	99	100	100	416	364	106	105	100	100	-	-	98	92	94
Solomon Islands	**113**	-	-	-	56x	141	6	104	90	-	-	-	-	81	21	14
Somalia	**8**	8x	1x	36x	14x	46	13	15x	8x	11x	6x	21x	13x	-	9x	5x
South Africa	**58**	78	75	84	82	316	118	117	115	93	95	-	-	65	76	91
Spain	**165**	97	92	98	96	328	406	106	105	100	100	-	-	98	114	128
Sri Lanka	**137**	91	79	94	87	210	83	110	108	-	-	-	-	83	71	78
Sudan	**43**	48	18	63	38	270	84	57	48	-	-	59x	52x	94	21	19
Suriname	**94**	92	84	95	91	683	144	129x	125x	100x	100x	-	-	99	50x	58x
Swaziland	**53**	64	56	78	75	170	23	132	125	95	95	-	-	74	52	52
Sweden	**189**	-	-	-	-	907	499	105	106	100	100	-	-	98	126	147
Switzerland	**175**	-	-	-	-	969	443	108	107	100	100	-	-	100	94	88
Syria	**102**	72	34	85	54	274	69	106	96	95	87	98	95	94	45	40
Tajikistan	**62**	97	92	99	98	-	-	95	92	-	-	-	-	-	81	72
Tanzania	**32**	65	34	80	59	278	3	67	66	47	49	61x	68x	83	6	5
TFYR Macedonia	**110**	-	-	-	-	184	230	90	87	86	84	-	-	99	58	58

	Under-5 mortality rank	Adult literacy rate 1980 male	Adult literacy rate 1980 female	Adult literacy rate 1995 male	Adult literacy rate 1995 female	No. of sets per 1000 population 1996 radio	No. of sets per 1000 population 1996 television	Primary school enrolment ratio 1990-97* (gross) male	Primary school enrolment ratio 1990-97* (gross) female	Primary school enrolment ratio 1990-96* (net) male	Primary school enrolment ratio 1990-96* (net) female	Net primary school attendance (%) 1990-98* male	Net primary school attendance (%) 1990-98* female	% of primary school entrants reaching grade 5 1990-95*	Secondary school enrolment ratio 1990-96* (gross) male	Secondary school enrolment ratio 1990-96* (gross) female
Thailand	**90**	92	83	96	92	204	189	99	96	-	-	-	-	88	38	37
Togo	**30**	48	18	67	35	217	17	140	99	93	69	73x	64x	71	40	14
Tonga	**120**	-	-	-	99x	612	20	-	-	-	-	-	-	92	-	-
Trinidad and Tobago	**140**	97	93	99	97	517	323	91	102	83	94	-	-	95	66	79
Tunisia	**102**	61	32	76	53	218	98	117	111	97	95	-	-	91	67	65
Turkey	**85**	81	50	92	72	178	333	107	102	98	94	74	71	89	67	45
Turkmenistan	**66**	-	-	99x	97x	96	193	-	-	-	-	81x	80x	-	-	-
Tuvalu	**71**	-	-	-	-	400	13	-	-	-	-	-	-	96	-	-
Uganda	**35**	60	31	74	50	123	15	79	67	58x	51x	65x	63x	55	15	9
Ukraine	**126**	-	-	98	99	872	349	87	86	-	-	-	-	-	88	94
United Arab Emirates	**153**	72	64	79	80	354	133	91	87	79	78	-	-	83	77	82
United Kingdom	**165**	-	-	-	-	1445	516	115	116	100	100	-	-	-	123	144
United States	**160**	99x	99x	-	-	2115	805	102	101	94	95	-	-	99	98	97
Uruguay	**137**	94	95	97	98	610	242	113	112	95	96	-	-	98	77	92
Uzbekistan	**70**	-	-	100	100	452	269	78	76	-	-	83	83	-	99	87
Vanuatu	**76**	-	-	-	60x	345	13	105	107	76x	72x	-	-	61	23	18
Venezuela	**115**	86	82	92	90	471	179	90	93	83	85	-	-	89	33	46
Viet Nam	**85**	92	76	95	88	106	47	106x	100x	-	-	-	-	-	44x	41x
Yemen	**38**	39	6	62	18	64	29	100	40	-	-	75x	40x	-	53	14
Yugoslavia	**130**	-	-	99	97	143	262	71	72	69	70	-	-	100	62	66
Zambia	**12**	73	50	86	71	121	42	92	86	76	75	74	74	84	34	21
Zimbabwe	**55**	83	68	90	80	96	31	115	111	-	-	91	90	79	52	44

Regional summaries

	Adult literacy rate 1980 male	1980 female	1995 male	1995 female	radio	television	Primary gross male	Primary gross female	Primary net male	Primary net female	Attendance male	Attendance female	Reaching grade 5	Secondary male	Secondary female
Sub-Saharan Africa	50	29	65	47	166	33	82	67	59	51	61	57	67	27	22
Middle East and North Africa	57	28	71	47	268	111	95	82	85	77	85	75	90	64	54
South Asia	52	24	62	33	99	50	105	81	65	50	74	62	56	52	33
East Asia and Pacific	80	56	90	75	207	249	117	115	99	99	93	93	91	67	61
Latin America and Caribbean	82	78	88	85	411	204	107	104	87	87	89	90	76	48	52
CEE/CIS and Baltic States	-	-	99	96	412	340	99	98	93	92	-	-	-	82	82
Industrialized countries	99	97	-	-	1319	638	104	103	97	97	-	-	99	105	107
Developing countries	68	46	79	61	199	154	105	92	86	81	81	75	74	55	46
Least developed countries	47	24	59	38	116	12	76	59	56	45	63	58	58	24	14
World	75	58	81	65	379	238	104	94	88	84	81	75	77	61	54

Countries in each region are listed on page 112.

Definitions of the indicators

Adult literacy rate – Percentage of persons aged 15 and over who can read and write.

Gross primary or secondary school enrolment ratio – The number of children enrolled in a level (primary or secondary), regardless of age, divided by the population of the age group which officially corresponds to the same level.

Net primary school enrolment ratio – The number of children enrolled in primary school, who belong to the age group that officially corresponds to primary schooling, divided by the total population of the same age group.

Net primary school attendance – Percentage of children in the age group that officially corresponds to primary schooling who attend primary school. These data come from national household surveys. While both the attendance and enrolment data should report on children going to primary school, the number of children of primary school age is uncertain for many countries, and this can lead to significant biases in the enrolment ratio.

Primary school entrants reaching grade five – Percentage of the children entering the first grade of primary school who eventually reach grade five.

Main data sources

Adult literacy – United Nations Educational, Scientific and Cultural Organization (UNESCO).

Radio and television – United Nations Educational, Scientific and Cultural Organization (UNESCO).

Primary and secondary school enrolment – United Nations Educational, Scientific and Cultural Organization (UNESCO).

Net primary school attendance – Demographic and Health Surveys (DHS) and Multiple Indicator Cluster Surveys (MICS).

Gross school enrolment and reaching grade five – United Nations Educational, Scientific and Cultural Organization (UNESCO).

Notes

- \- Data not available.
- x Indicates data that refer to years or periods other than those specified in the column heading, differ from the standard definition, or refer to only part of a country.
- * Data refer to the most recent year available during the period specified in the column heading.

Table 5: Demographic indicators

	Under-5 mortality rank	Population (thousands) 1998		Population annual growth rate (%)		Crude death rate		Crude birth rate		Life expectancy		Total fertility rate 1998	% of population urbanized 1998	Average annual growth rate of urban population (%)	
		under 18	under 5	1970-90	1990-98	1970	1998	1970	1998	1970	1998			1970-90	1990-98
Afghanistan	**4**	10321	4014	0.4	4.6	27	21	53	52	37	46	6.8	20	2.9	6.2
Albania	**90**	1117	314	2.2	-0.7	8	6	33	20	67	73	2.5	38	2.7	0.1
Algeria	**88**	13395	4022	3.0	2.3	16	6	49	29	53	69	3.8	56	4.3	3.3
Andorra	**165**	14	4	5.3	4.1	-	-	-	-	-	-	-	92	5.0	3.7
Angola	**2**	6542	2339	2.5	3.4	27	19	49	48	37	47	6.7	31	5.6	4.8
Antigua and Barbuda	**133**	24	7	0.6	0.6	7	5	26	18	67	76	1.7	36	1.0	0.5
Argentina	**126**	12175	3469	1.5	1.3	9	8	23	20	66	73	2.6	87	2.1	1.4
Armenia	**104**	1132	244	1.7	0.0	6	8	23	13	72	71	1.7	70	2.3	0.5
Australia	**175**	4675	1267	1.5	1.2	9	8	20	13	71	78	1.8	84	1.5	1.0
Austria	**175**	1708	444	0.2	0.7	13	10	15	10	70	77	1.4	64	0.2	0.5
Azerbaijan	**80**	2759	682	1.6	0.9	7	7	29	16	68	70	2.0	56	2.0	1.3
Bahamas	**130**	107	33	2.0	1.9	7	5	30	23	66	74	2.6	85	2.8	2.1
Bahrain	**133**	212	63	4.0	2.4	9	4	40	20	62	73	2.8	89	4.5	2.5
Bangladesh	**48**	55857	14697	2.5	1.6	21	10	48	28	44	58	3.1	19	5.9	3.8
Barbados	**146**	71	18	0.4	0.5	9	8	22	12	69	76	1.5	48	1.4	1.2
Belarus	**110**	2542	522	0.6	0.1	9	13	16	10	71	68	1.4	72	2.7	1.0
Belgium	**165**	2129	561	0.2	0.2	12	10	15	11	71	77	1.6	97	0.3	0.2
Belize	**83**	109	34	2.1	2.6	8	4	40	31	66	75	3.6	45	1.8	1.7
Benin	**22**	3109	1015	2.7	2.7	25	13	53	41	43	53	5.8	39	6.2	4.3
Bhutan	**41**	980	332	2.4	2.1	22	10	42	38	42	61	5.5	6	4.9	4.9
Bolivia	**57**	3694	1188	2.2	2.4	20	9	46	33	46	62	4.3	61	3.8	3.5
Bosnia and Herzegovina	**137**	905	192	0.9	-2.0	7	7	23	10	66	73	1.4	41	2.8	-1.2
Botswana	**77**	784	241	3.5	2.6	15	16	50	34	52	47	4.3	64	11.8	7.9
Brazil	**85**	60185	16008	2.2	1.4	10	7	35	20	59	67	2.3	78	3.6	2.0
Brunei Darussalam	**156**	122	36	3.4	2.5	7	3	36	22	67	76	2.8	69	3.7	3.0
Bulgaria	**144**	1776	381	0.1	-0.6	9	14	16	9	71	71	1.2	69	1.3	0.0
Burkina Faso	**22**	6128	2137	2.6	2.8	25	19	53	46	39	45	6.5	16	6.8	4.8
Burundi	**17**	3438	1150	2.2	2.1	20	20	44	42	44	43	6.2	8	7.7	6.2
Cambodia	**24**	5110	1602	1.1	2.7	19	13	42	34	43	53	4.6	21	2.8	5.2
Cameroon	**27**	7213	2416	2.8	2.8	21	12	45	39	44	55	5.3	46	6.2	4.4
Canada	**165**	7178	1857	1.3	1.2	7	7	17	11	73	79	1.6	76	1.4	1.1
Cape Verde	**65**	193	60	1.2	2.2	12	6	40	32	57	69	3.5	56	5.4	5.3
Central African Rep.	**18**	1723	557	2.3	2.1	22	19	43	37	42	45	4.9	39	3.4	2.8
Chad	**13**	3805	1314	2.3	2.9	26	18	49	44	38	47	6.0	22	5.1	3.7
Chile	**148**	5046	1455	1.6	1.5	10	6	29	20	62	75	2.4	83	2.1	1.6
China	**79**	380453	98570	1.6	1.0	8	7	33	16	61	70	1.8	31	3.8	3.4
Colombia	**104**	16113	4793	2.2	1.9	9	6	38	24	61	71	2.8	72	3.2	2.4
Comoros	**53**	332	104	3.2	2.8	18	9	50	36	48	59	4.8	31	5.2	3.8
Congo	**47**	1470	513	2.8	2.8	20	16	46	44	46	49	6.0	59	5.2	4.1
Congo, Dem. Rep.	**9**	26744	9554	3.1	3.4	20	15	48	46	45	51	6.4	29	2.7	3.7
Cook Islands	**104**	8	2	-0.8	0.7	-	-	-	-	-	-	-	63	0.0	1.1
Costa Rica	**145**	1515	432	2.8	2.9	6	4	34	23	67	76	2.8	49	3.6	3.4
Côte d'Ivoire	**28**	7340	2266	3.7	2.6	20	16	52	37	44	47	5.0	44	5.7	3.7
Croatia	**156**	988	234	0.4	-0.1	10	11	15	11	69	73	1.6	57	1.9	0.5
Cuba	**160**	2861	746	1.1	0.6	7	7	30	13	69	76	1.6	76	2.1	1.1
Cyprus	**156**	223	57	0.5	1.6	10	7	19	14	71	78	2.0	54	1.6	2.4
Czech Rep.	**165**	2226	503	0.2	0.0	13	11	16	9	70	74	1.2	65	1.4	0.1
Denmark	**175**	1098	329	0.2	0.3	10	12	16	12	73	76	1.7	85	0.5	0.3
Djibouti	**26**	298	97	6.3	2.3	24	15	48	37	40	51	5.3	82	7.5	2.6
Dominica	**133**	25	7	0.1	0.0	11	6	26	22	-	76	1.9	69	1.9	0.3
Dominican Rep.	**75**	3292	948	2.4	1.8	11	5	42	24	58	71	2.8	62	4.2	2.7
Ecuador	**89**	5036	1463	2.7	2.1	12	6	42	25	58	70	3.1	59	4.3	3.0
Egypt	**68**	28569	8024	2.3	2.0	17	7	40	26	51	67	3.3	45	2.6	2.1
El Salvador	**97**	2588	786	1.8	2.1	12	6	44	28	57	69	3.1	45	2.4	2.3
Equatorial Guinea	**20**	213	74	1.0	2.5	24	16	40	41	40	50	5.5	44	2.4	4.9
Eritrea	**45**	1814	616	2.3	2.7	21	14	47	40	43	51	5.7	17	4.2	3.6
Estonia	**126**	334	65	0.7	-1.2	11	14	15	9	70	69	1.3	74	1.2	-0.8

	Under-5 mortality rank	Population (thousands) 1998 under 18	Population (thousands) 1998 under 5	Population annual growth rate (%) 1970-90	Population annual growth rate (%) 1990-98	Crude death rate 1970	Crude death rate 1998	Crude birth rate 1970	Crude birth rate 1998	Life expectancy 1970	Life expectancy 1998	Total fertility rate 1998	% of population urbanized 1998	Average annual growth rate of urban population (%) 1970-90	Average annual growth rate of urban population (%) 1990-98
Ethiopia	**18**	31275	10815	2.6	2.7	24	20	50	44	40	43	6.3	16	4.4	5.2
Fiji	**120**	317	84	1.7	1.2	7	4	34	22	64	73	2.7	41	2.2	1.8
Finland	**175**	1154	307	0.4	0.4	10	10	15	11	70	77	1.7	64	1.4	0.9
France	**175**	13467	3589	0.6	0.4	11	9	17	12	72	78	1.7	75	0.8	0.6
Gabon	**30**	527	185	3.1	2.8	21	16	33	38	44	52	5.4	51	6.0	4.3
Gambia	**59**	570	200	3.4	3.6	28	17	50	40	36	47	5.2	29	6.1	5.1
Georgia	**120**	1393	357	0.7	-1.0	10	9	19	14	68	73	1.9	60	1.6	-0.1
Germany	**175**	15790	3919	0.1	0.4	12	11	14	9	71	77	1.3	87	0.4	0.7
Ghana	**49**	9709	3144	2.8	3.0	17	9	47	37	49	60	5.1	36	3.6	3.6
Greece	**162**	2079	501	0.8	0.5	8	10	17	9	72	78	1.3	59	1.3	0.5
Grenada	**109**	33	9	-0.2	0.3	-	7	-	26	-	72	3.6	37	0.2	1.2
Guatemala	**74**	5537	1787	2.6	2.6	15	7	45	36	52	64	4.9	38	2.8	2.8
Guinea	**14**	3779	1234	1.9	3.0	27	17	51	42	37	47	5.5	30	5.0	5.0
Guinea-Bissau	**11**	567	196	3.1	2.2	28	20	42	42	36	45	5.7	22	4.5	3.6
Guyana	**60**	313	89	0.6	0.8	11	7	38	22	60	65	2.3	36	1.2	1.9
Haiti	**36**	3897	1122	2.1	1.7	19	12	39	32	47	54	4.3	33	4.0	3.3
Holy See	-	-	-	-	-	-	-	-	-	-	-	-	100	-	-
Honduras	**81**	3039	959	3.2	2.9	15	5	49	33	52	70	4.2	44	4.9	3.8
Hungary	**149**	2177	537	0.0	-0.3	11	14	15	10	69	71	1.4	66	1.2	0.5
Iceland	**175**	78	22	1.1	1.0	7	7	22	16	74	79	2.1	91	1.5	0.9
India	**49**	395791	115615	2.1	1.8	17	9	39	25	49	63	3.1	27	3.4	2.2
Indonesia	**71**	77808	21967	2.1	1.5	18	7	41	23	48	65	2.5	37	5.1	3.6
Iran	**100**	30375	7283	3.4	1.9	16	5	45	21	55	69	2.8	59	4.9	2.6
Iraq	**37**	10593	3327	3.3	2.3	16	8	49	36	55	63	5.2	74	4.6	2.7
Ireland	**162**	1010	253	0.9	0.6	11	8	22	14	71	76	1.9	58	1.3	0.8
Israel	**165**	2011	579	2.2	3.1	7	6	27	20	71	78	2.7	89	2.6	2.9
Italy	**165**	10068	2670	0.3	0.1	10	10	17	9	72	78	1.2	67	0.5	0.1
Jamaica	**149**	963	276	1.2	0.9	8	6	35	22	68	75	2.5	54	2.2	1.7
Japan	**189**	23653	6097	0.8	0.3	7	8	19	10	72	80	1.4	78	1.3	0.5
Jordan	**93**	3088	999	3.5	3.9	18	5	52	35	54	70	4.8	70	4.9	4.3
Kazakhstan	**83**	5584	1431	1.2	-0.3	9	9	26	18	64	68	2.3	61	2.0	0.3
Kenya	**40**	15025	4435	3.6	2.6	18	12	53	34	50	52	4.4	30	8.0	5.4
Kiribati	**62**	37	12	1.8	1.5	-	8	41	32	-	60	4.5	36	3.3	1.9
Korea, Dem. People's Rep.	**104**	7415	2387	1.8	1.6	10	5	41	21	60	72	2.0	61	2.3	1.8
Korea, Rep. of	**175**	12496	3430	1.5	0.9	10	6	30	15	60	73	1.7	82	4.4	2.2
Kuwait	**147**	779	195	5.3	-2.1	5	2	47	22	66	76	2.9	97	6.3	-2.0
Kyrgyzstan	**69**	1953	562	2.0	0.7	11	7	31	25	62	68	3.2	39	2.1	1.1
Lao People's Dem. Rep.	**41**	2606	875	2.1	2.7	23	13	44	39	40	53	5.7	21	5.1	4.8
Latvia	**126**	568	111	0.6	-1.3	11	14	14	8	70	69	1.3	75	1.3	-0.7
Lebanon	**94**	1249	372	0.2	2.8	11	6	35	23	64	70	2.7	86	1.9	3.1
Lesotho	**33**	960	311	2.4	2.3	20	12	43	35	48	56	4.7	25	6.4	5.1
Liberia	**6**	1453	432	3.1	0.4	21	15	49	44	46	48	6.3	44	5.5	1.0
Libya	**117**	2489	699	4.0	2.4	16	5	50	29	52	70	3.8	84	7.0	2.7
Liechtenstein	**149**	7	2	1.6	1.2	-	-	-	-	-	-	-	19	2.0	0.0
Lithuania	**120**	916	201	0.9	-0.1	9	12	17	10	71	70	1.4	73	2.5	0.6
Luxembourg	**175**	90	27	0.6	1.3	12	9	13	12	70	77	1.7	89	1.8	1.6
Madagascar	**25**	7577	2704	2.6	3.2	20	11	47	40	45	58	5.4	27	5.1	5.2
Malawi	**7**	5580	1948	3.6	1.3	24	23	56	47	40	39	6.7	14	7.1	2.9
Malaysia	**153**	8781	2685	2.5	2.3	10	5	37	25	61	72	3.1	54	4.6	3.3
Maldives	**56**	138	42	2.9	2.8	17	7	40	35	50	65	5.3	27	6.3	3.1
Mali	**5**	5745	1965	2.4	2.4	26	16	51	47	42	54	6.5	28	5.1	4.2
Malta	**162**	98	25	0.8	1.0	9	8	16	13	70	77	1.9	89	1.5	1.1
Marshall Islands	**52**	27	9	3.0	3.3	-	-	-	-	-	-	-	68	3.1	3.9
Mauritania	**16**	1277	431	2.5	2.8	22	13	45	40	43	54	5.5	53	8.1	5.3
Mauritius	**120**	362	98	1.2	1.0	7	6	28	16	62	72	1.9	40	1.0	1.0
Mexico	**97**	38751	11224	2.5	1.8	10	5	45	24	61	72	2.7	72	3.5	1.8
Micronesia, Fed. States of	**117**	52	17	2.3	2.0	-	6	-	28	-	67	4.0	28	2.6	3.1

Table 5: Demographic indicators

	Under-5 mortality rank	Population (thousands) 1998		Population annual growth rate (%)		Crude death rate		Crude birth rate		Life expectancy		Total fertility rate 1998	% of population urbanized 1998	Average annual growth rate of urban population (%)	
		under 18	under 5	1970-90	1990-98	1970	1998	1970	1998	1970	1998			1970-90	1990-98
Moldova, Rep. of	**94**	1315	296	1.0	0.0	10	11	18	13	65	68	1.7	53	3.0	1.3
Monaco	**175**	7	2	1.1	1.2	-	-	-	-	-	-	-	100	1.1	1.2
Mongolia	**28**	1113	283	2.8	1.9	14	6	42	23	53	66	2.6	61	4.1	2.6
Morocco	**67**	10997	3131	2.2	1.7	17	7	47	26	52	67	3.0	52	3.8	2.8
Mozambique	**10**	9670	3365	2.1	3.6	22	19	46	43	42	44	6.2	35	9.6	7.0
Myanmar	**44**	15978	4179	2.0	1.2	17	9	41	21	49	60	2.4	27	2.4	1.9
Namibia	**62**	801	261	2.7	2.6	18	14	43	36	47	51	4.9	37	5.1	4.8
Nauru	**104**	-	-	2.6	1.2	-	-	-	-	-	-	-	100	2.6	1.2
Nepal	**51**	11066	3449	2.5	2.5	22	11	45	34	42	58	4.4	11	6.6	4.5
Netherlands	**175**	3410	946	0.7	0.6	8	9	17	11	74	78	1.5	89	0.9	0.5
New Zealand	**165**	1030	288	0.9	1.5	9	8	22	15	72	77	2.0	85	1.1	1.6
Nicaragua	**77**	2445	796	2.9	2.8	14	6	48	36	54	68	4.4	62	4.1	3.4
Niger	**3**	5526	1997	3.1	3.3	26	17	59	48	38	49	6.8	19	6.0	5.3
Nigeria	**15**	53769	17607	2.8	2.5	22	15	50	39	43	50	5.1	41	5.6	4.4
Niue	**-**	1	0	-	-	-	-	-	-	-	-	-	50	-	-
Norway	**189**	1020	295	0.4	0.5	10	10	18	13	74	78	1.9	73	1.0	0.7
Oman	**140**	1228	388	4.5	3.6	22	4	51	35	47	71	5.8	77	13.1	6.3
Pakistan	**33**	71952	23470	3.0	2.7	19	8	48	36	49	64	5.0	34	4.2	3.6
Palau	**97**	9	3	2.0	3.0	-	-	-	-	-	-	-	68	3.0	2.1
Panama	**133**	1051	303	2.3	1.8	8	5	38	22	65	74	2.6	56	2.9	2.2
Papua New Guinea	**45**	2089	657	2.3	2.3	18	10	42	32	46	58	4.6	16	4.3	3.1
Paraguay	**100**	2458	757	2.9	2.7	9	5	37	31	65	70	4.1	52	4.3	3.5
Peru	**73**	10146	2900	2.5	1.7	14	6	42	25	54	68	2.9	71	3.4	2.0
Philippines	**81**	32012	9692	2.4	2.3	10	6	39	28	57	68	3.6	55	4.4	3.7
Poland	**149**	10069	2225	0.8	0.2	8	10	17	11	70	73	1.5	65	1.7	0.7
Portugal	**156**	2056	536	0.4	0.0	11	11	20	10	67	75	1.4	37	1.6	1.4
Qatar	**140**	180	50	7.4	2.2	13	4	35	18	61	72	3.7	90	8.0	2.2
Romania	**117**	5267	1056	0.7	-0.4	9	11	21	9	69	70	1.2	57	1.9	0.3
Russian Federation	**115**	35628	7003	0.6	-0.1	9	14	15	10	69	67	1.3	77	1.5	0.4
Rwanda	**21**	3513	1156	3.1	-0.7	21	17	53	43	44	41	6.1	6	5.7	0.9
Saint Kitts and Nevis	**90**	14	4	-0.6	-0.9	11	12	26	21	-	70	2.4	36	-0.3	-0.9
Saint Lucia	**130**	54	15	1.4	1.4	-	7	41	21	62	70	2.4	37	1.1	0.9
Saint Vincent/Grenadines	**120**	40	11	1.0	0.7	-	7	40	21	63	73	2.2	51	5.9	3.8
Samoa	**110**	80	23	0.5	1.0	11	5	43	29	57	71	4.1	21	0.8	1.1
San Marino	**165**	5	1	1.2	1.5	-	-	-	-	-	-	-	96	3.2	2.2
Sao Tome and Principe	**61**	75	26	2.4	2.1	-	10	-	33	-	64	4.7	44	5.0	3.7
Saudi Arabia	**113**	9556	3135	5.1	2.9	19	4	48	34	52	72	5.7	82	7.5	3.3
Senegal	**38**	4648	1571	2.8	2.6	25	13	49	40	41	53	5.5	44	3.8	3.8
Seychelles	**140**	40	13	1.4	1.0	-	7	-	21	-	71	2.1	55	4.6	2.3
Sierra Leone	**1**	2304	808	2.0	1.7	30	25	49	46	34	38	6.0	34	4.6	3.2
Singapore	**175**	904	273	1.9	1.8	5	5	23	14	69	77	1.7	98	1.9	1.6
Slovakia	**153**	1396	314	0.7	0.3	10	10	19	10	70	73	1.4	60	2.3	1.1
Slovenia	**175**	425	96	0.7	0.5	10	10	17	9	70	74	1.3	52	2.2	0.9
Solomon Islands	**113**	210	68	3.5	3.3	10	4	46	35	60	72	4.8	18	6.2	5.4
Somalia	**8**	5024	1847	3.8	2.2	24	18	50	52	40	47	7.2	26	4.8	3.0
South Africa	**58**	16413	4906	2.2	1.8	14	12	35	27	53	54	3.2	49	2.3	1.7
Spain	**165**	7540	1848	0.8	0.1	9	9	20	9	72	78	1.1	77	1.4	0.4
Sri Lanka	**137**	6233	1590	1.5	1.0	8	6	30	18	65	73	2.1	23	1.3	1.9
Sudan	**43**	13456	4095	2.8	2.0	21	11	47	33	43	55	4.6	33	5.4	4.3
Suriname	**94**	162	41	0.4	0.4	8	6	37	20	63	70	2.2	50	0.5	1.1
Swaziland	**53**	477	158	2.9	2.9	19	9	48	38	46	60	4.7	32	7.7	5.6
Sweden	**189**	1940	508	0.3	0.5	10	11	14	10	74	79	1.6	83	0.4	0.4
Switzerland	**175**	1532	421	0.5	0.8	9	9	16	11	73	79	1.5	61	1.0	1.1
Syria	**102**	7660	2146	3.4	2.7	14	5	47	30	56	69	4.0	52	4.2	3.1
Tajikistan	**62**	2877	859	2.9	1.6	10	7	40	32	63	67	4.1	32	2.2	1.5
Tanzania	**32**	16870	5643	3.1	2.9	20	15	50	41	45	48	5.4	25	8.6	5.1
TFYR Macedonia	**110**	571	152	1.0	0.6	8	8	25	16	66	73	2.1	60	2.0	1.1

	Under-5 mortality rank	Population (thousands) 1998 under 18	Population (thousands) 1998 under 5	Population annual growth rate (%) 1970-90	Population annual growth rate (%) 1990-98	Crude death rate 1970	Crude death rate 1998	Crude birth rate 1970	Crude birth rate 1998	Life expectancy 1970	Life expectancy 1998	Total fertility rate 1998	% of population urbanized 1998	Average annual growth rate of urban population (%) 1970-90	Average annual growth rate of urban population (%) 1990-98
Thailand	**90**	19264	4826	2.2	1.0	10	7	39	17	58	69	1.7	21	4.1	2.0
Togo	**30**	2313	788	2.8	2.8	20	15	45	41	44	49	6.0	31	6.6	4.1
Tonga	**120**	41	12	0.8	0.3	-	6	-	28	-	71	3.6	43	3.5	2.6
Trinidad and Tobago	**140**	435	94	1.1	0.7	7	6	27	14	66	74	1.6	72	1.6	1.3
Tunisia	**102**	3586	927	2.3	1.7	14	7	39	20	54	70	2.5	63	3.6	2.7
Turkey	**85**	22972	6611	2.3	1.7	12	6	37	22	56	69	2.5	70	4.7	3.5
Turkmenistan	**66**	1936	573	2.6	2.0	11	7	37	28	60	66	3.6	45	2.3	1.9
Tuvalu	**71**	5	1	2.0	2.5	-	-	-	-	-	-	-	45	6.9	2.8
Uganda	**35**	11668	4215	2.6	2.8	18	21	49	51	46	40	7.1	13	4.2	5.0
Ukraine	**126**	11798	2546	0.5	-0.3	9	14	15	10	71	69	1.4	71	1.5	0.4
United Arab Emirates	**153**	803	211	10.8	2.5	12	3	39	18	61	75	3.4	83	12.5	2.8
United Kingdom	**165**	13367	3581	0.2	0.2	12	11	16	12	72	77	1.7	89	0.2	0.2
United States	**160**	71222	19623	1.0	0.9	9	8	17	14	71	77	2.0	76	1.0	1.1
Uruguay	**137**	974	283	0.5	0.7	10	9	21	18	69	74	2.4	90	0.9	0.8
Uzbekistan	**70**	10609	3068	2.7	1.7	10	7	36	28	63	68	3.4	41	3.2	1.7
Vanuatu	**76**	89	27	2.7	2.5	14	6	46	32	53	68	4.3	19	4.5	2.9
Venezuela	**115**	9585	2784	3.0	2.2	7	5	37	25	65	72	3.0	85	3.8	2.3
Viet Nam	**85**	32058	8755	2.2	1.9	15	7	38	22	49	68	2.6	19	2.8	1.3
Yemen	**38**	9187	3355	3.0	4.7	23	10	53	48	41	58	7.5	34	7.0	6.9
Yugoslavia	**130**	2699	673	0.8	0.6	9	10	18	13	68	73	1.8	58	2.3	1.7
Zambia	**12**	4844	1584	2.7	2.4	19	20	49	42	46	40	5.5	43	4.4	2.7
Zimbabwe	**55**	5625	1637	3.1	1.8	16	18	50	31	50	44	3.8	33	5.6	3.7

Regional summaries

	Under-5 mortality rank	Population (thousands) 1998 under 18	Population (thousands) 1998 under 5	Population annual growth rate (%) 1970-90	Population annual growth rate (%) 1990-98	Crude death rate 1970	Crude death rate 1998	Crude birth rate 1970	Crude birth rate 1998	Life expectancy 1970	Life expectancy 1998	Total fertility rate 1998	% of population urbanized 1998	Average annual growth rate of urban population (%) 1970-90	Average annual growth rate of urban population (%) 1990-98
Sub-Saharan Africa		298834	100036	2.8	2.6	21	16	48	41	44	48	5.5	32	4.4	4.2
Middle East and North Africa		147923	42576	2.9	2.3	17	7	45	28	52	66	3.8	56	4.2	3.0
South Asia		552338	163209	2.2	1.9	18	9	41	27	48	62	3.4	27	3.6	2.6
East Asia and Pacific		599090	160477	1.7	1.2	10	7	35	18	58	69	2.0	34	3.9	3.2
Latin America and Caribbean		192738	54841	2.2	1.7	10	6	37	23	60	69	2.7	73	3.2	2.0
CEE/CIS and Baltic States		133507	31712	0.9	0.3	9	11	20	14	66	69	1.8	67	1.9	1.0
Industrialized countries		189861	50598	0.7	0.6	10	9	17	12	72	78	1.6	77	0.9	0.7
Developing countries		1844149	536105	2.1	1.7	14	9	38	25	53	62	3.0	38	3.7	2.9
Least developed countries		303946	98575	2.5	2.5	22	15	48	38	43	50	5.0	23	4.4	4.3
World		2114291	603449	1.7	1.4	12	9	33	22	56	64	2.7	45	2.4	2.1

Countries in each region are listed on page 112.

Definitions of the indicators

Life expectancy at birth – The number of years newborn children would live if subject to the mortality risks prevailing for the cross-section of population at the time of their birth.

Crude death rate – Annual number of deaths per 1,000 population.

Crude birth rate – Annual number of births per 1,000 population.

Total fertility rate – The number of children that would be born per woman if she were to live to the end of her childbearing years and bear children at each age in accordance with prevailing age-specific fertility rates.

Urban population – Percentage of population living in urban areas as defined according to the national definition used in the most recent population census.

Main data sources

Life expectancy – United Nations Population Division.

Child population – United Nations Population Division.

Crude death and birth rates – United Nations Population Division.

Fertility – United Nations Population Division.

Urban population – United Nations Population Division.

Notes

- \- Data not available.
- x Indicates data that refer to years or periods other than those specified in the column heading, differ from the standard definition, or refer to only part of a country.

Table 6: Economic indicators

	Under-5 mortality rank	GNP per capita (US$) 1997	GNP per capita average annual growth rate (%) 1965-80*	GNP per capita average annual growth rate (%) 1990-97*	Annual rate of inflation (%) 1990-97*	% of population below $1 a day 1990-96*	% of central government expenditure allocated to (1992-98*) health	education	defence	ODA inflow in millions US$ 1997	ODA inflow as a % of recipient GNP 1997	Debt service as a % of exports of goods and services 1970	1997
Afghanistan	**4**	250x	0.6	-	-	-	-	-	-	279	5	-	-
Albania	**90**	760	-	2.2	58	-	6	2	7	155	7	-	5
Algeria	**88**	1500	4.2	-1.6	24	2	-	-	-	248	1	3	24
Andorra	**165**	d	-	-	-	-	-	-	-	-	-	-	-
Angola	**2**	260	-	-10.0	1091	-	6x	15x	34x	436	14	-	15
Antigua and Barbuda	**133**	7380	-	1.8	3	-	-	-	-	4	1	-	2x
Argentina	**126**	8950	1.7	4.2	12	-	3	6	5	222	0	22	54
Armenia	**104**	560	-	-10.7	483	-	-	-	-	168	8	-	5
Australia	**175**	20650	2.2	2.4	2	-	14	8	7	-	-	-	-
Austria	**175**	27920	4.0	1.1	3	-	13	9	2	-	-	-	-
Azerbaijan	**80**	510	-	-16.0	448	-	-	-	-	182	5	-	6
Bahamas	**130**	11830x	-	-2.0	3	-	15	19	3	4x	0x	-	-
Bahrain	**133**	8640x	-	2.6	1	-	10	14	18	84	2	-	2x
Bangladesh	**48**	360	-0.3	3.3	4	-	5x	11x	10x	1009	2	0	9
Barbados	**146**	6590x	-	-0.9	1	-	-	-	-	3	0	-	5x
Belarus	**110**	2150	-	-5.6	561	2	4	5	4	-	-	-	2
Belgium	**165**	26730	3.6	1.3	3	-	2x	12x	5x	-	-	-	-
Belize	**83**	2670	-	0.3	4	-	8	20	5	14	2	-	8
Benin	**22**	380	-0.3	1.7	11	-	6x	31x	17x	225	10	2	8
Bhutan	**41**	430	-	2.0	10	-	10	11	-	70	8	-	5
Bolivia	**57**	970	1.7	2.0	10	7x	3	19	8	717	9	11	29
Bosnia and Herzegovina	**137**	a	-	-	-	-	-	-	-	863	-	-	0x
Botswana	**77**	3310	9.9	1.3	10	33x	5	26	8	125	2	1	5x
Brazil	**85**	4790	6.3	1.9	476	24	6	4	3	487	0	12	55
Brunei Darussalam	**156**	25160x	-	-2.1	2	-	-	-	-	4x	0x	-	-
Bulgaria	**144**	1170	-	-2.0	110	3	6	6	8	-	-	-	12
Burkina Faso	**22**	250	1.7	0.8	7	-	7	17	14	370	13	4	11
Burundi	**17**	140	2.4	-5.9	11	-	3	14	26	119	13	4	21
Cambodia	**24**	300	-	2.7	38	-	-	-	-	372	12	-	1
Cameroon	**27**	620	2.4	-3.3	6	-	4	15	12	501	6	3	18
Canada	**165**	19640	3.3	0.8	1	-	5	3	6	-	-	-	-
Cape Verde	**65**	1090	-	1.0	5	-	-	-	-	110	25	-	5
Central African Rep.	**18**	320	0.8	-1.0	6	-	-	-	-	92	8	5	2
Chad	**13**	230	-1.9	1.0	7	-	8x	8x	-	225	13	4	8
Chile	**148**	4820	0.0	6.4	10	15	12	16	8	136	0	19	18
China	**79**	860	4.1	10.0	11	22	0	2	13	2040	0	0x	8
Colombia	**104**	2180	3.7	2.6	22	7	5	19	9	274	0	12	25
Comoros	**53**	400	-	-3.1	4	-	-	-	-	28	11	-	3
Congo	**47**	670	2.7	-2.9	9	-	-	-	-	268	14	11	5
Congo, Dem. Rep.	**9**	110	-1.3	-9.6	2013	-	1	1	4	168	3	5	0
Cook Islands	**104**	-	-	-	-	-	-	-	-	10	16x	-	-
Costa Rica	**145**	2680	3.3	2.3	18	19x	22	17	-	0	0	10	11
Côte d'Ivoire	**28**	710	2.8	0.9	9	18x	4x	21x	4x	444	4	7	25
Croatia	**156**	4060	-	2.7	218	-	14	7	12	44	0	-	12
Cuba	**160**	1170x	-	-	-	-	23x	10x	-	67	1	-	-
Cyprus	**156**	10260x	-	2.6	4	-	6	12	4	30x	0x	-	-
Czech Rep.	**165**	5240	-	-0.3	17	3	18	11	5	-	-	-	13
Denmark	**175**	34890	2.2	2.5	2	-	1	9	4	-	-	-	-
Djibouti	**26**	b	-	-	5	-	-	-	-	87	-	-	3
Dominica	**133**	3040	-	0.7	4	-	-	-	-	14	6	-	7
Dominican Rep.	**75**	1750	3.8	3.5	12	20x	11	13	4	76	1	4	5
Ecuador	**89**	1570	5.4	0.9	33	30	11x	18x	13x	172	1	9	29
Egypt	**68**	1200	2.8	2.8	11	8	3	14	9	1947	2	26	8
El Salvador	**97**	1810	1.5	3.5	10	-	10	20	7	294	3	4	6
Equatorial Guinea	**20**	1060	-	12.1	15	-	-	-	-	24	5	-	0
Eritrea	**45**	230	-	2.9	13	-	-	-	-	123	15	-	0
Estonia	**126**	3360	-	-2.8	92	6	16	10	5	-	-	-	1

	Under-5 mortality rank	GNP per capita (US$) 1997	GNP per capita average annual growth rate (%) 1965-80*	GNP per capita average annual growth rate (%) 1990-97*	Annual rate of inflation (%) 1990-97*	% of population below $1 a day 1990-96*	% of central government expenditure allocated to (1992-98*) health	education	defence	ODA inflow in millions US$ 1997	ODA inflow as a % of recipient GNP 1997	Debt service as a % of exports of goods and services 1970	1997
Ethiopia	**18**	110	0.4	2.2	9	46x	5	14	9	637	10	11	9
Fiji	**120**	2460	-	0.4	4	-	9	18	6	44	2	-	3
Finland	**175**	24790	3.6	0.9	2	-	3	10	4	-	-	-	-
France	**175**	26300	3.7	1.0	2	-	16x	7x	6x	-	-	-	-
Gabon	**30**	4120	5.6	-0.1	9	-	-	-	-	40	1	6	12
Gambia	**59**	340	-	-0.6	5	-	7x	12x	4x	40	10	1	8
Georgia	**120**	860	-	-14.9	1033	-	4	6	10	246	6	-	5
Germany	**175**	28280	3.0x	0.7	3	-	17x	1x	7x	-	-	-	-
Ghana	**49**	390	-0.8	1.4	29	-	7	22	5	493	7	5	18
Greece	**162**	11640	4.8	1.0	12	-	7	10	7	-	-	9	17x
Grenada	**109**	3140	-	1.3	3	-	10	17	-	8	3	-	5x
Guatemala	**74**	1580	3.0	1.5	12	53x	11	17	11	302	2	7	8
Guinea	**14**	550	1.3	2.7	6	26	3x	11x	29x	382	9	-	19
Guinea-Bissau	**11**	230	-2.7	1.0	45	88	1x	3x	4x	125	47	-	14
Guyana	**60**	800	-	12.9	27	-	-	-	-	272	40	-	14
Haiti	**36**	380	0.9	-4.4	25	-	-	-	-	332	11	5	13
Holy See	**-**	-	-	-	-	-	-	-	-	-	-	-	-
Honduras	**81**	740	1.1	1.0	20	47	10x	19x	7x	308	7	3	20
Hungary	**149**	4510	5.1	0.2	23	2	6	2	2	-	-	-	29
Iceland	**175**	26470x	-	0.4	3	-	23	13	-	-	-	-	-
India	**49**	370	1.5	4.3	9	47	2	2	15	1678	0	21	19
Indonesia	**71**	1110	5.2	5.9	9	8	3	9	7	832	0	7	28
Iran	**100**	1780	2.9	1.9	33	-	6	15	8	196	0	-	31
Iraq	**37**	b	-	-	-	-	-	-	-	281	-	-	-
Ireland	**162**	17790	2.8	5.6	2	-	15	13	3	-	-	-	-
Israel	**165**	16180	3.7	2.6	11	-	14	14	18	2217x	2x	3	-
Italy	**165**	20170	3.2	1.0	5	-	11x	8x	4x	-	-	-	-
Jamaica	**149**	1550	-0.1	0.8	33	4	7x	11x	8x	71	2	3	14
Japan	**189**	38160	5.1	1.4	1	-	2	6	4	-	-	-	-
Jordan	**93**	1520	5.8x	2.8	3	3	9	14	17	462	5	4	10
Kazakhstan	**83**	1350	-	-7.4	440	2	-	-	-	131	1	-	6
Kenya	**40**	340	3.1	-0.3	16	50	6	20	6	457	5	6	18
Kiribati	**62**	910	-	-0.6	7	-	-	-	-	16	22	-	-
Korea, Dem. People's Rep.	**104**	970x	-	-	-	-	-	-	-	202	1	-	-
Korea, Rep. of	**175**	10550	7.3	6.0	5	-	1	21	17	-160	0	20	7
Kuwait	**147**	20190x	0.6x	17.5	-1x	-	8	11	23	6x	0x	-	-
Kyrgyzstan	**69**	480	-	-9.7	199	19	-	-	-	240	11	-	4
Lao People's Dem. Rep.	**41**	400	-	3.9	12	-	-	-	-	341	17	-	5
Latvia	**126**	2430	-	-7.3	88	2	11	6	2	-	-	-	3
Lebanon	**94**	3350	-	4.9	28	-	2	6	10	239	2	-	13
Lesotho	**33**	680	6.8	2.5	8	49x	13	21	6	93	7	1	6
Liberia	**6**	490x	0.5	-	-	-	5x	11x	9x	95	7	8	3x
Libya	**117**	5540x	0.0	-	-	-	-	-	-	9	0	-	-
Liechtenstein	**149**	d	-	-	-	-	-	-	-	-	-	-	-
Lithuania	**120**	2260	-	-7.1	140	2	14	7	3	-	-	-	5
Luxembourg	**175**	44690x	-	0.2	2	-	2	10	2	-	-	-	-
Madagascar	**25**	250	-0.4	-1.6	24	72	7	9	5	838	22	32	25
Malawi	**7**	210	3.2	0.8	34	-	7x	12x	5x	350	16	8	9
Malaysia	**153**	4530	4.7	5.8	5	4	6	23	11	-241	0	4	6
Maldives	**56**	1180	-	4.3	9	-	11	17	18	26	8	-	7
Mali	**5**	260	2.1x	0.3	10	-	2x	9x	8x	455	16	1	9
Malta	**162**	9330	-	3.0	4	-	9	11	2	22	1	-	1
Marshall Islands	**52**	1610	-	-4.0x	7	-	-	-	-	63	65	-	-
Mauritania	**16**	440	-0.1	1.5	6	31x	4x	23x	-	250	22	3	22
Mauritius	**120**	3870	3.7	3.7	6	-	8	18	1	42	1	3	10
Mexico	**97**	3700	3.6	0.2	19	15	3	25	4	108	0	24	28
Micronesia, Fed. States of	**117**	1920	-	-1.8	3	-	-	-	-	96	44	-	-

Table 6: Economic indicators

	Under-5 mortality rank	GNP per capita (US$) 1997	GNP per capita average annual growth rate (%)		Annual rate of inflation (%) 1990-97*	% of population below $1 a day 1990-96*	% of central government expenditure allocated to (1992-98*)			ODA inflow in millions US$ 1997	ODA inflow as a % of recipient GNP 1997	Debt service as a % of exports of goods and services	
			1965-80*	1990-97*			health	education	defence			1970	1997
Moldova, Rep. of	**94**	460	-	-10.8	223	7	-	-	-	63	3	-	8
Monaco	**175**	d	-	-	-	-	-	-	-	-	-	-	-
Mongolia	**28**	390	-	-1.4	89	-	4x	7x	12x	248	25	-	11
Morocco	**67**	1260	2.7	0.2	4	2	3	17	14	462	1	8	27
Mozambique	**10**	140	-	2.6	46	-	5x	10x	35x	963	36	-	15
Myanmar	**44**	220x	1.6	3.9x	24	-	4	12	36	45	0	18	8
Namibia	**62**	2110	-	1.1	9	-	10x	22x	7x	166	5	-	-
Nauru	**104**	-	-	-	-	-	-	-	-	3	-	-	-
Nepal	**51**	220	-	2.2	10	50	7	14	5	414	8	3	6
Netherlands	**175**	25830	2.7	1.9	2	-	15	10	4	-	-	-	-
New Zealand	**165**	15830	1.7	1.2	2	-	16	16	3	-	-	-	-
Nicaragua	**77**	410	-0.7	1.6	68	44	13	15	6	421	21	11	30
Niger	**3**	200	-2.5	-1.9	7	62	-	-	-	341	17	4	14
Nigeria	**15**	280	4.2	0.7	43	31	1x	3x	3x	202	1	4	8
Niue	**-**	-	-	-	-	-	-	-	-	5	-	-	-
Norway	**189**	36100	3.6	3.8	2	-	4	7	7	-	-	-	-
Oman	**140**	4940x	9.0	-0.4	-3	-	7	15	36	20	0	-	5
Pakistan	**33**	500	1.8	2.0	11	12	1x	2x	31x	597	1	22	30
Palau	**97**	c	-	-	-	-	-	-	-	39	-	-	-
Panama	**133**	3080	2.8	3.0	3	26x	21	17	4	124	1	8	16
Papua New Guinea	**45**	930	-	2.5	7	-	9	18	3	349	8	1	15
Paraguay	**100**	2000	4.1	0.0	16	-	7	22	11	116	1	12	5
Peru	**73**	2610	0.8	4.6	40	49x	5x	16x	11x	488	1	12	26
Philippines	**81**	1200	3.2	1.6	9	27	3	20	8	689	1	8	8
Poland	**149**	3590	-	4.2	30	7	10	6	4	-	-	-	6
Portugal	**156**	11010	4.6	2.0	6	-	9x	11x	6x	-	-	7	16x
Qatar	**140**	11340x	-	-5.3	-	-	-	-	-	3x	0x	-	-
Romania	**117**	1410	-	-0.1	124	18	7	10	6	-	-	0x	14
Russian Federation	**115**	2680	-	-7.9	299	2	2	2	12	-	-	-	5
Rwanda	**21**	210	1.6	-5.7	19	46x	5x	26x	-	592	43	1	10
Saint Kitts and Nevis	**90**	6260	-	4.0	4	-	-	-	-	7	3	-	4
Saint Lucia	**130**	3510	-	2.8	3	-	-	-	-	24	5	-	3x
Saint Vincent/Grenadines	**120**	2420	-	1.8	3	-	11	14	-	6	2	-	5x
Samoa	**110**	1140	-	0.7	3	-	-	-	-	28	14	-	4
San Marino	**165**	-	-	-	-	-	-	-	-	-	-	-	-
Sao Tome and Principe	**61**	290	-	-1.7	57	-	-	-	-	33	81	-	44
Saudi Arabia	**113**	7150	4.0x	-2.5	2	-	6x	14x	36x	15	0	-	1x
Senegal	**38**	540	-0.5	0.0	7	54	-	-	-	427	9	4	11
Seychelles	**140**	6910	-	1.7	1	-	8	12	4	15	3	-	4
Sierra Leone	**1**	160	0.7	-5.7	35	-	10x	13x	10x	130	18	11	20
Singapore	**175**	32810	8.3	6.7	3	-	7	19	29	16x	0x	1	-
Slovakia	**153**	3680	-	0.3	13	13	-	-	-	-	-	-	10
Slovenia	**175**	9840	-	4.2	32	2	-	-	-	97	0	-	9x
Solomon Islands	**113**	870	-	1.0	10	-	-	-	-	42	12	-	2
Somalia	**8**	110x	-0.1	-2.3x	75x	-	1x	2x	38x	104	10	2	25x
South Africa	**58**	3210	3.2	-0.2	10	24	-	-	-	497	0	-	10
Spain	**165**	14490	4.1	1.3	5	-	6	4	3	-	-	-	-
Sri Lanka	**137**	800	2.8	4.0	10	4	5	10	16	345	2	11	5
Sudan	**43**	290	0.8	3.7	82	-	-	-	-	187	2	11	0
Suriname	**94**	1320	-	-0.5	138	-	-	-	-	77	14	-	-
Swaziland	**53**	1520	-	-0.6	13	-	-	-	-	27	2	-	2
Sweden	**189**	26210	2.0	0.2	3	-	2	6	5	-	-	-	-
Switzerland	**175**	43060	1.5	-0.5	2	-	16	3	6	-	-	-	-
Syria	**102**	1120	5.1	3.3	9	-	4	10	26	199	1	11	7
Tajikistan	**62**	330	-	-16.1	394	-	-	-	-	101	5	-	4
Tanzania	**32**	210	0.8	0.9	25	11x	6x	8x	16x	963	14	1	10
TFYR Macedonia	**110**	1100	-	-2.1	61	-	-	-	-	149	7	-	8

	Under-5 mortality rank	GNP per capita (US$) 1997	GNP per capita average annual growth rate (%) 1965-80*	1990-97*	Annual rate of inflation (%) 1990-97*	% of population below $1 a day 1990-96*	% of central government expenditure allocated to (1992-98*) health	education	defence	ODA inflow in millions US$ 1997	ODA inflow as a % of recipient GNP 1997	Debt service as a % of exports of goods and services 1970	1997
Thailand	**90**	2740	4.4	5.9	5	2	9	22	12	626	0	3	13
Togo	**30**	340	1.7	-1.2	9	-	5x	20x	11x	124	8	3	6
Tonga	**120**	1810	-	1.4	4	-	7x	13x	-	28	16	-	7
Trinidad and Tobago	**140**	4250	3.1	0.5	7	-	9	15	2	33	1	5	16
Tunisia	**102**	2110	4.7	2.0	5	4	7	19	6	194	1	18	15
Turkey	**85**	3130	3.6	2.3	79	-	2	11	8	-1	0	16	17
Turkmenistan	**66**	640	-	-14.6	1074	5	-	-	-	11	0	-	32
Tuvalu	**71**	-	-	-	-	-	-	-	-	10	-	-	-
Uganda	**35**	330	-2.2	4.4	18	69	2x	15x	26x	840	12	3	15
Ukraine	**126**	1040	-	-12.6	591	2	-	-	-	-	-	-	6
United Arab Emirates	**153**	18240x	-	-3.8	-	-	7	17	37	8x	0x	-	-
United Kingdom	**165**	20870	2.0	1.9	3	-	14	5	8	-	-	-	-
United States	**160**	29080	1.8	1.7	2	-	20	2	16	-	-	-	-
Uruguay	**137**	6130	2.5	3.5	45	-	6	7	4	57	0	22	13
Uzbekistan	**70**	1020	-	-5.6	443	-	-	-	-	130	1	-	12
Vanuatu	**76**	1340	-	-3.5	5	-	-	-	-	27	11	-	1
Venezuela	**115**	3480	2.3	-0.2	50	12	10x	20x	6x	28	0	3	29
Viet Nam	**85**	310	-	6.1	20	-	-	-	-	997	4	-	7
Yemen	**38**	270	-	-1.5	27	-	4	18	17	366	8	-	2
Yugoslavia	**130**	b	-	-	-	-	-	-	-	97	-	-	-
Zambia	**12**	370	-1.2	-0.9	72	85	10	18	5	618	19	6	19
Zimbabwe	**55**	720	1.7	-0.7	22	41	8x	24x	17x	327	4	2	19

Regional summaries

	GNP per capita (US$) 1997	GNP growth 1965-80*	1990-97*	Inflation 1990-97*	% below $1 a day	health	education	defence	ODA inflow (US$ millions)	ODA % of GNP	Debt service 1970	1997
Sub-Saharan Africa	513	2.8	-0.1	62	39	5	14	10	13924	4	6	11
Middle East and North Africa	2078	3.1	0.4	15	-	5	14	19	5043	1	12	17
South Asia	385	1.4	3.9	9	42	2	4	17	4418	0	17	18
East Asia and Pacific	1273	4.9	7.7	9	19	2	11	14	6771	0	6	10
Latin America and Caribbean	3894	4.0	2.2	209	22	6	11	5	5266	0	13	32
CEE/CIS and Baltic States	2339	-	-3.3	212	4	5	6	8	-	-	-	10
Industrialized countries	27146	2.9	1.4	2	-	13	4	9	-	-	-	-
Developing countries	1299	3.7	4.1	86	28	4	11	11	38847	1	11	17
Least developed countries	256	-0.1	1.2	118	-	5	12	13	13544	9	6	9
World	5132	3.1	1.8	25	26	11	6	9	40337	1	11	16

Countries in each region are listed on page 112.

Definitions of the indicators

GNP per capita – Gross national product (GNP) is the sum of gross value added by all resident producers, plus any taxes that are not included in the valuation of output, plus net receipts of primary income from non-resident sources. GNP per capita is the gross national product, converted to United States dollars using the World Bank Atlas method, divided by the mid-year population.

% of population below $1 a day – Percentage of population living on less than $1 a day at 1985 international prices, adjusted for purchasing power parity.

ODA – Official development assistance.

Debt service – The sum of interest payments and repayments of principal on external public and publicly guaranteed long-term debts.

Main data sources

GNP per capita – World Bank.

% of population below $1 a day – World Bank.

Expenditure on health, education and defence – International Monetary Fund (IMF).

ODA – Organisation for Economic Co-operation and Development (OECD).

Debt service – World Bank.

Notes

a: Range $785 or less.
b: Range $786 to $3125.
c: Range $3126 to $9655.
d: Range $9656 or more.

\- Data not available.
x Indicates data that refer to years or periods other than those specified in the column heading, differ from the standard definition, or refer to only part of a country.
* Data refer to the most recent year available during the period specified in the column heading.

	Under-5 mortality rank	Life expectancy females as a % of males 1998	Adult literacy rate females as a % of males 1995	Enrolment ratios females as a % of males 1990-97*		Contraceptive prevalence (%) 1990-99*	% of pregnant women immunized against tetanus 1995-98*	% of births attended by trained health personnel 1990-99*	Maternal mortality ratio† reported 1980-98*
				primary school	secondary school				
Afghanistan	**4**	102	35	50	34	2x	19	8x	-
Albania	**90**	109	-	102	100	-	65	99x	-
Algeria	**88**	103	64	89	95	57	52	77	220
Andorra	**165**	-	-	-	-	-	-	-	-
Angola	**2**	107	52x	93	-	8	24	-	-
Antigua and Barbuda	**133**	-	-	-	-	53x	-	100	150
Argentina	**126**	110	100	99	111	74x	-	97	38
Armenia	**104**	110	99	105	107	60	-	96	35
Australia	**175**	107	-	100	100	76x	-	100	-
Austria	**175**	108	-	101	96	71x	-	100	-
Azerbaijan	**80**	112	99	97	111	-	-	99	37
Bahamas	**130**	108	101	99	103	62x	-	100x	-
Bahrain	**133**	106	89	102	108	62	80	98	46
Bangladesh	**48**	100	53	86	50	49	86	8	440
Barbados	**146**	107	99	101	89x	55x	-	100	0
Belarus	**110**	119	98	95	104	50	-	100x	22
Belgium	**165**	109	-	99	107	79	-	100x	-
Belize	**83**	104	100x	95	111	47	65	77	140
Benin	**22**	106	43	58	43	37	66	60	500
Bhutan	**41**	103	50	61x	29x	19	80	15	380
Bolivia	**57**	105	84	91	85	48	27	59	390
Bosnia and Herzegovina	**137**	107	-	-	-	-	-	97	10
Botswana	**77**	104	107	101	110	48	54	78x	330
Brazil	**85**	113	99	96x	116x	77	30	92	160
Brunei Darussalam	**156**	107	91	95	115	-	52	98	0
Bulgaria	**144**	110	99	98	99	76x	-	100x	15
Burkina Faso	**22**	102	34	65	55	12	54	27	-
Burundi	**17**	107	63	84	56	9x	9	24	-
Cambodia	**24**	106	66x	84	60	13	31	31	470
Cameroon	**27**	106	69	90	69	19	49	58	430
Canada	**165**	108	-	98	99	73x	-	100x	-
Cape Verde	**65**	108	75	98	93	53	51	54	55
Central African Rep.	**18**	109	51	65	40	15	37	46	1100
Chad	**13**	107	56	52	25	4	27	15	830
Chile	**148**	108	99	97	108	43x	-	100	23
China	**79**	106	80	99	91	83	13	89	65
Colombia	**104**	110	100	99	107	72	57x	85	80
Comoros	**53**	103	79	84	81	21	22	52	500
Congo	**47**	111	81	92	73	-	30	-	-
Congo, Dem. Rep.	**9**	106	78	69	59	8	-	-	-
Cook Islands	**104**	-	-	-	-	50	29	99	-
Costa Rica	**145**	107	100	99	108	75	-	98	29
Côte d'Ivoire	**28**	102	63	74	48	15	44	47	600
Croatia	**156**	112	97	99	102	-	-	-	12
Cuba	**160**	105	100	96	112	82	70	99	27
Cyprus	**156**	105	94	100	103	-	-	100	0
Czech Rep.	**165**	111	-	99	103	69	-	99	9
Denmark	**175**	107	-	99	104	78x	-	100x	10
Djibouti	**26**	106	54	73	71	-	16	79x	-
Dominica	**133**	-	-	-	-	50x	-	98	65
Dominican Rep.	**75**	106	99	101	138	64	77	99	230
Ecuador	**89**	109	95	89	104	57	3	64	160
Egypt	**68**	105	60	86	88	55	61	56	170
El Salvador	**97**	109	92	100	117	60	-	87	160
Equatorial Guinea	**20**	106	75	-	-	-	70	5	-
Eritrea	**45**	108	-	83	71	8	34	21	1000
Estonia	**126**	119	100	98	108	70	-	-	50

	Under-5 mortality rank	Life expectancy females as a % of males 1998	Adult literacy rate females as a % of males 1995	Enrolment ratios females as a % of males 1990-97*		Contraceptive prevalence (%) 1990-99*	% of pregnant women immunized against tetanus 1995-98*	% of births attended by trained health personnel 1990-99*	Maternal mortality ratio† reported 1980-98*
				primary school	secondary school				
Ethiopia	**18**	105	66	57	77	4	30	8	-
Fiji	**120**	106	95	99	102	32x	-	-	38
Finland	**175**	111	-	100	117	80x	-	100	6
France	**175**	111	-	98	99	75	83	99	10
Gabon	**30**	106	72	-	-	-	4	80x	600
Gambia	**59**	107	47	77	63	12	96	44	-
Georgia	**120**	112	99	99	97	-	-	-	70
Germany	**175**	108	-	99	98	75	80	100x	8
Ghana	**49**	105	72	84	64	22	45	39	210
Greece	**162**	107	96	99	100	-	-	99x	1
Grenada	**109**	-	-	-	-	54	-	99	0
Guatemala	**74**	108	79	88	92	31	38	35	190
Guinea	**14**	102	44	54	33	29	48	31	670
Guinea-Bissau	**11**	107	34	58	44x	1x	46	25	910
Guyana	**60**	111	98	99	107	-	88	95	190
Haiti	**36**	110	89	93	96	18	38	21	-
Holy See	**-**	-	-	-	-	-	-	-	-
Honduras	**81**	106	98	102	128	50	-	55	220
Hungary	**149**	112	100	98	103	73x	-	99x	15
Iceland	**175**	105	-	98	97	-	-	100x	-
India	**49**	102	55	82	66	41	80	34	410
Indonesia	**71**	105	87	96	85	57	53	43	450
Iran	**100**	101	80	95	87	73	75	86	37
Iraq	**37**	105	63	85	63	18x	45	54x	-
Ireland	**162**	107	-	100	107	-	-	100	6
Israel	**165**	105	95	100	106	-	-	99x	5
Italy	**165**	108	99	99	101	78x	-	100x	7
Jamaica	**149**	105	111	100	113	66	52	95	120
Japan	**189**	108	-	101	102	59	-	100	8
Jordan	**93**	104	89	101	104	53	22	97	41
Kazakhstan	**83**	116	99	101	111	59	-	100	70
Kenya	**40**	104	81	100	85	39	51	44	590
Kiribati	**62**	-	-	-	-	28	74	72	-
Korea, Dem. People's Rep.	**104**	109	-	94x	-	-	5	100x	110
Korea, Rep. of	**175**	110	96	100	100	79	-	98	20
Kuwait	**147**	105	92	97	100	35x	8	98x	5
Kyrgyzstan	**69**	113	96	97	112	60	-	98	65
Lao People's Dem. Rep.	**41**	106	64	78	64	19	32	14	650
Latvia	**126**	117	100	94	104	-	-	100	45
Lebanon	**94**	106	85	96	109	63	-	89	100
Lesotho	**33**	106	131	111	148	23	-	50	-
Liberia	**6**	104	46	55x	39x	6x	14	58x	-
Libya	**117**	106	69	100	100	45	-	94	75
Liechtenstein	**149**	-	100x	-	-	-	-	-	-
Lithuania	**120**	117	99	97	104	-	-	-	18
Luxembourg	**175**	110	-	107	106	-	-	100x	0
Madagascar	**25**	105	53	96	100	19	30	47	490
Malawi	**7**	103	58	90	57	22	81	55	620
Malaysia	**153**	106	89	102	114	48x	71	99	39
Maldives	**56**	97	100	97	100	17	91	90	350
Mali	**5**	106	63	66	50	7	62	24	580
Malta	**162**	105	101	98	92	-	-	98	-
Marshall Islands	**52**	-	-	-	-	37	-	-	-
Mauritania	**16**	106	55	90	52	4	63	40	550
Mauritius	**120**	110	91	99	105	75	78	97	50
Mexico	**97**	109	95	97	100	69	70	68	48
Micronesia, Fed. States of	**117**	-	-	-	-	-	-	90x	-

Table 7: Women

	Under-5 mortality rank	Life expectancy females as a % of males 1998	Adult literacy rate females as a % of males 1995	Enrolment ratios females as a % of males 1990-97*: primary school	Enrolment ratios females as a % of males 1990-97*: secondary school	Contraceptive prevalence (%) 1990-99*	% of pregnant women immunized against tetanus 1995-98*	% of births attended by trained health personnel 1990-99*	Maternal mortality ratio† reported 1980-98*
Moldova, Rep. of	**94**	113	98	99	104	74	-	-	42
Monaco	**175**	-	-	-	-	-	-	-	-
Mongolia	**28**	105	87	106	135	-	-	100	150
Morocco	**67**	106	53	76	77	59	33	43	230
Mozambique	**10**	107	42	71	56	10	41	44	1100
Myanmar	**44**	105	88	97	103	33	78	56	230
Namibia	**62**	102	96	102	118	29	70	68	230
Nauru	**104**	-	-	-	-	-	-	-	-
Nepal	**51**	98	35	71	51	30	65	9	540
Netherlands	**175**	108	-	98	94	80	-	100	7
New Zealand	**165**	108	-	100	105	70x	-	95	15
Nicaragua	**77**	108	103	103	116	60	42	65	150
Niger	**3**	106	32	61	56	8	19	18	590
Nigeria	**15**	106	72	79	85	6	29	31	-
Niue	**-**	-	-	-	-	-	40	99	-
Norway	**189**	108	-	100	94	76x	-	100x	6
Oman	**140**	106	68	94	96	40	96	91	19
Pakistan	**33**	103	44	45	52	17	58	18	-
Palau	**97**	-	-	-	-	38x	-	99	-
Panama	**133**	106	99	96	108	58x	-	86	85
Papua New Guinea	**45**	104	77	85	65	26	11	53	370
Paraguay	**100**	106	97	97	107	59	32	61	190
Peru	**73**	108	88	97	89	64	57	56	270
Philippines	**81**	104	99	102	106x	47	38	56	170
Poland	**149**	113	100	98	99	75x	-	99x	8
Portugal	**156**	110	94	95	109	66x	-	98x	8
Qatar	**140**	109	101	98	98	32x	-	98	10
Romania	**117**	112	97	98	100	57	-	99	41
Russian Federation	**115**	120	99	99	108	-	-	99	50
Rwanda	**21**	108	76	98	75	21	43	26	-
Saint Kitts and Nevis	**90**	-	-	-	-	41x	-	100	130
Saint Lucia	**130**	-	-	-	-	47x	-	100	30
Saint Vincent/Grenadines	**120**	-	-	-	-	58x	-	96	43
Samoa	**110**	107	-	93	112	21	99	76	-
San Marino	**165**	-	-	-	-	-	-	-	-
Sao Tome and Principe	**61**	-	-	-	-	10x	31	86x	-
Saudi Arabia	**113**	106	75	97	88	-	66	90	-
Senegal	**38**	106	54	82	60	13	34	47	560
Seychelles	**140**	-	104x	-	-	-	100	99x	-
Sierra Leone	**1**	108	40	69	59	4x	42	-	-
Singapore	**175**	105	90	98	110	74x	-	100x	6
Slovakia	**153**	112	-	100	104	74	-	-	9
Slovenia	**175**	110	100	99	102	-	-	100	11
Solomon Islands	**113**	106	-	87	67	25	55	85	550
Somalia	**8**	107	39x	53x	56x	1x	41	2x	-
South Africa	**58**	112	98	98	120	50x	26	82	-
Spain	**165**	109	98	99	112	59x	99	96x	6
Sri Lanka	**137**	107	93	98	110	66	78	94	60
Sudan	**43**	106	60	84	90	8	55	69	550
Suriname	**94**	107	96	97x	116x	-	-	91x	110
Swaziland	**53**	109	96	95	100	21x	79	56	230
Sweden	**189**	107	-	101	117	78x	-	100x	5
Switzerland	**175**	109	-	99	94	71x	-	99x	5
Syria	**102**	106	63	91	89	36	53	67	110
Tajikistan	**62**	109	99	97	89	-	-	79	65
Tanzania	**32**	104	74	99	83	18	27	38	530
TFYR Macedonia	**110**	106	-	97	100	-	91x	95	11

	Under-5 mortality rank	Life expectancy females as a % of males 1998	Adult literacy rate females as a % of males 1995	Enrolment ratios females as a % of males 1990-97* primary school	Enrolment ratios females as a % of males 1990-97* secondary school	Contraceptive prevalence (%) 1990-99*	% of pregnant women immunized against tetanus 1995-98*	% of births attended by trained health personnel 1990-99*	Maternal mortality ratio† reported 1980-98*
Thailand	**90**	109	96	97	97	74	88	71x	44
Togo	**30**	104	53	71	35	24	41	51	480
Tonga	**120**	-	-	-	-	39	93	92	-
Trinidad and Tobago	**140**	106	98	112	120	53x	-	98x	-
Tunisia	**102**	103	70	95	97	60	80	81	70
Turkey	**85**	107	79	95	67	64	32	81	130
Turkmenistan	**66**	111	98x	-	-	-	-	96	110
Tuvalu	**71**	-	-	-	-	-	71	100	-
Uganda	**35**	105	68	85	60	15	38	38	510
Ukraine	**126**	116	101	99	107	-	-	100	25
United Arab Emirates	**153**	104	101	96	106	28	-	99	3
United Kingdom	**165**	107	-	101	117	82	-	98x	7
United States	**160**	110	-	99	99	74x	-	99x	8
Uruguay	**137**	110	101	99	119	84	-	96x	21
Uzbekistan	**70**	111	100	97	88	56	-	98	21
Vanuatu	**76**	106	-	102	78	15	78	79	-
Venezuela	**115**	109	98	103	139	49x	-	-	65
Viet Nam	**85**	108	93	94x	93x	75	92	77	160
Yemen	**38**	102	29	40	26	21	26	22	350
Yugoslavia	**130**	109	98	101	106	-	-	93	10
Zambia	**12**	103	83	93	62	26	-	47	650
Zimbabwe	**55**	102	88	97	85	66	58	69	400

Regional summaries

Sub-Saharan Africa		106	72	82	80	17	37	36	-
Middle East and North Africa		104	67	86	85	50	54	66	-
South Asia		102	54	77	64	39	64	28	-
East Asia and Pacific		106	83	98	92	76	58	78	-
Latin America and Caribbean		110	97	97	108	68	46	78	-
CEE/CIS and Baltic States		113	97	98	99	65	-	94	-
Industrialized countries		109	-	99	102	72	-	99	-
Developing countries		105	77	89	84	56	49	54	-
Least developed countries		104	63	78	59	22	48	26	-
World		106	80	90	88	59	51	58	-

Countries in each region are listed on page 112.

Definitions of the indicators

Life expectancy at birth – The number of years newborn children would live if subject to the mortality risks prevailing for the cross-section of population at the time of their birth.

Adult literacy rate – Percentage of persons aged 15 and over who can read and write.

Primary or secondary enrolment ratios – The number of children enrolled in a schooling level (primary or secondary), regardless of age, divided by the population of the age group which officially corresponds to that level.

Contraceptive prevalence – Percentage of married women aged 15-49 years currently using contraception.

Births attended – Percentage of births attended by physicians, nurses, midwives, or primary health care workers trained in midwifery skills.

Maternal mortality ratio – Annual number of deaths of women from pregnancy-related causes per 100,000 live births. This 'reported' column shows country reported figures which are not adjusted for underreporting and misclassification.

Main data sources

Life expectancy – United Nations Population Division.

Adult literacy – United Nations Educational, Scientific and Cultural Organization (UNESCO).

School enrolment – Demographic and Health Surveys (DHS) and United Nations Educational, Scientific and Cultural Organization (UNESCO).

Immunization – Demographic and Health Surveys (DHS), Multiple Indicator Cluster Surveys (MICS), World Health Organization (WHO) and UNICEF.

Contraceptive prevalence – Demographic and Health Surveys (DHS), United Nations Population Division and UNICEF.

Births attended – World Health Organization (WHO) and UNICEF.

Maternal mortality – World Health Organization (WHO) and UNICEF.

† The maternal mortality data provided in this table are those reported by national authorities. Periodically, UNICEF and WHO evaluate these data and make adjustments to account for the well-documented problems of underreporting and misclassification of maternal deaths, and to develop estimates for countries with no data. Such an exercise is currently in progress and results are expected shortly. Regional and global totals will be calculated once the results become available.

Notes

- \- Data not available.
- x Indicates data that refer to years or periods other than those specified in the column heading, differ from the standard definition, or refer to only part of a country.
- * Data refer to the most recent year available during the period specified in the column heading.

Regional summaries country list

Regional averages given at the end of each table are calculated using data from the countries as grouped below.

Sub-Saharan Africa

Angola; Benin; Botswana; Burkina Faso; Burundi; Cameroon; Cape Verde; Central African Rep.; Chad; Comoros; Congo; Congo, Dem. Rep.; Côte d'Ivoire; Equatorial Guinea; Eritrea; Ethiopia; Gabon; Gambia; Ghana; Guinea; Guinea-Bissau; Kenya; Lesotho; Liberia; Madagascar; Malawi; Mali; Mauritania; Mauritius; Mozambique; Namibia; Niger; Nigeria; Rwanda; Sao Tome and Principe; Senegal; Seychelles; Sierra Leone; Somalia; South Africa; Swaziland; Tanzania; Togo; Uganda; Zambia; Zimbabwe

Middle East and North Africa

Algeria; Bahrain; Cyprus; Djibouti; Egypt; Iran; Iraq; Jordan; Kuwait; Lebanon; Libya; Morocco; Oman; Qatar; Saudi Arabia; Sudan; Syria; Tunisia; United Arab Emirates; Yemen

South Asia

Afghanistan; Bangladesh; Bhutan; India; Maldives; Nepal; Pakistan; Sri Lanka

East Asia and Pacific

Brunei Darussalam; Cambodia; China; Cook Islands; Fiji; Indonesia; Kiribati; Korea, Dem. People's Rep.; Korea, Rep. of; Lao People's Dem. Rep.; Malaysia; Marshall Islands; Micronesia, Fed. States of; Mongolia; Myanmar; Nauru; Niue; Palau; Papua New Guinea; Philippines; Samoa; Singapore; Solomon Islands; Thailand; Tonga; Tuvalu; Vanuatu; Viet Nam

Latin America and Caribbean

Antigua and Barbuda; Argentina; Bahamas; Barbados; Belize; Bolivia; Brazil; Chile; Colombia; Costa Rica; Cuba; Dominica; Dominican Rep.; Ecuador; El Salvador; Grenada; Guatemala; Guyana; Haiti; Honduras; Jamaica; Mexico; Nicaragua; Panama; Paraguay; Peru; Saint Kitts and Nevis; Saint Lucia; Saint Vincent/Grenadines; Suriname; Trinidad and Tobago; Uruguay; Venezuela

CEE/CIS and Baltic States

Albania; Armenia; Azerbaijan; Belarus; Bosnia and Herzegovina; Bulgaria; Croatia; Czech Rep.; Estonia; Georgia; Hungary; Kazakhstan; Kyrgyzstan; Latvia; Lithuania; Moldova, Rep. of; Poland; Romania; Russian Federation; Slovakia; Tajikistan; TFYR Macedonia; Turkey; Turkmenistan; Ukraine; Uzbekistan; Yugoslavia

Industrialized countries

Andorra; Australia; Austria; Belgium; Canada; Denmark; Finland; France; Germany; Greece; Holy See; Iceland; Ireland; Israel; Italy; Japan; Liechtenstein; Luxembourg; Malta; Monaco; Netherlands; New Zealand; Norway; Portugal; San Marino; Slovenia; Spain; Sweden; Switzerland; United Kingdom; United States

Developing countries

Afghanistan; Algeria; Angola; Antigua and Barbuda; Argentina; Armenia; Azerbaijan; Bahamas; Bahrain; Bangladesh; Barbados; Belize; Benin; Bhutan; Bolivia; Botswana; Brazil; Brunei Darussalam; Burkina Faso; Burundi; Cambodia; Cameroon; Cape Verde; Central African Rep.; Chad; Chile; China; Colombia; Comoros; Congo; Congo, Dem. Rep.; Cook Islands; Costa Rica; Côte d'Ivoire; Cuba; Cyprus; Djibouti; Dominica; Dominican Rep.; Ecuador; Egypt; El Salvador; Equatorial Guinea; Eritrea; Ethiopia; Fiji; Gabon; Gambia; Georgia; Ghana; Grenada; Guatemala; Guinea; Guinea-Bissau; Guyana; Haiti; Honduras; India; Indonesia; Iran; Iraq; Israel; Jamaica; Jordan; Kazakhstan; Kenya; Kiribati; Korea, Dem. People's Rep.; Korea, Rep. of; Kuwait; Kyrgyzstan; Lao People's Dem. Rep.; Lebanon; Lesotho; Liberia; Libya; Madagascar; Malawi; Malaysia; Maldives; Mali; Marshall Islands; Mauritania; Mauritius; Mexico; Micronesia, Fed. States of; Mongolia; Morocco; Mozambique; Myanmar; Namibia; Nauru; Nepal; Nicaragua; Niger; Nigeria; Niue; Oman; Pakistan; Palau; Panama; Papua New Guinea; Paraguay; Peru; Philippines; Qatar; Rwanda; Saint Kitts and Nevis; Saint Lucia; Saint Vincent/Grenadines; Samoa; Sao Tome and Principe; Saudi Arabia; Senegal; Seychelles; Sierra Leone; Singapore; Solomon Islands; Somalia; South Africa; Sri Lanka; Sudan; Suriname; Swaziland; Syria; Tajikistan; Tanzania; Thailand; Togo; Tonga; Trinidad and Tobago; Tunisia; Turkey; Turkmenistan; Tuvalu; Uganda; United Arab Emirates; Uruguay; Uzbekistan; Vanuatu; Venezuela; Viet Nam; Yemen; Zambia; Zimbabwe

Least developed countries

Afghanistan; Angola; Bangladesh; Benin; Bhutan; Burkina Faso; Burundi; Cambodia; Cape Verde; Central African Rep.; Chad; Comoros; Congo, Dem. Rep.; Djibouti; Equatorial Guinea; Eritrea; Ethiopia; Gambia; Guinea; Guinea-Bissau; Haiti; Kiribati; Lao People's Dem. Rep.; Lesotho; Liberia; Madagascar; Malawi; Maldives; Mali; Mauritania; Mozambique; Myanmar; Nepal; Niger; Rwanda; Samoa; Sao Tome and Principe; Sierra Leone; Solomon Islands; Somalia; Sudan; Tanzania; Togo; Tuvalu; Uganda; Vanuatu; Yemen; Zambia

Measuring human development

An introduction to table 8

If development in the 1990s is to assume a more human face, then there arises a corresponding need for a means of measuring human as well as economic progress. From UNICEF's point of view, in particular, there is a need for an agreed method of measuring the level of child well-being and its rate of change.

The under-five mortality rate (U5MR) is used in table 8 (next page) as the principal indicator of such progress.

The U5MR has several advantages. First, it measures an end result of the development process rather than an 'input' such as school enrolment level, per capita calorie availability, or the number of doctors per thousand population — all of which are means to an end.

Second, the U5MR is known to be the result of a wide variety of inputs: the nutritional health and the health knowledge of mothers; the level of immunization and ORT use; the availability of maternal and child health services (including prenatal care); income and food availability in the family; the availability of clean water and safe sanitation; and the overall safety of the child's environment.

Third, the U5MR is less susceptible than, say, per capita GNP to the fallacy of the average. This is because the natural scale does not allow the children of the rich to be one thousand times as likely to survive, even if the man-made scale does permit them to have one thousand times as much income. In other words, it is much more difficult for a wealthy minority to affect a nation's U5MR, and it therefore presents a more accurate, if far from perfect, picture of the health status of the majority of children (and of society as a whole).

For these reasons, the U5MR is chosen by UNICEF as its single most important indicator of the state of a nation's children. That is why the tables rank the nations of the world not in ascending order of their per capita GNP but in descending order of their under-five mortality rates.

The speed of progress in reducing the U5MR can be measured by calculating its average annual reduction rate (AARR). Unlike the comparison of absolute changes, the AARR reflects the fact that the lower limits to U5MR are approached only with increasing difficulty. As lower levels of under-five mortality are reached, for example, the same absolute reduction obviously represents a greater percentage of reduction. The AARR therefore shows a higher rate of progress for, say, a 10-point reduction if that reduction happens at a lower level of under-five mortality. (A fall in U5MR of 10 points from 100 to 90 represents a reduction of 10 per cent, whereas the same 10-point fall from 20 to 10 represents a reduction of 50 per cent).

When used in conjunction with GNP growth rates, the U5MR and its reduction rate can therefore give a picture of the progress being made by any country or region, and over any period of time, towards the satisfaction of some of the most essential of human needs.

As table 8 shows, there is no fixed relationship between the annual reduction rate of the U5MR and the annual rate of growth in per capita GNP. Such comparisons help to throw the emphasis on to the policies, priorities, and other factors which determine the ratio between economic and social progress.

Finally, the table gives the total fertility rate for each country and its average annual rate of reduction. It will be seen that many of the nations that have achieved significant reductions in their U5MR have also achieved significant reductions in fertility.

Table 8: The rate of progress

	Under-5 mortality rank	Under-5 mortality rate			Average annual rate of reduction (%)			GNP per capita average annual growth rate (%)		Total fertility rate			Average annual rate of reduction (%)	
		1960	1990	1998	1960-90	1990-98	required† 1998-2000	1965-80	1990-97	1960	1990	1998	1960-90	1990-98
Afghanistan	**4**	360	260	257	1.1	0.1	65.0	0.6	-	6.9	6.9	6.8	0.0	0.2
Albania	**90**	151	41	37	4.3	1.3	15.2	-	2.2	5.9	3.0	2.5	2.3	2.3
Algeria	**88**	255	48	40	5.6	2.3	11.2	4.2	-1.6	7.3	4.6	3.8	1.5	2.4
Andorra	**165**	-	-	6	-	-	-	-	-	-	-	-	-	-
Angola	**2**	345	297	292	0.5	0.2	71.4	-	-10.0	6.4	7.2	6.7	-0.4	0.9
Antigua and Barbuda	**133**	-	-	20	-	-	-	-	1.8	-	2.6	1.7	-	5.3
Argentina	**126**	72	28	22	3.1	3.0	8.1	1.7	4.2	3.1	2.9	2.6	0.2	1.4
Armenia	**104**	48	31	30	1.5	0.4	18.6	-	-10.7	4.5	2.4	1.7	2.1	4.3
Australia	**175**	24	10	5	2.9	8.7	-14.6	2.2	2.4	3.3	1.9	1.8	1.8	0.7
Austria	**175**	43	9	5	5.2	7.3	-9.1	4.0	1.1	2.7	1.5	1.4	2.0	0.9
Azerbaijan	**80**	74	44	46	1.7	-0.6	22.6	-	-16.0	5.5	2.7	2.0	2.4	3.8
Bahamas	**130**	68	29	21	2.8	4.0	4.2	-	-2.0	4.4	2.6	2.6	1.8	0.0
Bahrain	**133**	203	23	20	7.3	1.7	13.4	-	2.6	7.1	3.8	2.8	2.1	3.8
Bangladesh	**48**	247	140	106	1.9	3.5	20.7	-0.3	3.3	6.7	4.3	3.1	1.5	4.1
Barbados	**146**	90	15	15	6.0	0.0	20.3	-	-0.9	4.5	1.7	1.5	3.2	1.6
Belarus	**110**	47	19	27	3.0	-4.4	37.7	-	-5.6	2.7	1.9	1.4	1.2	3.8
Belgium	**165**	35	9	6	4.5	5.1	0.0	3.6	1.3	2.6	1.6	1.6	1.6	0.0
Belize	**83**	104	49	43	2.5	1.6	13.7	-	0.3	6.5	4.4	3.6	1.3	2.5
Benin	**22**	300	185	165	1.6	1.4	42.9	-0.3	1.7	6.9	6.6	5.8	0.1	1.6
Bhutan	**41**	300	166	116	2.0	4.5	25.3	-	2.0	5.9	5.8	5.5	0.1	0.7
Bolivia	**57**	255	122	85	2.5	4.5	9.7	1.7	2.0	6.7	4.9	4.3	1.0	1.6
Bosnia and Herzegovina	**137**	160	22	19	6.6	1.8	12.8	-	-	4.0	1.7	1.4	2.9	2.4
Botswana	**77**	170	62	48	3.4	3.2	7.5	9.9	1.3	6.8	5.1	4.3	1.0	2.1
Brazil	**85**	177	60	42	3.6	4.5	2.4	6.3	1.9	6.2	2.7	2.3	2.8	2.0
Brunei Darussalam	**156**	87	11	9	6.9	2.5	10.5	-	-2.1	6.9	3.2	2.8	2.6	1.7
Bulgaria	**144**	70	18	17	4.5	0.7	17.4	-	-2.0	2.2	1.7	1.2	0.9	4.4
Burkina Faso	**22**	315	196	165	1.6	2.2	42.9	1.7	0.8	6.7	7.3	6.5	-0.3	1.5
Burundi	**17**	255	180	176	1.2	0.3	46.1	2.4	-5.9	6.8	6.8	6.2	0.0	1.2
Cambodia	**24**	217	193	163	0.4	2.1	42.3	-	2.7	6.3	5.0	4.6	0.8	1.0
Cameroon	**27**	255	139	153	2.0	-1.2	39.1	2.4	-3.3	5.8	5.9	5.3	-0.1	1.3
Canada	**165**	33	9	6	4.3	5.1	0.0	3.3	0.8	3.8	1.7	1.6	2.7	0.8
Cape Verde	**65**	164	73	73	2.7	0.0	20.2	-	1.0	7.0	4.3	3.5	1.6	2.6
Central African Rep.	**18**	327	177	173	2.0	0.3	45.2	0.8	-1.0	5.6	5.5	4.9	0.1	1.4
Chad	**13**	325	198	198	1.7	0.0	52.0	-1.9	1.0	6.0	6.6	6.0	-0.3	1.2
Chile	**148**	138	20	12	6.4	6.4	-5.1	0.0	6.4	5.3	2.6	2.4	2.4	1.0
China	**79**	209	47	47	5.0	0.0	20.3	4.1	10.0	5.7	2.2	1.8	3.2	2.5
Colombia	**104**	130	40	30	3.9	3.6	5.8	3.7	2.6	6.8	3.1	2.8	2.6	1.3
Comoros	**53**	265	120	90	2.6	3.6	12.6	-	-3.1	6.8	6.0	4.8	0.4	2.8
Congo	**47**	220	110	108	2.3	0.2	21.7	2.7	-2.9	5.9	6.3	6.0	-0.2	0.6
Congo, Dem. Rep.	**9**	302	207	207	1.3	0.0	54.2	-1.3	-9.6	6.0	6.7	6.4	-0.4	0.6
Cook Islands	**104**	-	32	30	-	0.8	17.1	-	-	-	-	-	-	-
Costa Rica	**145**	112	16	16	6.5	0.0	20.1	3.3	2.3	7.0	3.2	2.8	2.6	1.7
Côte d'Ivoire	**28**	300	150	150	2.3	0.0	38.1	2.8	0.9	7.2	6.3	5.0	0.4	2.9
Croatia	**156**	98	13	9	6.7	4.6	1.7	-	2.7	2.3	1.7	1.6	1.0	0.8
Cuba	**160**	54	13	8	4.7	6.1	-4.2	-	-	4.2	1.7	1.6	3.0	0.8
Cyprus	**156**	36	12	9	3.7	3.6	5.9	-	2.6	3.5	2.4	2.0	1.3	2.3
Czech Rep.	**165**	25	11	6	2.7	7.6	-9.8	-	-0.3	2.3	1.8	1.2	0.8	5.1
Denmark	**175**	25	9	5	3.4	7.3	-9.1	2.2	2.5	2.6	1.6	1.7	1.6	-0.8
Djibouti	**26**	289	164	156	1.9	0.6	40.1	-	-	7.0	6.0	5.3	0.5	1.6
Dominica	**133**	-	23	20	-	1.7	13.4	-	0.7	-	5.5	1.9	-	13.3
Dominican Rep.	**75**	149	65	51	2.8	3.0	8.2	3.8	3.5	7.4	3.3	2.8	2.7	2.1
Ecuador	**89**	180	50	39	4.3	3.1	7.9	5.4	0.9	6.7	3.8	3.1	1.9	2.5
Egypt	**68**	282	106	69	3.3	5.4	-0.7	2.8	2.8	7.0	4.2	3.3	1.7	3.0
El Salvador	**97**	210	54	34	4.5	5.8	-2.9	1.5	3.5	6.8	3.7	3.1	2.0	2.2
Equatorial Guinea	**20**	316	206	171	1.4	2.3	44.7	-	12.1	5.5	5.9	5.5	-0.2	0.9
Eritrea	**45**	250	160	112	1.5	4.5	23.5	-	2.9	6.9	6.2	5.7	0.4	1.1
Estonia	**126**	52	22	22	2.9	0.0	20.2	-	-2.8	2.0	1.9	1.3	0.2	4.7

	Under-5 mortality rank	Under-5 mortality rate			Average annual rate of reduction (%)			GNP per capita average annual growth rate (%)		Total fertility rate			Average annual rate of reduction (%)	
		1960	1990	1998	1960-90	1990-98	required[†] 1998-2000	1965-80	1990-97	1960	1990	1998	1960-90	1990-98
Ethiopia	**18**	280	190	173	1.3	1.2	45.2	0.4	2.2	6.9	6.8	6.3	0.0	1.0
Fiji	**120**	97	31	23	3.8	3.7	5.3	-	0.4	6.4	3.1	2.7	2.4	1.7
Finland	**175**	28	7	5	4.6	4.2	3.1	3.6	0.9	2.7	1.7	1.7	1.5	0.0
France	**175**	34	9	5	4.4	7.3	-9.1	3.7	1.0	2.8	1.8	1.7	1.5	0.7
Gabon	**30**	287	164	144	1.9	1.6	36.1	5.6	-0.1	4.1	5.1	5.4	-0.7	-0.7
Gambia	**59**	364	127	82	3.5	5.5	7.9	-	-0.6	6.4	5.9	5.2	0.3	1.6
Georgia	**120**	70	29	23	2.9	2.9	8.8	-	-14.9	2.9	2.2	1.9	0.9	1.8
Germany	**175**	40	9	5	5.0	7.3	-9.1	3.0x	0.7	2.4	1.4	1.3	1.8	0.9
Ghana	**49**	215	127	105	1.8	2.4	20.3	-0.8	1.4	6.9	6.0	5.1	0.5	2.0
Greece	**162**	64	11	7	5.9	5.6	-2.1	4.8	1.0	2.2	1.5	1.3	1.3	1.8
Grenada	**109**	-	37	28	-	3.5	6.3	-	1.3	-	-	3.6	-	-
Guatemala	**74**	202	81	52	3.0	5.5	-1.9	3.0	1.5	6.9	5.6	4.9	0.7	1.7
Guinea	**14**	380	237	197	1.6	2.3	51.7	1.3	2.7	7.0	6.3	5.5	0.4	1.7
Guinea-Bissau	**11**	336	246	205	1.0	2.3	53.7	-2.7	1.0	5.1	6.0	5.7	-0.5	0.6
Guyana	**60**	126	90	79	1.1	1.6	13.8	-	12.9	6.5	2.6	2.3	3.1	1.5
Haiti	**36**	253	148	130	1.8	1.6	31.0	0.9	-4.4	6.3	5.4	4.3	0.5	2.8
Holy See	**-**	-	-	-	-	-	-	-	-	-	-	-	-	-
Honduras	**81**	204	61	44	4.0	4.1	3.9	1.1	1.0	7.5	5.1	4.2	1.3	2.4
Hungary	**149**	57	16	11	4.2	4.7	1.4	5.1	0.2	2.0	1.8	1.4	0.4	3.1
Iceland	**175**	22	5	5	4.9	0.0	20.8	-	0.4	4.0	2.2	2.1	2.0	0.6
India	**49**	236	131	105	2.0	2.8	20.3	1.5	4.3	5.9	3.8	3.1	1.5	2.5
Indonesia	**71**	216	91	56	2.9	6.1	-4.0	5.2	5.9	5.5	3.1	2.5	1.9	2.7
Iran	**100**	233	59	33	4.6	7.3	-8.7	2.9	1.9	7.2	4.9	2.8	1.3	7.0
Iraq	**37**	171	50	125	4.1	-11.5	66.1	-	-	7.2	5.9	5.2	0.7	1.6
Ireland	**162**	36	9	7	4.6	3.1	7.7	2.8	5.6	3.8	2.1	1.9	2.0	1.3
Israel	**165**	39	12	6	3.9	8.7	-14.4	3.7	2.6	3.9	3.0	2.7	0.9	1.3
Italy	**165**	50	10	6	5.4	6.4	-5.5	3.2	1.0	2.5	1.3	1.2	2.2	1.0
Jamaica	**149**	76	16	11	5.2	4.7	1.4	-0.1	0.8	5.4	2.8	2.5	2.2	1.4
Japan	**189**	40	6	4	6.3	5.1	0.0	5.1	1.4	2.0	1.6	1.4	0.7	1.7
Jordan	**93**	139	38	36	4.3	0.7	17.6	5.8x	2.8	7.7	5.8	4.8	0.9	2.4
Kazakhstan	**83**	74	48	43	1.4	1.4	14.8	-	-7.4	4.5	2.8	2.3	1.6	2.5
Kenya	**40**	205	97	117	2.5	-2.3	29.6	3.1	-0.3	8.0	6.1	4.4	0.9	4.1
Kiribati	**62**	-	88	74	-	2.2	11.6	-	-0.6	-	-	4.5	-	-
Korea, Dem. People's Rep.	**104**	120	35	30	4.1	1.9	12.6	-	-	5.8	2.2	2.0	3.2	1.2
Korea, Rep. of	**175**	127	9	5	8.8	7.3	-9.1	7.3	6.0	6.0	1.7	1.7	4.2	0.0
Kuwait	**147**	128	16	13	6.9	2.6	9.7	0.6x	17.5	7.3	3.6	2.9	2.4	2.7
Kyrgyzstan	**69**	180	83	66	2.6	2.9	8.8	-	-9.7	5.1	3.8	3.2	1.0	2.1
Lao People's Dem. Rep.	**41**	235	163	116	1.2	4.3	25.3	-	3.9	6.2	6.5	5.7	-0.2	1.6
Latvia	**126**	44	20	22	2.6	-1.2	25.2	-	-7.3	1.9	1.9	1.3	0.0	4.7
Lebanon	**94**	85	40	35	2.5	1.7	13.5	-	4.9	6.3	3.3	2.7	2.2	2.5
Lesotho	**33**	203	148	136	1.1	1.1	33.2	6.8	2.5	5.8	5.1	4.7	0.4	1.0
Liberia	**6**	288	235	235	0.7	0.0	60.6	0.5	-	6.6	6.8	6.3	-0.1	1.0
Libya	**117**	270	42	24	6.2	7.0	-7.7	0.0	-	7.1	4.9	3.8	1.2	3.2
Liechtenstein	**149**	-	-	11	-	-	-	-	-	-	-	-	-	-
Lithuania	**120**	70	21	23	4.0	-1.1	24.8	-	-7.1	2.5	1.9	1.4	0.9	3.8
Luxembourg	**175**	41	9	5	5.1	7.3	-9.1	-	0.2	2.3	1.6	1.7	1.2	-0.8
Madagascar	**25**	364	168	157	2.6	0.8	40.4	-0.4	-1.6	6.6	6.2	5.4	0.2	1.7
Malawi	**7**	361	230	213	1.5	1.0	55.6	3.2	0.8	6.9	7.3	6.7	-0.2	1.1
Malaysia	**153**	105	21	10	5.4	9.3	-16.8	4.7	5.8	6.8	3.8	3.1	1.9	2.5
Maldives	**56**	300	115	87	3.2	3.5	10.9	-	4.3	7.0	6.4	5.3	0.3	2.4
Mali	**5**	517	254	237	2.4	0.9	61.0	2.1x	0.3	7.1	7.1	6.5	0.0	1.1
Malta	**162**	42	14	7	3.7	8.7	-14.2	-	3.0	3.4	2.0	1.9	1.8	0.6
Marshall Islands	**52**	-	92	92	-	0.0	20.3	-	-4.0x	-	-	-	-	-
Mauritania	**16**	310	183	183	1.8	0.0	48.0	-0.1	1.5	6.5	6.0	5.5	0.3	1.1
Mauritius	**120**	92	25	23	4.3	1.0	16.0	3.7	3.7	5.8	2.2	1.9	3.2	1.8
Mexico	**97**	134	46	34	3.6	3.8	5.1	3.6	0.2	6.9	3.4	2.7	2.4	2.9
Micronesia, Fed. States of	**117**	-	31	24	-	3.2	7.4	-	-1.8	-	-	4.0	-	-

Table 8: The rate of progress

	Under-5 mortality rank	Under-5 mortality rate			Average annual rate of reduction (%)			GNP per capita average annual growth rate (%)		Total fertility rate			Average annual rate of reduction (%)	
		1960	1990	1998	1960-90	1990-98	required† 1998-2000	1965-80	1990-97	1960	1990	1998	1960-90	1990-98
Moldova, Rep. of	**94**	88	37	35	2.9	0.7	17.4	-	-10.8	3.3	2.4	1.7	1.1	4.3
Monaco	**175**	-	-	5	-	-	-	-	-	-	-	-	-	-
Mongolia	**28**	185	150	150	0.7	0.0	38.1	-	-1.4	6.0	4.1	2.6	1.3	5.7
Morocco	**67**	220	83	70	3.2	2.1	11.8	2.7	0.2	7.2	3.8	3.0	2.1	3.0
Mozambique	**10**	313	235	206	1.0	1.6	54.0	-	2.6	6.3	6.5	6.2	-0.1	0.6
Myanmar	**44**	252	130	113	2.2	1.8	23.9	1.6	3.9x	6.0	3.2	2.4	2.1	3.6
Namibia	**62**	206	84	74	3.0	1.6	13.9	-	1.1	6.0	5.4	4.9	0.4	1.2
Nauru	**104**	-	-	30	-	-	-	-	-	-	-	-	-	-
Nepal	**51**	297	138	100	2.6	4.0	17.8	-	2.2	5.8	5.4	4.4	0.2	2.6
Netherlands	**175**	22	8	5	3.4	5.9	-2.9	2.7	1.9	3.1	1.6	1.5	2.2	0.8
New Zealand	**165**	26	11	6	2.9	7.6	-9.8	1.7	1.2	3.9	2.1	2.0	2.1	0.6
Nicaragua	**77**	193	66	48	3.6	4.0	4.4	-0.7	1.6	7.3	5.0	4.4	1.3	1.6
Niger	**3**	354	320	280	0.3	1.7	69.3	-2.5	-1.9	7.3	7.6	6.8	-0.1	1.4
Nigeria	**15**	207	190	187	0.3	0.2	49.1	4.2	0.7	6.5	6.0	5.1	0.3	2.0
Niue	**-**	-	-	-	-	-	-	-	-	-	-	-	-	-
Norway	**189**	23	9	4	3.1	10.1	-20.3	3.6	3.8	2.9	1.8	1.9	1.6	-0.7
Oman	**140**	280	30	18	7.4	6.4	-5.3	9.0	-0.4	7.2	7.0	5.8	0.1	2.4
Pakistan	**33**	226	138	136	1.6	0.2	33.2	1.8	2.0	6.9	5.8	5.0	0.6	1.9
Palau	**97**	-	34	34	-	0.0	20.2	-	-	-	-	-	-	-
Panama	**133**	104	21	20	5.3	0.6	17.8	2.8	3.0	5.9	3.0	2.6	2.3	1.8
Papua New Guinea	**45**	204	112	112	2.0	0.0	23.5	-	2.5	6.3	5.1	4.6	0.7	1.3
Paraguay	**100**	90	37	33	3.0	1.4	14.5	4.1	0.0	6.5	4.7	4.1	1.1	1.7
Peru	**73**	234	75	54	3.8	4.1	3.8	0.8	4.6	6.9	3.7	2.9	2.1	3.0
Philippines	**81**	110	66	44	1.7	5.1	0.0	3.2	1.6	6.9	4.2	3.6	1.7	1.9
Poland	**149**	70	19	11	4.3	6.8	-7.2	-	4.2	3.0	2.0	1.5	1.4	3.6
Portugal	**156**	112	15	9	6.7	6.4	-5.3	4.6	2.0	3.1	1.6	1.4	2.2	1.7
Qatar	**140**	239	36	18	6.3	8.7	-14.4	-	-5.3	7.0	4.4	3.7	1.5	2.2
Romania	**117**	82	32	24	3.1	3.6	6.0	-	-0.1	2.3	1.9	1.2	0.6	5.7
Russian Federation	**115**	64	26	25	3.0	0.5	18.4	-	-7.9	2.6	1.8	1.3	1.2	4.1
Rwanda	**21**	210	161	170	0.9	-0.7	44.4	1.6	-5.7	7.5	6.8	6.1	0.3	1.4
Saint Kitts and Nevis	**90**	-	44	37	-	2.2	11.7	-	4.0	-	3.5	2.4	-	4.7
Saint Lucia	**130**	-	24	21	-	1.7	13.6	-	2.8	-	5.5	2.4	-	10.4
Saint Vincent/Grenadines	**120**	-	26	23	-	1.5	14.2	-	1.8	-	5.0	2.2	-	10.3
Samoa	**110**	210	42	27	5.4	5.5	-1.8	-	0.7	8.3	4.7	4.1	1.9	1.7
San Marino	**165**	-	10	6	-	6.4	-5.5	-	-	-	-	-	-	-
Sao Tome and Principe	**61**	-	90	77	-	2.0	12.5	-	-1.7	-	-	4.7	-	-
Saudi Arabia	**113**	292	45	26	6.2	6.9	-7.2	4.0x	-2.5	7.2	6.6	5.7	0.3	1.8
Senegal	**38**	300	147	121	2.4	2.4	27.4	-0.5	0.0	7.0	6.3	5.5	0.4	1.7
Seychelles	**140**	-	21	18	-	1.9	12.6	-	1.7	-	-	2.1	-	-
Sierra Leone	**1**	390	323	316	0.6	0.3	75.4	0.7	-5.7	6.2	6.5	6.0	-0.2	1.0
Singapore	**175**	40	8	5	5.4	5.9	-2.9	8.3	6.7	5.5	1.7	1.7	3.9	0.0
Slovakia	**153**	40	15	10	3.3	5.1	0.0	-	0.3	3.1	2.0	1.4	1.5	4.5
Slovenia	**175**	45	9	5	5.4	7.3	-9.1	-	4.2	2.4	1.5	1.3	1.6	1.8
Solomon Islands	**113**	185	36	26	5.5	4.1	4.0	-	1.0	6.4	5.7	4.8	0.4	2.1
Somalia	**8**	294	215	211	1.0	0.2	55.2	-0.1	-2.3x	7.3	7.3	7.2	0.0	0.2
South Africa	**58**	130	81	83	1.6	-0.3	21.5	3.2	-0.2	6.5	3.7	3.2	1.9	1.8
Spain	**165**	57	9	6	6.2	5.1	0.0	4.1	1.3	2.8	1.4	1.1	2.3	3.0
Sri Lanka	**137**	133	23	19	5.8	2.4	10.8	2.8	4.0	5.3	2.4	2.1	2.6	1.7
Sudan	**43**	210	125	115	1.7	1.0	24.8	0.8	3.7	6.7	5.2	4.6	0.8	1.5
Suriname	**94**	98	44	35	2.7	2.9	8.9	-	-0.5	6.6	2.7	2.2	3.0	2.6
Swaziland	**53**	233	115	90	2.4	3.1	12.6	-	-0.6	6.5	5.4	4.7	0.6	1.7
Sweden	**189**	20	6	4	4.0	5.1	0.0	2.0	0.2	2.3	2.0	1.6	0.5	2.8
Switzerland	**175**	27	8	5	4.1	5.9	-2.9	1.5	-0.5	2.4	1.5	1.5	1.6	0.0
Syria	**102**	201	44	32	5.1	4.0	4.4	5.1	3.3	7.3	5.7	4.0	0.8	4.4
Tajikistan	**62**	140	78	74	1.9	0.7	17.6	-	-16.1	6.3	4.9	4.1	0.8	2.2
Tanzania	**32**	240	150	142	1.6	0.7	35.4	0.8	0.9	6.8	6.1	5.4	0.4	1.5
TFYR Macedonia	**110**	177	41	27	4.9	5.2	-0.6	-	-2.1	4.2	2.2	2.1	2.2	0.6

	Under-5 mortality rank	Under-5 mortality rate			Average annual rate of reduction (%)			GNP per capita average annual growth rate (%)		Total fertility rate			Average annual rate of reduction (%)	
		1960	1990	1998	1960-90	1990-98	required† 1998-2000	1965-80	1990-97	1960	1990	1998	1960-90	1990-98
Thailand	**90**	148	41	37	4.3	1.3	15.2	4.4	5.9	6.4	2.3	1.7	3.4	3.8
Togo	**30**	267	152	144	1.9	0.7	36.1	1.7	-1.2	6.6	6.6	6.0	0.0	1.2
Tonga	**120**	-	27	23	-	2.0	12.3	-	1.4	-	-	3.6	-	-
Trinidad and Tobago	**140**	73	24	18	3.7	3.6	5.9	3.1	0.5	5.1	2.5	1.6	2.4	5.6
Tunisia	**102**	254	52	32	5.3	6.1	-4.1	4.7	2.0	7.1	3.6	2.5	2.3	4.6
Turkey	**85**	219	70	42	3.8	6.4	-5.3	3.6	2.3	6.3	3.2	2.5	2.3	3.1
Turkmenistan	**66**	150	76	72	2.3	0.7	17.5	-	-14.6	6.4	4.3	3.6	1.3	2.2
Tuvalu	**71**	-	56	56	-	0.0	20.3	-	-	-	-	-	-	-
Uganda	**35**	224	165	134	1.0	2.6	32.5	-2.2	4.4	6.9	7.1	7.1	-0.1	0.0
Ukraine	**126**	53	22	22	2.9	0.0	20.2	-	-12.6	2.2	1.8	1.4	0.7	3.1
United Arab Emirates	**153**	223	14	10	9.2	4.2	3.6	-	-3.8	6.9	4.2	3.4	1.7	2.6
United Kingdom	**165**	27	9	6	3.7	5.1	0.0	2.0	1.9	2.7	1.8	1.7	1.4	0.7
United States	**160**	30	10	8	3.7	2.8	8.9	1.8	1.7	3.5	2.0	2.0	1.9	0.0
Uruguay	**137**	56	24	19	2.8	2.9	8.6	2.5	3.5	2.9	2.5	2.4	0.5	0.5
Uzbekistan	**70**	120	58	58	2.4	0.0	20.2	-	-5.6	6.3	4.1	3.4	1.4	2.3
Vanuatu	**76**	225	70	49	3.9	4.5	2.4	-	-3.5	7.2	4.9	4.3	1.3	1.6
Venezuela	**115**	75	27	25	3.4	1.0	16.4	2.3	-0.2	6.6	3.5	3.0	2.1	1.9
Viet Nam	**85**	219	55	42	4.6	3.4	6.7	-	6.1	6.1	3.8	2.6	1.6	4.7
Yemen	**38**	340	142	121	2.9	2.0	27.4	-	-1.5	7.6	7.6	7.5	0.0	0.2
Yugoslavia	**130**	120	30	21	4.6	4.5	2.4	-	-	2.7	2.1	1.8	0.8	1.9
Zambia	**12**	213	192	202	0.3	-0.6	53.0	-1.2	-0.9	6.6	6.2	5.5	0.2	1.5
Zimbabwe	**55**	159	80	89	2.3	-1.3	25.6	1.7	-0.7	7.5	5.0	3.8	1.4	3.4

Regional summaries

Sub-Saharan Africa	261	180	173	1.2	0.5	46.2	2.8	-0.1	6.7	6.2	5.5	0.3	1.5
Middle East and North Africa	241	76	66	3.8	1.7	15.9	3.1	0.4	7.1	4.9	3.8	1.3	3.1
South Asia	239	135	114	1.9	2.1	24.6	1.4	3.9	6.1	4.1	3.4	1.3	2.5
East Asia and Pacific	201	57	50	4.2	1.8	14.2	4.9	7.7	5.8	2.5	2.0	2.8	2.5
Latin America and Caribbean	154	53	39	3.5	3.8	6.0	4.0	2.2	6.1	3.2	2.7	2.2	2.0
CEE/CIS and Baltic States	101	40	35	3.1	1.9	9.7	-	-3.3	3.1	2.3	1.8	1.1	3.1
Industrialized countries	37	9	6	4.7	4.7	1.7	2.9	1.4	2.8	1.7	1.6	1.6	0.7
Developing countries	216	104	95	2.5	1.2	27.5	3.7	4.1	6.0	3.5	3.0	1.8	2.2
Least developed countries	282	182	167	1.5	1.1	43.5	-0.1	1.2	6.6	5.7	5.0	0.5	1.6
World	193	94	86	2.4	1.1	27.2	3.1	1.8	5.1	3.1	2.7	1.6	1.9

Countries in each region are listed on page 112.

Definitions of the indicators

Under-five mortality rate – Probability of dying between birth and exactly five years of age expressed per 1,000 live births.

GNP per capita – Gross national product (GNP) is the sum of gross value added by all resident producers, plus any taxes that are not included in the valuation of output, plus net receipts of primary income from non-resident sources. GNP per capita is the gross national product, converted to United States dollars using the World Bank Atlas method, divided by the mid-year population.

Total fertility rate – The number of children that would be born per woman if she were to live to the end of her childbearing years and bear children at each age in accordance with prevailing age-specific fertility rates.

† Average annual rate of reduction required 1998-2000 – The average annual reduction rate required, for the period 1998-2000, to achieve an under-five mortality rate in the year 2000 of 70 per 1,000 live births or two thirds the 1990 rate, whichever is less.

Main data sources

Under-five mortality – United Nations Population Division, United Nations Statistics Division and UNICEF.

GNP per capita – World Bank.

Fertility – United Nations Population Division.

Notes

- Data not available.

x Indicates data that refer to years or periods other than those specified in the column heading, differ from the standard definition, or refer to only part of a country.

Index

unicef

UNICEF Headquarters
UNICEF House
3 United Nations Plaza
New York, NY 10017, USA

UNICEF Regional Office for Europe
Palais des Nations
CH-1211 Geneva 10, Switzerland

UNICEF Regional Office for Central and Eastern Europe, Commonwealth of Independent States, and Baltic States
Palais des Nations
CH-1211 Geneva 10, Switzerland

UNICEF Regional Office for Eastern and Southern Africa
P.O. Box 44145
Nairobi, Kenya

UNICEF Regional Office for West and Central Africa
P.O. Box 443
Abidjan 04, Côte d'Ivoire

UNICEF Regional Office for the Americas and Caribbean
Apartado Aéreo 89829
Santafé de Bogotá, Colombia

UNICEF Regional Office for East Asia and the Pacific
P.O. Box 2-154
Bangkok 10200, Thailand

UNICEF Regional Office for the Middle East and North Africa
P.O. Box 1551
Amman 121821, Jordan

UNICEF Regional Office for South Asia
P.O. Box 5815
Lekhnath Marg
Kathmandu, Nepal

UNICEF Office for Japan
United Nations University
Headquarters Building, 8th floor
53-70, Jingumae 5-chome
Shibuya-ku
Tokyo 150-0001, Japan

UNICEF Web site:
www.unicef.org